Pinter's Odd Man Out

Our Fragile Universe, by David Homan.

Pinter's Odd Man Out
Staging and Filming
Old Times

Sidney Homan

With
Stephanie Dugan,
Sandra Langsner
and Thomas Pender

Lewisburg
Bucknell University Press
London and Toronto: Associated University Presses

Associated University Presses
440 Forsgate Drive
Cranbury, NJ 08512

Associated University Presses
25 Sicilian Avenue
London WC1A 2QH, England

Associated University Presses
P.O. Box 338, Port Credit
Mississauga, Ontario
Canada L5G 4L8

The paper used in this publication meets the requirements
of the American National Standard for Permanence of Paper
for Printed Library Materials Z39.48-1984.

Library of Congress Cataloging-in-Publication Data

Homan, Sidney, 1938–
   Pinter's odd man out : staging and filming Old times / Sidney
Homan with Stephanie Dugan, Sandra Langsner, and Thomas Pender.
    p. cm.
   Includes bibliographical references (p.) and index.
   ISBN 0-8387-5238-1 (alk. paper)
   1. Pinter, Harold, 1930– Old times. 2. Pinter, Harold, 1930–
—Film and video adaptations. 3. Pinter, Harold, 1930– —Stage
history. I. Title.
PR6066.I530434 1993
792.9'5—dc20   91-58962
                                        CIP

PRINTED IN THE UNITED STATES OF AMERICA

for my "Kate," "Anna," and "Deeley"—Stephanie, Sandy, and Tom
for my "twin stars"—Patricia and Judith
and, as always, for my own "Maddie Rooney"—Norma

Contents

Preface

To invoke that wonderfully flexible and hence fruitful phrase from the critic's vocabulary, "on the surface" this book is about a single play. That *Old Times* is one of the major works of someone who ranks among a handful (at most two) of the most important playwrights of the modern theatre is, I would hope, sufficient to justify a book-length study. *Old Times* has even been called Pinter's major work; clearly, it is his most commercially successful. Since the first chapter places *Old Times* within a critical and theatrical history of Pinter's canon, the work thereby stands as a microcosm for all his plays, a mirror to put in context a career that began with *The Room* and continues to this day, on the screen as well as the stage. Therefore, while concentrating on a single play, the book is no less about its playwright.

But that "on the surface" is flexible in a more direct way, for this study of *Old Times* is an account of an actual production of the play that I directed in the fall of 1989. The study is, properly, a piece of performance criticism, and hence the subsequent scholarly approach to *Old Times* either led to or evolves from all the practical, theatrical business involved in translating a script to the stage.

Among current scholarship on the theatre, performance criticism has taken a central, sometimes controversial position. Some of its advocates would hold that such criticism effectively displaces what they dismiss as a "mere literary" approach to the theatre, that in focusing on an actual production it duplicates the "real" process by which a play's text is enacted and then received by the audience, and that unlike approaches confined to the scholar's study, performance criticism can treat the visual as well as the verbal nature of a play. Moreover, performance criticism recognizes, so the argument goes, the collaborative nature of production, one where the authority passes from playwright to director to actor to audience, rather than being limited to the author/reader axis of nondramatic literature. Some would even hold that only those who have participated in a performance have a special pipeline to the play's meaning, and that actual theatrical practice is a prerequisite to a full, responsible understanding of a text.

This exclusive attitude has, predictably, spawned a counter-reaction. One contention is that the performance criticism is never broad enough, chained as it is to a specific performance that, by definition, represents a choice among what are often equally valid options for interpretation. It is said that performance criticism lacks the breadth, the sensitivity to cultural or historical forces outside the theatre. Nor can it slow down and, in so doing, draw out all the implications of a text the way literary criticism can do. Moreover, performance criticism, it is suggested, speaks not about the performance itself, in any real sense, but only about an idiosyncratic critical reaction to that performance.

Thus, on one hand we are told that in treating the play as if it were a novel or poem, traditional scholarship misses the boat—entirely. On the other hand, so-called performance criticism is nothing but recycled new criticism, privileging the text as staged rather than as printed.

As someone who works both in the academy and the theatre, I cannot resolve this quarrel for the simple fact that, for me, there is, indeed, should be, no such opposition. For me, there are many avenues to the so-called heart of a play, each in its way, by its own principles, constituting a dramatization or recreation of the text. And if there is much to be learned from focusing on the actual performance of a text, that same text is also a document, a piece of literature. Both dramatic and nondramatic literature imply an audience.

A dear friend, who is both a fine Shakespearean scholar and actor, tells me that very little of what he does as a scholar influences his work onstage—and that the reverse is no less true. He claims that as an actor he sees the "world" of the play from the limited nature of the character in his charge, that, in fact, as a character, his worldview, his very presence, is in competition with those of other characters. While as an actor he knows the particular character's "history" in the play, as that character he must give the illusion of experiencing each moment serially, for the first and only time. However, as a scholar he has the leisure, the vantage point, indeed the obligation to see the play as a whole, to develop an interpretation of its world that is not only "after the fact," but catholic, all-embracing, beyond the provincial view of any single character.

Yet as someone who works primarily as a director in the theatre, I find my situation very different. What is called the director's concept is, I think, very close to that interpretation developed in one's private study or in the classroom with students. Indeed, my Shakespearean friend concedes that for him the rehearsal period resembles what goes on in the classroom and, by implication, that more private process by which a scholar develops an interpretation. All three are times for weighing options and balancing competing readings of a scene or a line; all three provide a "free space" where alternative views can still exist. In the theatre, it is usually only in the final stages of rehearsals that commitments must be made.

It is surely true that, as opposed to the scholar concentrating on the text, the word, the director working in the theatre must perforce give much more attention to the physical, nonverbal dimensions of a play—to blocking and movement, to "what happens" between the lines or to characters who are not speaking, to the "look" of a production as that word embraces set, props, costumes, lighting, and technical effects. Nor will the director usually talk with actors about the symbolic, thematic, let alone cultural dimensions of the text. An actor, rather, will want to know the psychological reason a character says this or that, or moves here as opposed to there. For the actor, the character does not stand for, or represent something but is, instead, a psychological being, an actual person whose enactment itself draws on the actor's own real-life experiences or observations.

But if the audience is the ultimate recipient of the play, the witness whose presence ratifies a performance and for whom that performance is designed, then the scholar speaks just as meaningfully to the goal of any text or of its performance. For the play, so received by the audience, goes into the individual mind and heart, into the thinking and emotions of each spectator, and is subject there to a context already established by the spectator's life experiences, even by his or her attending earlier productions. Enactment exists not for itself but for its reception, and that reception, open to interpretation, is the legitimate topic of the scholar, be his or her approach new historical, psychological, Marxist, or even that of the performance critic.

This is why the present study moves back and forth from scholarship to performance, and shows, I hope, the ways in which one activity influences, indeed, sustains the other. Commentary on the rehearsal period, changes in blocking, the director's concept as it influenced the set, the ways in which Pinter's silences were interpreted, the psychological as well as the practi-

cal considerations for an interchange between two of the characters coexist with and are inseparable from commentary on the
place of *Old Times* in Pinter's canon, the conflicting scholarly
readings of the ending, the work's stage history, or the ways in
which the film *Odd Man Out* served as Pinter's "source." For
this reason, the concern here goes beyond *Old Times* itself to
such issues as the peculiar role in the theater of a scholar who
doubles as a director, the relationship between performance
criticism and more traditional approaches to theatre, and that
between the text as literature and as the basis for enactment.

Such broad issues are expanded further by the fact that I directed *Old Times* for both the stage and television. I am therefore
concerned with the similarities, no less than the differences between those two productions, the added control given a director
by the use of a camera, the unique roles of the audience in the
two media, the aesthetic issues raised by the filming of a live
performance, what happens when a play translated into a television film is then remounted for the stage. The two media, one
ancient, the other peculiar to the twentieth century, are also a
subject of the study.

Chapter 1 first surveys the stage history and then the critical
and scholarly writings on the play, while in chapter 2 *Old Times*
is placed within the context of Pinter's work for the stage, television, and cinema. The material in these first two chapters, then,
constitutes my own preparation for directing *Old Times*. Chapter
3 records the activities connected with, as well as the various
dimensions of the stage and television productions, starting with
the director's concept (as it embraces everything from the design
of the play to the psychological profile of its three characters),
continuing with detailed accounts of the blocking and movement, set, props, lighting, costumes, and music, and concluding
with an analysis of the rehearsal process. In chapter 4, I talk
about some of the things that happened, as well as what we
learned, during performance; the focus here is on the aural and
visual dimensions of the play as it was witnessed by the audience. Complementing this description, chapter 5 is devoted to
commentary by my colleagues in the Theatre Department who
were my actors, Stephanie Dugan (Kate), Thomas Pender
(Deeley), and Sandra Langsner (Anna). From their individual
perspectives, and in their own way, they talk about their conception of the character, their collaboration with both their director
and fellow actors, the rehearsal process, and the experience of
portraying that character in two media. In chapter 6, I analyze

our television film of *Old Times*. Here, through a discussion of
the actual process of filming as well as the media of film itself, I
consider the "role" of the camera, those larger ways in which
this special technological medium influenced my director's concept—in effect, the degree to which the medium was the message—and the context provided by the television production for
the subsequent stage version. The afterword, "Doing Pinter," offers a few, brief thoughts on "presence" in the play and the theatre generally. In the Appendix, I look at *Old Times* from the
perspective of *Odd Man Out*, the film to which the characters
refer in the play itself, indeed which becomes a motif in *Old
Times*. In a very profound way, *Odd Man Out* was one of Pinter's
"sources" for the play, and thus a consideration of the film involves the larger issue of the process of artistic creation.

I am responsible, then, for six of the seven chapters; the faults
here are entirely my own. Nor will my actors and I always, or
even consistently, see the two productions of *Old Times* in the
same way. We worked closely together, but our understandings
of Pinter remain our own. While I was responsible for the television and stage productions in the sense that I was their director, that title is inaccurate, as it usually is in the theatre. The
buck may stop with the director since he or she is technically
"in charge," but one of the excruciating joys of working in the
theatre is that one works with others, in collaboration with them,
as an ensemble. The production is everyone's, and no one's in
particular. My practice, for example, is that if an actor suggests
something—a way of delivering a line, a notion about some aspect of his or her character, a particular bit of stage business, a
change in blocking or movement—that is at least as good as whatever I have had in mind (it doesn't need to be better), I always go
with the actor's suggestion for in this way I can underscore the
collaborative nature of the theatre. Not all directors, of course,
work this way, and there are actors who prefer to be told what
to do, at least to a point. In the case of *Old Times*, however,
my three actors were also my colleagues, close personal friends,
directors themselves, and there is no way in the following pages
that I could, or would want to separate what I contributed, my
ideas from their own. They themselves are responsible for a single chapter, but, in full measure, they are equally responsible for
staging *Old Times*.

And this sense of collaboration extended to the others connected with this production: Donald Loftus, who headed the
television studio in which we filmed *Old Times* and was my

technical director; Ericka Hansen, the stage manager; Stuart Ho-
rowitz who doubled as stage manager and camera operator, with
his fellow operator, Bob Rankin; and Al Wehlburg, who designed
the lights for the stage production. Judith Williams, chairperson
of the Theatre Department of the University of Florida, was my
consultant, as she is on many issues and situations in life, inside
and outside the theater.

One night, while on a ship sailing between Shanghai and Hong
Kong, I found myself all alone on deck, staring at the China
moon and remembering a summer, just completed, of teaching
and directing plays in the People's Republic. Suddenly, for some
inexplicable reason, I decided to pay a visit to the ship's captain.
After knocking on the door, I entered a room to discover five men
seated about a table. When I asked for the captain, they laughed,
politely, and told me that on Chinese vessels there is no captain,
no one individual who bears that title. Rather, the ship is steered
by committee! Chalk this up to the peculiarities of the commu-
nist system, their avoidance of the cult of personality, or, more
profoundly, to the ancient Chinese virtue of valuing the other
over the self. Still, working on this production of *Old Times*, as
well as the writing of this very book based on that experience,
is analogous to what I learned that night from those five men
seated around a table, on a boat making its way down the coast
of China. Four of those collaborators are recognized in the dedication, along with a fifth, who for the performances of *Old Times*
lent us her tea service, her drum-table, her Persian rug, and a
robe bought in Shanghai.

Acknowledgments

Quotations from Pinter's plays are through the kind permission of Grove Weidenfeld.

The object of a dedication in an early book on *Filming Beckett's Television Plays*, Don Loftus, my technical director for the filming of Pinter—and, more, my friend—knows how grateful I am.

Patricia Craddock, Chairperson of the English Department, generously allows me to move between two departments. Judith Williams, Chairperson of the Theatre Department, generously allows me to translate the visions of my study to the stage. Both know what they mean to me.

As always, I owe much to the theatres for which I work and have worked: the Hippodrome State Theatre, the Acrosstown Repertory Theatre, and the University of Florida's Department of Theatre.

Pinter's Odd Man Out

1

Old Times in the Theatre and Among the Scholars

In the Theatre

As with any other Pinter play, the reaction from critics and audiences to the London and New York premiers in 1971 has been—to invoke the inevitable adjectives—mixed, divided, complex, wide-ranging. Old Times marked a "new phase" in Pinter's career;[1] others saw here a combination of the "new and old Pinter"[2] or someone under the influence of film directors like Ingmar Bergman, melding the principles of the stage and screen.[3]

Old Times was said to be Pinter's "best play."[4] If it represented no new departure, it was the most critically distinguished play of the 1970s, one that was Pinter's "most commercially viable,"[5] for here, in characterization, situations, and language, he had "achieved an effect unlike those of any other author now writing."[6] This "chamber play"[7] or "little fugue for three instruments"[8] was distinguished by "beautiful symmetry,"[9] whether that symmetry be defined by a musical or theatrical metaphor.

Others were more restrained. The frequent appellation of "most enigmatic"[10] damned with faint praise. There were few moments of sharp alarm, and in taking more away than he gave, making his play "less real" as a consequence, Pinter had honed, but perhaps honed too much his "nakedness formula."[11] Almost without fail, he was praised for his technical mastery, but could he go beyond this achievement, was he becoming "too mannered"? Confessing that he himself preferred "less aesthetic art," Harold Clurman found the playwright too withdrawn from "external tumult," from the political and social issues of the day.[12] More than one critic noted that members of the audience frequently walked out of the productions.[13] And in the New York Times, Jean Kerr, on the heels of her husband's bad review, offered a parody of Pinter, where a man and a woman bandy about the same few words, as if defying the audience to find deeper meanings behind their cryptic monosyllables.[14]

There was also much about the play to like. The acting in both productions was uniformly described as "splendid,"[15] Peter Hall's direction as "impeccable,"[16] characterized by its "loving reverence" and the "minimum of movement and gesture."[17] The song-contest between Deeley and Anna was a clear highlight.[18] For one critic Anna's counter-story about seeing *Odd Man Out* led to "unnerving reverberations."[19]

There was also much to dislike. The reviewer in *The New Statesman* found the performances "precious at times."[20] A London critic described the pauses as "sometimes drawn out almost to the limits of tolerance."[21] The abrupt changes from short lines to operatic-like speeches seemed grating and unnatural. *Time* gave an especially harsh review: the play was a bore; Pinter here had fallen on his face; the trio seemed flaccid, lethargic. Those famous pauses were nothing more than "toothless gaps" in the text, and apparently there was a good "deal of grumbling" as audiences left the theater.[22]

The reviewers' various and conflicting interpretations of the play are especially revealing. Some suggested that *Old Times*, by accident or by design, refused "interpretation"; one critic then proceeded to offer a tentative interpretation: the three characters might be the same person.[23] The Italian director, Antonio Visconti, took *Old Times* to the extreme, and in a production condemned by the playwright himself, showed Kate and Anna in a series of lesbian lovemaking scenes.[24] A majority of critics, sometimes affirmatively, sometimes negatively, found that the "real" play was below the surface, "between the lines."[25] The contest itself was inconclusive, and an ambiguous Pirandello-like mood was pervasive.[26] Several stressed the element of game playing. The overriding fear of each of the three characters is that of becoming the odd man out. *Old Times* was a "field of game playing, social poise, confidence, and power."[27] While one of the tasks of a reviewer is to offer a capsule summary of the plot, it is interesting that many of the reviews of *Old Times* offered a disproportionately large amount of space to this task, as if the reviewer, faced with such an enigmatic work, hesitated to go beyond the mechanics of its plot, or was struggling, as the characters within the play appear to be doing, to make sense of what happened.

Charles Marowitz in the *New York Times* argued that the three characters do not involve the audience, that they prohibit us from entering into their experiences the ways characters in Beckett do so intensely.[28] A New York critic dismissed the characters as consistently ambiguous, whether dimly presented or fully illuminated.[29] Just as often, if not more, they were found to be fascinating precisely because their motives or even backgrounds were not so clear-cut. Yet for every critic who found the characters sterile, mannered, or too enigmatic, there was one who, for example, described them as palpably human, as "vulnerable but capable of emotional outbursts."[30]

Kate was, easily, the most puzzling of the three. One reviewer found her "so determinately there" that, even though she said very little, he couldn't keep his eyes off her.[31] One saw her as sitting cross-legged like a "tiny Buddha in a white bathrobe."[32] Inert, her presence impassive, she also seemed "luxuriously witty, like an amused cat."[33] Dorothy Tuten was at once "withdrawing yet omnipresent," like some earth-mother, with a certain "voraciousness" in her silence.[34] In her longest speech she seemed given to the "unconscious cruelty of indifference."[35] Her final lines presented special difficulties, for they sounded so out of place in the play, a stylistic oddity, or, conversely, an aria overpowering the rest of the play.

Deeley presented less problems, and with exceptions, received very little sympathy. His curiosity was "obsessional," that of a man needing "emotional certainty."[36] Robert Shaw was praised for the "thunderous explosion" of his "Stop that" when he interrupted the women as Kate lit Anna's cigarette. His Deeley was surly, resentful, a man headed for "defeat."[37] Colin Blakeley's Deeley, on the other hand, was "alert to . . . every shift from favor,"[38] at times "blessedly funny,"[39] and, in his final moments, deserving of our sympathy.

Vivian Merchant's Anna was described as an "erotic stage personality."[40] She was the "most immediately showy" of the three characters, combining a "prim sexiness" with a "slightly sinister undertow."[41] In the New York production, Rosemary Harris displayed "grace in her rigidity,"[42] balancing "sapphic intricacies" with "cool eroticism."[43] In both productions her most noticeable quality was a certain detachment most evident in her abilities as the "mistress of the delayed response."[44]

In these reviews one misses discussion of elements of production other than the acting and directing—the sets, costumes, props, lighting, and so on. However, John Bury's set was said to have a "cold, clean luxury,"[45] at once "striking and restful,"[46] although one reviewer complained that it resembled nothing more than a summer cottage that, oddly, came to a point at the

footlights.[47] In a later New York production, the same furniture
was used for both acts: two elegant white armchairs balanced on
either end of the single sofa. In the Saint Louis production of
1985—and in most productions of *Old Times*—different furniture was used for each act.

In the New York production Anna wore an "icily warm, green
outfit," that was at once "immaculate and sensuous." Deeley was
in a fashionable suit that became rumpled, as he did, during the
course of the evening. Kate was in a "non-committal sweater
and slacks." Gerald Weales confessed to being intrigued by the
outline of her underpants whenever she crossed upstage![48]

Among the Scholars

While he has spoken elsewhere about *Old Times*, Pinter has
made some extraordinary observations about the work in a 1971
interview with Mel Gussow in the *New York Times*.[49] Pro-
nouncing the play "very closely grained," the playwright also
denied the frequent charge that he "willfully keep[s] a secret"
from the audience. Any difficulties here come not from the playwright but from the issue of the past as it bears on the present:
how to define what happened yesterday. If the characters are
involved with, perhaps even overwhelmed by the past, as it
stretches from Deeley's boyhood days to Anna's life with Kate in
London twenty years ago, the fact is that the theater, as Pinter
conceives it, is also a present-tense event: "it is entirely taking
place before your very eyes," and the characters, therefore, "are
sharing something in the present." Hence, "the past is not past"
and the issue, for the audience, is "who's feeling what at what
time."

Nor are the famous pauses and silences gaps in the text, man-
nerisms on Pinter's part, or a deliberate burying of dialogue,
withholding information from the audience. The pauses, he insists, cover "what has just happened in the minds and guts of
the characters," and they thereby "spring out of the text." During
a silence, "something has happened to create the impossibility
of anyone speaking for a certain amount of time."

Even if the question of time seems "to absorb" him "more and
more," the "one thing about *Old Times*" for the playwright, at
least, is that "it happens. It all happens." While *Old Times* may
resist a consensus of interpretations, it is still there—"it happens"—with all the material we need in place ready for interpre-

tations, however idiosyncratic, however much they may reveal about the interpreter rather than the work itself. *Old Times* may well be "very dangerous territory" for all of us locked in time, and for whom "the past is not past," yet it is not dangerous in the sense of being obscure, or purposely enigmatic on the part of the playwright.

Time even played a part in its composition. Pinter wrote the first draft in just three days, although it was not until a few months later that the second draft was completed. The title came last, displacing the working title of *And Others with Dancers*. Even the names of the characters were something of an after-thought, and when Pinter's wife, the actress Vivian Merchant, read an early draft where Kate, Deeley, and Anna were simply called A, B, and C, she confessed that she could not tell the genders of the three. Admitting that he was "a little tough, some-times" with those characters, Pinter maintained that he tried to see them "as clearly as possibly," and, further, that his motive in writing *Old Times* was to create interesting, albeit complex characters, rather than—as he is sometimes accused of doing—merely good parts for actors. Indeed, he argues that the actors should bring real-life experiences to the three roles.

Even the language, which is alternately simplistic (to the level of being banal) and tortured, at once sensible and cryptic, while it has a double purpose, still points toward meaning and, there-fore, comprehension. In an earlier interview Pinter observed that "the speech we hear is an indication of what we don't hear . . . a necessary avoidance, a violent, sly, anguished or mocking smoke-screen. . . . When true silence falls, we are still left with echo but are near nakedness. One way of looking at speech is to say it is a constant stratagem to cover nakedness."[50]

In effect, the playwright's own reading of *Old Times* here is at variance with some of the theater critics' judgments just sur-veyed. For him, *Old Times* is about "real" people facing an im-portant problem: what we see is what we see—"It is all happening."

Pinter's purpose in writing *Old Times*, his intentions—in ef-fect—regarding the function of the play, its characters, and mean-ing, are both sustained and qualified, even attacked by the considerable amount of scholarly commentary on this work. Si-mon Trussler labeled the characters' efforts to revive and then impose memories on the present as little more than "tricks" played by the dramatist. Why, he argued, should the characters' accounts of the past be any more at variance now than twenty years ago.[51] A more recent feminist reading, however, sees the play as a success, particularly with its two women characters. By adopting a "totally amoral stance" toward Kate and Anna, Pinter allows for their "complete sexual freedom," and the result is "a more mellow and human image of the world."[52]

David Thompson links this sense of "freedom" in the work's "humane image" with Pinter's "desire to remove himself from the position of the omniscient author."[53] Peter Briggs suggests that Pinter's stance is inseparable from the play's own structural principle, which is to combine "disparate modes," a "blatant" tactic allowing for a "sudden juxtaposition of sections of the dialogue," some of which are motivated, while others are not.[54] Yet Pinter has also been faulted for being too distant from the action, which, however skillfully presented, is at length nothing but the "lucid spectacle of a failure."[55]

The question of the work's meaning is inseparable from that of the playwright's purpose, or the way he functions as an artist. Elizabeth Sakellandou, for example, outlines five options for understanding the conflict. *Old Times* may be a reenactment of Deeley's nightmares, an expression of his own fears as he projects them upon a neurotic, fantasy world he himself has fashioned. Or, at the heart of the play is Kate's relationship with Anna that stands between her and Deeley. On a less realistic level, Kate and Anna may be part of the same composite woman. Or we may be observing a ritualized game between Deeley and Kate, one in which Anna becomes the pawn. A fifth possibility is that Deeley is dead, and that everything is happening in the minds of Anna and Kate.[56] Another reading suggests that in seeing her as an "extension" of themselves, Anna and Deeley are "more vulnerable" than Kate.[57]

This rivalry has been described as a "process of triangular desire: a point-by-point opposition between two symmetrical and opposite figures."[58] For any of the three, aggression is the only option whenever one's verbal space is uncertain or threatened.[59] The battle here is not metaphysical, as in Beckett, but literal and metaphorical as in Ibsen. Each of the three has a desire for power and yet is "held back in a state of psychic paralysis."[60] Other readings would make the conflict more archetypal. Here Pinter takes the "sub-text of human experience" and makes it textual.[61]

Several interpretations stress the act of interpretation itself. Each of the characters is a "perceiver who distorts," and, fashioning a world through a private language "straining further from

reality," resembles an artist engaged in the "process of creation."[62] Two modes of perception and, hence, creation may be in
operation: what we see of others and what we insist others see
of us. In the evening's "game of light," each character is a "force
to be reckoned with," strongest when he or she is alone, silent,
or when only dimly perceived by others.[63] Under such limitations man is an "artificer" of the past; reality itself "is thus an
artifact."[64] As such, *Old Times* underscores the elusiveness of
objectivity itself: everything we see and hear in the play may be
taking place in the mind.[65] With its reality below the surface, in
the midst of a game of perceptions and fashionings, both of the
self and of others, there is, for the audience, a "simultaneous
scarcity and abundance of facts."[66]

Pinter's purpose, in this light, is to "release his audience's
imagination into the sexual consciousness of each of his characters," in a theatrically based world where the spectator is "free
from the pressure to judge."[67] It is the audience who is forced to
compare these versions of the past. They can do this without
ethical obligations, for in *Old Times* there are "words, echoing
silences, and images which ought to be enjoyed as such."[68] The
play's first director, Peter Hall, expresses the same sentiment
when he suggests that the key line is "Normal, what's normal?"[69]
Theatrical presence, game playing (albeit serious), and relative
perceptions supersede ethical or even political considerations.

Though their judgments, not to mention interpretations, differ,
almost all commentators agree that *Old Times* is about language—the word. Elin Diamond calls Deeley and Anna "dazzling
word performers," who, viewing past and present as "matters of
linguistic choice," seduce the audience "into voyeuristic acts of
the imagination." In this comedy of "verbal resiliency," words
are the only commodity, and are capable of being "echoed or
stolen" by the traders.[70] Katharine Worth describes Anna and
Deeley as "pouncing on each other's vocabulary."[71] This sharing
and stealing of language bonds the rivals. Language thereby becomes "an essentially pluralistic activity,"[72] or, from the perspective of performance, a "theatrical collage," the product of the
ensemble onstage.[73]

The darker side of this verbal comedy is that the participants
are also subject to what one commentator terms their own "vic-
timizing narratives."[74] It is Kate's narrative, her final speech, that
demolishes everything her rivals have tried to establish by verbal
fiat. Language is here a double-edged sword that, at length,
wounds the players themselves, betraying them because it is

"endlessly and hopelessly significant."[75] The very act of remembering rebounds on a character when "he or she fully accepts an authorized history which then proves vulnerable."[76] Deeley, in particular, tries to recreate his youth with the portraits of his father buying him his first and only bicycle and his mother disapproving of the practice of powdering someone after a bath.[77]

Speech is thus an attempt to bring what Pinter himself has called the "mistiness of the past" into the present.[78] Anna cannot "live in the present"; only Kate can live there.[79] Lucina Gabbard describes the rivals as "reaping the arid harvest of their neurotic pasts."[80]

Whether the perspective be philosophical, psychological, theatrical, even theological, efforts to define the "meaning" of *Old Times*—or even its lack of meaning—usually give way to accounts of its three characters, of what has happened and—no less—is happening between and among them. In essence, the play, as an object for discussion, seems to insist on being taken for what it is: three people, during the course of an evening, talking and interacting with each other, in an isolated, converted farmhouse, removed from the larger, seemingly more real world surrounding it—from London, Sicily, even China of the Cultural Revolution. In similar fashion, the stage itself, while a mirror for reality, also insists on its own presence.

From this perspective, the relationships among the characters—the ways they resemble and differ from each other—have been variously defined. Despite their rivalry, Anna and Deeley are often seen as doubles, both "restless" and "volcanic type[s]."[81] Barbara Kreps calls them "literally and metaphorically bed fellows."[82] Anna, in fact, may be "attracted" to Deeley.[83] At the same time, both are driven by the twin desires of winning Kate and defeating each other. Although they may protest otherwise, both lack "self-sufficiency" because, more than they understand, they are dependent on Kate.[84] Each mistakes the "restless, dreamlike quality" in Kate as a sign of her weakness,[85] but it is they who become "impotent" after she asserts herself when she enters refreshed from the bath in act 2. Unlike Kate, the rivals are too "terrified by a shifting sense of the self to confront the reality of death."[86]

The relationship between Kate and Anna, of course, has been the subject of much discussion. Anna has been seen as Kate's other half, her past, a mother-figure against whom the daughter rebels, a demon, one who would remove Kate from the world and alone possess her, Kate's more passionate side, that Kate who is physically dependent on men, a part of Kate's nature that is sexually attracted to women, that despises men. Anna is a regressive or infantile Kate who seeks only the friendship of her own gender. She is Kate as a little girl resisting the attention of boys, all the past, all that has happened and needs to be exorcised, a shameful period of Kate's life, of her life as a prostitute, or the Kate that Deeley has some chance of fashioning or controlling. She represents all those forces, both benign and malignant, that Kate must, indeed, that all of us must reject, or, at the very least, put in place so that an authentic self can develop. On the other hand, Kate, for Anna, is all that she loves and hates, even as Kate occupies this same paradoxical position for Deeley. Thus, at the end of the play, when Kate breaks this balance, these twin, conflicting emotions are transferred by Anna and Deeley from the object to the rival.[87] In recognizing a part of herself, in assimilating it, Kate at once absorbs Anna and is then prepared to fashion her own self.

Kate's is the final, authentic performance of the play, built as it is on what she observes in the two "flawed performers" before her during the course of the evening.[88] Kate is the one who "nullifies" the attempts by the rivals to define her,[89] and in her final speech we see that nullification in the "nightmare poetry of [her] fantasy."[90] She is, in a way, the hero of *Old Times* who, at the end, shows an "absolute acceptance of herself."[91] If, in removing herself from others, she is guilty of a "narcissistic self-love," the fact is that she frees herself from the "infantile self" represented by Anna and from an equally "infantile husband."[92]

Christopher Hudgins reads the play as a series of "filmically or directly presented memories" on Kate's part.[93] In this approach, Anna's opening speech becomes Kate's "dim memory" of the past, and when she tries to convince Kate not to go into the park, Anna materializes as a "frightened homebody." By the time Kate asks if it is raining outside, the question that initiates a second flashback to the London days, Kate's self is stronger, and she is strengthened further when she recalls that she herself made the decision on what man will come over to their apartment. In her final speech Kate directly presents her memory of Deeley's part in her "unsatisfactory London life," even as she accuses Anna of stealing not just her underwear but "elements of her personality." At the end, as she accepts the death of this past, Kate's revolt against the rivals is "justified and vital," for her actions here announce "a limited freedom and a continuing passionate revolt" against the claim of others. She has at last, exorcised a "negative part of herself," and the images of dirt are those of both death and rebirth: She no longer needs "husband or friend."[94]

A very different image of Kate has also been advanced. If her images are "heroic," they are also "trite romantic" ones.[95] She is little more than someone who "occasionally surfaces to make a feeble protest." Kate is an exhibitionist bound by her own "self-contained narcissistic dreams."[96] In her search for an authentic self, she invariably drives Deeley back to a regressive posture as a child.[97]

Deeley has been branded an "egocentric fool,"[98] and, as a consequence, is the "least aware" of the three characters. For Deeley, the evening is a kind of "dream game"[99] that turns into a nightmare. His hope is that if he can successfully "remember a sexual relationship with Anna, she cannot maintain her claim to an exclusive intimacy with Kate in the past."[100] He may even see Kate and Anna as "two opposite aspects of the female principle."[101] Driven by his own "homosexual fantasies," Deeley is the outsider who plays "the memory game with greater intensity." "Like a practiced raconteur," he tries to reshape the reality of both past and present; for him as a consequence, the real Kate is "spatially non-existent."[102] In the final moments Deeley "can no longer pretend objectivity about what he sees."[103] A feminist reading finds in him the "grain of sensitivity and vulnerability that Kate [herself] sees in his nature." His sobs, unmasculine by his own principles, are the proof of this.[104]

Anna is "Kate's passionate self," her "inner self," the embodiment of a powerful sexual passion" that is more concealed in Kate herself.[105] For Katherine Burkman, Anna is the double "who seeks Kate's damnation."[106] The "past incarnate,"[107] she "does not 'exist' until she is sufficiently remembered."[108] Or her psychological state is warped, for in her recollections Anna reveals that within her are the "seeds of jealousy and antagonism" for Kate. Like her playwright, Anna looks back into a relationship, not beyond it.[109] Driven by a desperate need to make Kate "conform" to her vision of their relationship, like Goldberg in *The Birthday Party* she "drowns details in clichés and inflates a stereotype to absurd proportions." Her comments that all she wanted was Kate's "happiness" represents a "language of sentiment [that] is invidious."[110]

Finally, several sections of the play have been afforded special commentary: Anna's presence at the start of act 1 as she stands silent upstage with her back to the audience, the opening dialogue of Anna and Deeley in act 2, Kate's "bath speech," several

of the longer speeches (especially Deeley's about the two usherettes), the song-contest, and the cinematic flashback of the two
women. However, none has been given more attention than the
mime at the end of *Old Times*, where first Anna, and then Deeley
try to leave the stage, and, once the silent stage movements are
finished, the three characters sit in silence in a dim light suddenly broken by a flash of full stage lights before the blackout.

The sudden bright light is said to be "like a photograph in
our memories" a "hellish bright light" interposing between the
"frustrated desires of the present and the troubling memory of
the past."[110] It underscores how the "verbal creativity" so dominant in the play "breaks down" into silence."[112] For one critic
the mime demonstrates the "repetitious compulsion" of old
times that lie forgotten in the unconscious. Anna lies dormant
on the divan until memory will again arouse her—at the next
performance—while Deeley's sobs reveal that he will suffer his
own loss until the evening of games is itself revived.[113] The silence reminds us that Anna and Deeley, in "seeking conclusive
victory over one another," have "relinquished further opportuni-
ties for verbal recreation." The stage action is a "palimpsestical
dialogue, fragments of Anna's memory, and Deeley's, and Kate's."
As with Beckett's *Endgame*, life ends when storytelling is over.[114]

Anna lies dead, or dormant, Deeley slumped, sobbing, humiliated in the chair. But it is Kate alone who sits upright, who does
not leave her place on the divan, and who, unlike her husband
and her friend, feels no need to try to escape. One observer argues that to be motionless in the mimes is to win.[115] Several
scholars have found in the mime an address to the audience.
Forced to look at the stage in bright light, we are "jolted to see
how we too lead our lives," and how there is no victory "for these
three half-concealed, half-revealed characters" who are now very
much like ourselves.[116]

The *Old Times* we have witnessed are those deep within us,
beyond, beneath the specific events that the three characters have
bandied about in the play. Perhaps the title comes from the song
itself, "Old Times," which recollects dinner dates, talking, "staying up for hours." Like the play itself, the song questions its own
events in the very first line—"Seems like old times."[117]

2

Within Pinter's World

Each of Pinter's plays is, of course, unique, autonomous, possessed of its own integrity.[1] *Old Times* is no exception as Pinter's first "woman's play," indeed, the only play by Pinter in which female characters outnumber the males. Compared to *The Homecoming*, it is one of Pinter's later "upscale" plays. The blue color world of *The Room*, the sleazy gentility of *The Birthday Party*, and the underworld characters of *The Dumb Waiter* have long been replaced by the sophistication of *The Betrayal* and *The Lover*, and now by Kate and Deeley residing comfortably in a converted farmhouse by the sea, visited by Anna who lives with her wealthy Italian husband in Sicily. Still, nothing changes in Pinter, and if no single play of his can be said to be "generic," there are, clearly, elements that almost all of his works share.

Most clearly, there is in Pinter a room fiercely guarded by its owner, or owners, an expression of the mind of its occupant. With his deceptively simple changes in grammar, Lenny in *The Dwarfs* cherishes his room: "There is my table. This is a table. There is my chair. There is my table" (p. 96). In *No Man's Land* it is, curiously, Spooner, the intruder on Hirst's room, who waxes most eloquently on his new surroundings, as if he wished the place were his own: "What a remarkably pleasant room. I feel at peace here. Safe from all danger" (p. 17). In her first long dialogue to a silent husband at the start of *The Room*, Rose expends her effort distinguishing her squalid apartment from the hostile world outside. Threatened by the intruder in *A Slight Ache*, Edward longs for a new room, even more isolated than his present one, a shelter where he could "compose himself, lying there and no longer hearing the world—a sort of serene death" (p. 198). While he has been away in prison, Walter's room in *Night School* has been lent out to a woman, and while Teddy has been in America, Lenny has given his brother's boyhood room to friends "passing through this part of the world" (p. 43). What particularly disturbs the mother (Voice 2) in *Family Voices* is that a rented room now seems more like home to her son than his real home. Here he has "found [his] home, [his] family" (p. 77).

The room, though, is seldom stable. Len in *The Dwarfs* knows that rooms often "change shape at their own will" (p. 99). In *The Basement* the room's metamorphosis is both literal and symbolic. In the course of this half-hour television drama, Law's room, initially resembling the comfortable den of a Victorian house, is converted to a streamlined apartment of Scandinavian design and then a bare playing area in which the two men stage their symbolic battles. In *The Collection* Mick has plans to convert the room into a penthouse, with "teal-blue, copper and parchment linoleum squares." In *Silence* Ellen recalls a room but is unsure if it existed today or "a long time ago" (p. 214). In *The Room* we hear of, but never see the rooms below and above Rose's apartment, yet what happens there threatens her hold on the room we do see onstage. She herself has once been to the basement, but that was "a long time ago" (p. 115).

The "outside" is literally that, but also generally a place to be avoided. Rose pleads with her silent husband Bert not "to go out" (p. 102) on the icy roads, and later the visitor, Mrs. Sands, delivers a long speech on their ordeal in making their way to Rose's apartment. Similarly, in *No Man's Land* Briggs offers a frustratingly detailed account on how he once gave street directions to Foster (p. 62). The Son (Voice 1) in *Family Voices* observes that "No-one seems to leave the house," and if Riley does, it is "but rarely" (p. 80). In *The Birthday Party* Lulu's basic advice to Stanley is that he should get out of the cottage, "go outside," but Meg only travels vicariously, inquiring of her essentially silent husband Petey if it "is nice out" (p. 20). In that same play, McCann's first interrogation of Stanley is a series of questions based on the world outside his seaside retreat.

The Basement opens with an exterior shot, where Stott and Jane wait to enter Law's apartment; then there is a cut to Law's comfortable bachelor apartment, an "interior" if there ever was one. Edward, in *A Slight Ache*, boasts of his worldwide travels, particularly in Africa, from the Gobi Desert to the Membunza Mountains, yet he clings to his living room, indeed is irritated when Flora insists she spotted him earlier that morning in the toolshed. He even boasts that from his window he can see "only a corner of the garden. A very small corner" (p. 177). Outside stands the Matchseller, and at the end Edward will exchange places with him. In *The Black and White* the outside waits and threatens, and the stay of the two women inside the milk bar can be only temporary. Even there one feels hounded by strangers who "come up and speak to you at the counter" (p. 241). A simple request for the time of day drives the women into rehashing bus schedules and routes, that inevitable drive through the night. The small comfort is that the same bus taking them away also returns at daylight to the milk bar. Davies in *The Caretaker* is also a transient, on his way to Sidcup, and like the women in *The Black and White*, he clings to the cluttered apartment, owned by the mercurial Mick and in which his brother Aston has given him temporary shelter. In *The Dumb Waiter* the outside world intrudes in the form of the items in a newspaper that Ben reads; later, that paper metamorphoses into the speaking tube which, once activated, initiates a series of impossible requests and pathetic answers between whoever is offstage—or, rather, above the stage—and the two characters onstage, whose grimy confidence in their occupation is quickly shattered. Sometimes that other place, the world outside, is home itself, although not always the mythical "Home Sweet Home." In *The Room* the black man, Riley, claiming to be Rose's father, brings a message from her "folks," that they want Rose "to come home." Here the messenger is savagely beaten by Bert, who, otherwise a silent, even sullen character, has just moments before delivered a highly charged sexual encomium to his van.

A defense against the outside world, indeed its claim on the occupant resting on its being the antithesis to all that is offstage, the larger "set" implied beyond the wings, the room in Pinter is not impregnable. Moreover, life there, in the room, is an increasingly difficult one. Spooner observes in *No Man's Land* that Hirst is in a "no man's land which never moves, which never changes, which never grows older, but which remains forever, icy and silent" (p. 95). If Hirst owns the room to which Spooner himself so desperately seeks admission, Hirst is also strangely depressed, given to excessive drinking, and plagued by a vision of a body "floating dead in the water," which he frantically dismisses as "nothing"—only to be contradicted by Spooner (p. 95).

The corollary to such rooms and such outsides is the relationship between the person (or persons) alone and the intruder. The former, as Rose defines them in *The Room*, are "we [who] keep ourselves to ourselves" (p. 115). Richard and Sarah in *The Lover* live in a place "far away from the main road" (p. 163). The Controller in *Victoria Station* defines his isolation as that of a "monk" (p. 50). And until the issue of the Matchseller enters their conversation, Flora and Edward can focus their attention on such reductive activities as suffocating a wasp in pot of marmalade. Here, the intruder waits within, in the form of a lowly insect, as well as without, in the silent person of the Matchseller.

When Riley opens the door in *Family Voices*, he brands the knockers as "imposter," even as the Matchseller is branded by the defensive Edward as "very false" (p. 179). Edward's first conversation with the intruder takes the form of an interrogation not unlike that in *The Birthday Party* which, in reverse fashion, the intruders, Goldberg and McCann, conduct with Stanley. In *The Caretaker* Davies cannot understand why his hosts would "invite [him] like this" (p. 76). At the start of *The Collection* the intruder is only a voice on the telephone whose call for Bill is intercepted by Harry. When James materializes and intrudes on Bill, the latter is outraged: "You can't just barge into someone's home like this" (p. 128). Stott tells his old friend Law that he is "looking for a place" (p. 154), and by the end of *The Basement* he himself will welcome Law as a guest into what used to be his own apartment. Spooner, the intruder, begs to be considered for a "post" in Hirst's household, vowing to become his host's "Chevalier" (pp. 88, 89). When Hirst demands that they "change the subject," and seconds later that the subject is "changed forever" (p. 90–92), Spooner, so assertive earlier in the play, goes to pieces. Willy in *The Tea Party* is the most subtle of intruders. Disson has lost his best man for the wedding, and so Wendy's brother, whom Disson has just met, replaces him. In the course of the play, Willy assumes Disson's role in the company. In *Night School*, Sally, who intrudes on Walter's room while he is in prison, quickly becomes the woman he desires, but this sought-after intruder suddenly vanishes, called away by "urgent matters." Rose, in contrast, resists Riley, the intruder: "You disturb my evening. You come in and sit down here" (p. 122).

Resisted, desired, simple in their mission, or—more often—not so simple, related or unrelated to those inside the room, at times an apparent psychological projection of, or doppleganger of the inhabitant—these are these "guests," as Stanley labels Goldberg and McCann. In the case of Teddy in *The Homecoming* the guest is a member of the family, and, for a time, even reclaims his boyhood room. Ruth's clichéd farewell, "Don't be a stranger," is wonderfully and—for Teddy at least—painfully ironic (p. 96). Only in *Family Voices* do potential intruders remain just that: Riley refuses entrance to the two women on the doorstop, who claim they are the mother and daughter of someone inside the house. In *The Dumb Waiter*, however, the two hoods go through a complicated comic rehearsal of just what to do and say if their victim should knock on the door. At the end of that play, the seeming victim becomes the temporary inhabitant of the abandoned cafe: "The door right opens sharply. BEN turns, his revolver leveled at the door. GUS stumbles in. . . . "They stare at each other" (p. 165). Earlier in that play the "intruder" is less than human when an envelope slides under the door.

The dichotomies of room/outside, inhabitant/intruder generate a feeling, variously defined by people who have seen or commented on Pinter's work, of something else, below the surface, beneath the lines, a subtext, or a subworld eager, even demanding to make an appearance yet somehow never quite arriving onstage or on the set. In *The Homecoming* Lenny first defines this "other," the strange child of the dichotomies, with a question, "How can the unknown merit reverence?" Then he suggests that it constitutes only half the world, indeed is dependent on its twin: "Apart from the known and the unknown, what else is there?" (p. 68). In *The Room* Kidd describes the mysterious Riley, who does make an ambiguous, unsettling appearance, as "just lying there. In the black dark. Hour after hour" (p. 121). Edward in *A Slight Ache* forces the fly down through the spout and into the airless, black, and sticky prison of the marmalade, almost as if he were repressing a dark side of himself. Goldberg and McCann in *The Birthday Party* have often been identified as a buried side of Stanley's self, or of his past, as being something more than literal intruders on his quiet life by the sea. Goldberg notes the inevitability of their arrival: "If we hadn't come today we'd have come tomorrow" (p. 42). Hirst puts the matter more directly in *No Man's Land*: "There are places in my heart . . . where no living soul . . . has . . . or can ever . . ,. trespass" (p. 84). In *A Kind of Alaska* Deborah has visited, indeed existed, in this world beyond what is visible onstage, there taking "a temporary habitation" in "foreign territories" (pp. 33, 35). Withers in *Family Voices* tries to seduce the son into such territory: "Are you prepared to follow me down the mountain. Look at me. My name's Withers. I'm there or thereabouts" (p. 77).

Such dualities and the mysterious trinity they hint at are supported in Pinter by the numbers one, two, three, and their combinations. The number three, the odd-man-out number, is especially pervasive. In *The Caretaker* Aston, Mick, and Davies are the three men in a single room, as are Len, Pete, and Mark in *The Dwarfs*. Two men, Stott and Law, and one woman, Jane, form the cast of *The Basement;* Sykes, the landlord talked about but unseen onstage, completes a trinity with Beth and Duff in *Landscape*. In *A Kind of Alaska* Deborah "returns" as both Pauline's sister and Hornby's patient. The narrator in *Monologue* thinks of his friend and the woman both men loved as "brother and sister." For him, there was "some kind of link-up, some kind of identical shimmer" between the two and hence with himself. The woman brought the two men together and then into contention; one loved her soul, the other her body. Such trinities become literal in Pinter's *Dialogue for Three*, where the short work is divided between the conversation of the men (during which the woman is relatively silent) and her long speech recalling her lovemaking with "First." After this, "First" returns to "Second" to recall a third man, Whipper Wallace, whom both knew.

These trinities almost invariably lead to a conflict in which two characters oppose the third. In *Silence* Ellen shifts her affections from the younger man, Bates, to an older man, Rumsey. By informing on Aston, Davies in *The Caretaker* tries to turn brother against brother, thereby strengthening his friendship with Mick, just as Mick earlier tricks Davies by confiding to him his disgust with his brother's laziness. Here, the odd-man-out motif is underscored by the presence of two beds in a set that houses three characters. Similarly, in *The Dwarfs*, Pete tries to take Len from the actor Mick, and in *The Collection* there are unions, real or imagined, that would exclude the third party, for example, Bill's alleged affair with James's wife, Stella or the growing romantic interest between Bill and James that would exclude Harry.

Uniting against the odd-man-out, often against the world, the couple becomes, at least for a time, a single entity. Or, as Meg says in *The Birthday Party*, "Oh, I've put you both together. Do you mind being both together?" (p. 43). Jew and Christian, brains and brawn, Goldberg and McCann, despite some tensions, form just such a couple. At one point Meg confuses Goldberg with Stanley, and we may wonder if in this second "couple" there is some undisclosed relation between guest and boarder. In a revealing bit of stage action in *The Collection*, James and Bill look at their mutual reflection in a single mirror. In *A Slight Ache*, when Flora gives Edward the Matchseller's tray, she, in effect, divorces one husband and finds another. In *The Basement*

Stott and Law are, in turn, Jane's lover. At the end, as Stott lies in bed dying, Jane wonders what they should do "with the body" (p. 166), as if the past, albeit present in only the most feeble way, threatened her new union with Law. Whatever differences in personality between the two brothers in *The Caretaker*, each has a co-equal right to the room; Mick informs the intruder Davies that "We take it in turns, once a fortnight" (p. 54). One personality can even be split, each with a separate name: in *The Lover* one actor plays both the stuffy husband Richard and his wife's exotic lover, Max. As they merge into a single, albeit complex personality, these tightly knit couples perforce exclude the odd-man-out, the "fifth-wheel," as Stanley ironically becomes at his own birthday party, in the presence of two couples, Goldberg and Lulu, Meg and McCann. In *The Homecoming* Lenny triumphantly informs Teddy, who used to be part of the family, "we do make a unit" (p. 81). In *Silence*, this unit is underscored physically when, violating the separate space otherwise given to the characters, Bates leaves his seat and crosses to Ellen.

These couples and couplings, the intruder or the person excluded, the specific room itself and the imagined, often threatening outside are the subject of and—no less—subject to the relativity of perception, to what both characters and audience see or think they see. To be sure, everything in the play is literal enough: a room is a room with recognizable, even mundane furniture, and a brandy served is a brandy served. Rather, the "stuff" of the play—the couple standing clearly before us, the single choir claimed by two potential occupants—is at the mercy of varying perceptions, from both on- and offstage. Lenny in *The Dwarfs* puts the issue in a somewhat pretentious series of corollaries: "What you are, or appear to be to me, or appear to be to you, changes so quickly, so horrifyingly." For him, each of us is the "sum of so many reflections" (p. 112). In *The Homecoming*, Teddy, albeit in sketchy fashion, defines his particular philosophic theory as "a way of being able to look at the world" (p. 77), and what is clear by the final act is that his "way" loses out to that of the family that has excluded him and, in turn, welcomes his wife as mother, mistress, and business associate.

The paradox is that when we assume our vision is clearest, we are most uncertain of just what we see. In *Silence* Rumsey comments on the phenomenon of people approaching him, "sharp at first sight ... then smudged ... then lost, then glimpsed again ... then gone" (p. 108). In *That's Your Trouble,*

A and B both observe a third man, invisible to the offstage audience, carrying a sandwich board, but then proceed to argue over the larger issue, for which his physical presence offers only conflicting evidence, of whether or not he is suffering.

Invariably, problems with the eyes, or even outright loss of sight, become a motif in the plays. At the end of The Room Rose, confronted by Riley, claims she cannot see, and Edward's problems with his eyes give the title to A Slight Ache. His guard down, he admits to the Matchseller that "sometimes [he has] viewed [him] through dark glasses" (p. 197). Hide-and-seek is Meg's first suggestion as a game to be played at Stanley's birthday party, but it is instead fitting that blindman's buff is substituted. At the climactic moment in act 2, when Stanley, excluded from his own party, is reduced to the role of a silent audience, the lights go out. As Disson's world tumbles in The Tea Party, his problems with vision increase; plagued by bad sight, he goes to a doctor friend who, from his examination, can find nothing wrong.

In Pinter, the perceiver and the perceived are locked in the past; the play thereby stands as a reaction to the facts. The relativity of memory, in turn, complicates an already relative present, or presence onstage. And memory is never neutral. In The Birthday Party Goldberg's seemingly innocuous recollections of his cosmopolitan Uncle Barney are, for the actor, a clue to the character's present "object," or motivation. Nor is a character's memory always inviolate: Rose doubts that Kidd's memories of his mother and sister are accurate. In A Slight Ache Flora's memories of her childhood are mythological rather than temporal, for they occurred "long before the flood" (p. 190). Hirst's recollections of the village church hung with garlands, and of the men and women who died virgins, is more psychological than factual, for he tries to recreate in the midst of Spooner's devouring presence an innocent time, in a dimension outside the corrupt city, long before the enervating present of his No Man's Land. Deborah in A Kind of Alaska has aged physically, yet mentally and socially she remains locked in the period of her childhood, just before her own sexual maturity.

Despite this relativity of perception, and a past that, through the vagaries of memory, intrudes upon the present, the characters in Pinter lust for certainty and are addicted to the facts, both historical and present. Even the most insignificant of facts can become all-consuming. In the revue piece, Last to Go, memories of their friend George are crowded out of the conversation among the barman, news-seller, and old man by a debate about which of the several London newspapers is the last to sell out. In *Night* Man and Woman offer conflicting but specific accounts about the facts of their meeting at a party and of making love afterwards. In *The Collection* there are several very different versions of precisely what happened, or did not happen, between Bill and Stella during a sales convention in Leeds. At the end James implores his wife, "That the truth . . . isn't it?—that nothing happened," but Pinter's final stage direction has Stella looking at him "neither confirming nor denying," although her face is "friendly, sympathetic" (p. 157). Briggs in *No Man's Land* confidently fills in details of Spooner's life—that he collects bear mugs at a local bar—which Spooner violently denies. Later Hirst, who has just met Spooner by accident this evening, claims to have had sexual relations with his wife. As if confirming what had been initially dismissed as a fiction, Spooner in turn recalls that both men knew Stella at one time and that she was later, or so he says, seduced by Hirst.

Sometimes these arguments concern the very recent past. Mr. and Mrs. Sacks in *The Room* argue over whether or not a few minutes earlier Mr. Sacks had sat down in a chair or has all this time remained standing. Conversely, such efforts to clarify the past can reach very far back: in *The Homecoming* Lenny wants to know the specific details of the moment when he was conceived. The major issues in the first extended conversation Stanley has with McCann in *The Birthday Party* is just where they have met, if they did meet, and just where in the city Stanley was raised as a child—or where his real home is (p. 49). In *The Basement* Jane, who has just recently met Law and is now his house guest, calls the apartment her place and insists that, if he demands that Stott leave, she and Law can be happy again "like we used to" (165). Law, curiously, challenges neither claim. Because her physician and sister do not provide her with the full facts of the present, nor of the period during which she has been in a coma, Deborah in *A Kind of Alaska*, not experiencing the present, interprets it in radically different ways from the audience. Simultaneously, she is privy to facts, to a past, of which we are only dimly aware. Her social development arrested for twenty-nine years, she encounters the events of the play in a way incomprehensible, at least at first, to anyone else onstage or off.

How to tell (and possibly control) time is the issue. The one household item that Davies in *The Caretaker* needs, he tells Mick, is a clock, and in *The Homecoming* Lenny's sleep is disturbed by "some kind of tick." Teddy sympathetically suggests that perhaps Lenny has a clock in his room (p. 41). When he returns home in the final act of *A Night Out*, Albert "violently raises [a clock] above his head," threatening to hurl it at his mother (p. 233); earlier, he has admired the clock in the prostitute's apartment.

The play itself provides a time frame, a past, on which the characters can speculate, and argue. In the final act of *The Birthday Party* Meg romantically recalls that at the party for Stanley in the previous act, the night before, she was the "belle of the ball." Our impressions of Meg at that same party may be very different. In *The Lover*, Sarah tells her husband, who doubles as her lover Max, that when she is with Max she retains a picture in her memory of her husband from the previous scene, that this recollection of the play's own immediate past makes her lovemaking more "piquant" (p. 165). Identifying herself as Hornby's wife at one moment, the next moment Pauline tells her sister that she is a widow, that, in effect, the man standing before her is Deborah's physician but not her husband.

Against this past, however, stands the "now" of the play, its theatrical presence: actors playing characters are speaking and moving about onstage, in time and in a definite space, and being witnessed, ratified by an audience offstage. And since the play's characters and events are illusions, fictive, even as the past referred to during the play is outside the immediate experience in the theater, this *now* or *presence* is, paradoxically, real, the one thing about the performance of which we can be sure. Given meaning by the context of the past, the stage's present tense, on its own terms, is simultaneously real and without larger meaning. However redundant the phrase, Max's basic advice in *The Homecoming* is to "live in the present" (p. 66). In *A Kind of Alaska*, Deborah, who has been caught in the past and, no less, removed from the present, can still feel upon awakening that "something is happening" (p. 5). Calling himself a poet, Spooner in *No Man's Land* claims that he is interested in "where I am eternally present and active" (p. 20), yet at the end he himself will be challenged by the unchanging presence, the *No Man's Land* of Hirst's house, a presence so internal, so rigid that the guest is denied entrance. Spooner's pleas, his offer to be a servant in this dead and present world are dismissed by Foster as reeking of the past, as the "previous subject" which, once open, is now closed, "forgotten" like yesterday's news.

Nor does this theatrical presence admit the future, or much of the future. Lenny alone uses the optative case—and then only once—when in *The Homecoming* he imagines that if he had been a soldier then at some distant date he would "have found" himself in Venice (p. 46). Len anticipates a future when *The Dwarfs* leave, when "all is bare. All is clear.—There is a shrub. There is a flower" (p. 147). Curiously, this blissful future is couched in present, rather than future, tense verbs.

Albeit to varying degrees of intensity, not to mention success, the characters are all fashioners of the past and present, artists taking material, from past or present, contested or agreed upon, weaving it into a pattern, and devising a scenario that passes for "fact" or the truth, motivated as they are by inner, private needs which they sometimes understand, at other times do not. This is why, I think, the figure of the artist, or the fashioner who makes fictions out of facts, looms so large in the plays. In *The Dwarfs* Mark is an actor, although Lenny, perhaps out of jealously, has a somewhat reductive opinion of the profession: "It is a time-honored profession—it's time honored. (Pause.) But what does it do?" (p. 96). Richard in *The Lover* is an actor—literally or figuratively, depending on one's perspective—who plays his wife's lover. Beth in *Landscape* is a painter, the subject for one of her portraits being a woman naked under a robe, with a man sitting in the background. She also experiences the frustrations of an artist. Her lover takes her to a desolate place so that she could "draw in peace," but once she has brought out her sketchbook and pencil, she finds there is "nothing to draw. Only the beach, the sun" (p. 186). Later Beth enumerates the "basic principles" of the profession, focusing on the relationship between object and shadow: "objects intercepting the light cast shadows. Shadow is deprivation of light. The shape of the shadow is determined by that of the object. But not always. Not always directly. Sometimes it is only indirectly affected by it. Sometimes the cause of the shadow cannot be found" (p. 196). Casey, a rival to both Jerry and Robert for Emma's love in *Betrayal*, is a writer, and even Stanley in *The Birthday Party* boasts of a career as a concert pianist. However, the unimaginative Petey in that same play brands a theatrical production at the Palace as a "show" where they "just talk." For the equally unimaginative, albeit desired, Sally in *Night School* Mozart and Brahms are little more than "that kind of stuff" (p. 219).

Behind these specific references to the theatre and to the world of art and music outside the confines of the play, there is a more profound, and also more subtle consideration of the creative process. Against their sterile present relationship, Emma in *The Betrayal* recalls how she and Jerry used their "imagination" in "the old days" (p. 53). In *The Lover*, of course, Richard and Sarah fabricate, with a mutual compliance, secondary roles, characters that counterbalance their stereotypical roles as the passionless couple of the English drawing-room comedy. In fact, their involvement in acting becomes so intense that Richard asks the (almost) impossible when he proposes that each be "utterly frank" with the other (p. 168). In *The Homecoming* it is often unclear just when the stories Lenny tells, such as beating the prostitute by the docks or of helping the old lady, are true, or whether they are conscious or unconscious fabrications.

Little wonder such artists and actors display a special addiction to language, the tools of the playwright. Stanley's most potent word in *The Birthday Party* is "succulent" (p. 27); Bill in *The Collection* employs "scrumptious" as one would a sharp instrument (p. 134). In *The Lover* "arrangement" is the couple's operative word (p. 193), the agreed-upon synonym for their role-playing, for the play of adultery they mutually fashion. Spooner in *No Man's Land* goes so far as to say that "all that England has is its language." The Officer in *Mountain Language* cites the official decree that since the language of the country people is "dead," they are forbidden to speak it; later the Guard in the scene "Visiting Room" announces that the rules have been changed, that the Woman can now speak "her own language" (p. 43). For two pages of dialogue (pp. 141–42), the hoods in *The Dumb Waiter* argue over the precise relationship between language and action: Does one "light the kettle" or "the gas"? After James in *The Collection* announces he is tired of words, he proposes instead a mock duel with Bill. Stanley's punishment in the final act of *The Birthday Party* is to lose his language: in his last appearance he is reduced to a baby's inarticulate sounds (p. 93).

Using language is equated with game playing. Tiring of his role in *The Lover*, Richard, as Max, announces he has played his "last game." A persuasive reading of *The Homecoming* holds that Max and his family are all playing a game, a con act, for their society as well as their audience, in which blue-collar crooks, whose professions range from con artist to pimp, pose as a respectable, middle-class family, with decent jobs—a charade that Ruth's arrival exposes and from which Teddy rightly shrinks. Lenny defines this acting game, this imposing of a impressive illusion on a shabby reality, as something transpiring in the "land of no holds barred" (p. 80). In *The Dwarfs* Mark, an actor, accuses Pete of playing "a double game," one in which his seeming friend has been "leading [him] up the garden" (p. 116). Davies in *The Caretaker* similarly charges Mick with "playing [him] about" (p. 56). Unable to play this game of language, caught in his own isolated world, Len is advised by Pete in *The Dwarfs* to be more "elastic" (p. 100). At the end of *The Lover* Richard begs Sarah to "change" their game, to play wife and lover simultaneously by becoming his "lovely whore" (p. 196).

A serious game, a play by Pinter for and with the audience, in turn encloses the characters' world of game-playing, where characters, comically or tragically, play with or against each other. In such a doubly charged world, everything, even the most commonplace or literal object becomes more than itself, part of the world of perception and fashioning, both for oneself and one's audience. In *The Lover* it is the high-heeled shoes, normally worn only on formal evening occasions, that Sarah wears solely for the afternoon tyrsts with her lover Max. When Richard becomes more like his rival character, the change is signaled by his playing the drum that the lovers used during the afternoons. *The Homecoming* opens with a violent argument between father and son over the scissors that Max needs to cut items out of the evening paper. Later in that play, the courtship between Lenny and Ruth revolves around a glass of water. Disson's focus during his sexual taunting of the secretary Wendy is on a lighter that, like a football, he keeps out of her grasp. And when language breaks down in *The Basement*, the two men express their rivalry by hurling marbles at each other. In *A Kind of Alaska* Deborah's most graphic hold on the past is the memory of her father playing with "balloons." And the crisis in *Trouble in the Works* revolves around the workers' dislike of the product they manufacture.

As in *Old Times*, furniture, in particular, plays a decisive "role" in these highly charged worlds. In *Night School* Annie's suggestion that Walter sleep in the "put-u-up," since his former bedroom is now occupied, proves especially threatening. He insists that he be allowed to sleep in his own bed, since he "bought it," even arguing that the bed was the reason why his Aunt Grace, who was "the only person who ever slept" on it, "went to America" (p. 215). The serving hatch, ominously stationed between the twin beds located at the ends of the stage, stands oddly unused for the opening half of *The Dumb Waiter*, and, since nothing on stage, no part of the set, is irrelevant, can remain unused, we know that at some point the hatch will figure as a "character" in the performance. Kidd in *The Room* challenges Rose's neurotic hold on her apartment with the mere speculation that the rocking chair may have been already there when she first moved in.

Even food and drink plays a "role." In *The Birthday Party* Goldberg's romantic portrait of his mother, a counterpoint to Meg's relationship with Stanley, is built on memories of her making gefiltefish and pancakes, and serving her boy hot milk. Meg makes a fuss over the fried bread, cornflakes, and tea she serves Petey and then Stanley for breakfast. *The Dumb Waiter*, of course, revolves around demands for complex exotic meals sent from above, via the dumb waiter, to Ben and Gus, who are cursed with meager and very commonplace supplies. Edward's manhood, to be questioned later in the play when the couple interacts with the silent Matchseller, is asserted in ridiculous fashion by his strategy for dealing with a wasp stuck in the pot of marmalade. In *The Collection* James's predilection for olives is first a bone of contention and later a sign of affection between Bill and himself, while the "arrangement" between Richard and Sarah in *The Lover* begins to crumble when, tired from an afternoon of love-making with Max, the wife fails to have dinner ready for her husband when he returns from a hard day at the office. Angered by Richard's jealously and hence by his inability to separate the roles of husband and lover, Sarah taunts him with the "news" that, while he is at work, she entertains numerous lovers, including strangers, offering them "strawberries in season" and cream. They come, she claims, on the pretext of seeing the hollyhocks, but "then they stay for tea" (p. 193). The "interlude" between Richard's departure and Max's arrival involves one John who comes to deliver some cream. Later to be excluded from the sealed, dead world of *No Man's Land*, Spooner is tricked into believing that he has been accepted when Briggs offers him the untasted breakfast that had been prepared for Hirst's financial adviser.

Along with location, the intruder, perception, and the imagination, gender is a pervasive issue in Pinter's worlds. At times as a defense from women, or as an attempt to return to some idyllic, often revisionist past, men in Pinter seek to bond with their fellows or to return to the nonsexual days of their childhood. In his uneasy marriage to Flora, Edward in *A Slight Ache* calls up boyhood memories of playing cricket, and in *The Birthday Party*

Goldberg asks what has "happened to the love, the bonhomie, the unashamed expression of affection of the day before yesterday," of that boyhood where the only important women were "our mums" (p. 66). McCann fondly remembers "one time" when he "stayed all night with the boys. Singing and drinking all night." He even identifies the bar as Mother Nolan's in Roscrea (p. 70). In *A Night Out* that all-male bar is the transitional place between Albert's time at home with his mother and the aborted evening with the prostitute, posing as a mother. Duff in *Landscape* also recounts his time spent in a bar, where he challenged a fellow drinker with his own knowledge of the proper way to brew beer. For Jerry in *Betrayal* the times spent "with a fellow in a pub" or "playing squash with one's buddy" are practically sacred occasions, not understood by women; in *No Man's Land* Spooner has met Hirst in a pub. And while he delights in putting down his brother, Max in *The Homecoming* revels in memories of the days the two brothers went to bars or bet on the horses.

In a world complicated by women, the men also cling to what they think is certain. Len in *The Dwarfs* likes calculus, the science of "mechanics and determinants" (p. 98). Pete in *The Dwarfs* cherishes a "good table and a good chair" because they are "solid stuff," and he envisions buying such furniture for a houseboat on which he and Len would sail down a river. Even if they had to park the boat, there would be "not a soul in sight" (p. 100). Spooner in *No Man's Land* distinguishes himself from weaker men who "inhabit the idea and not the fact" (p. 16). Pete in *The Dwarfs*, while acknowledging that "thinking got [him] into" his present predicament, insists that "thinking's got to get me out" (p. 105).

Just as often, men fantasize about a role or a profession that confers status on them. In *A Night Out* Albert lies to the Girl that he is an assistant director for a movie company (p. 237), and Edward in *A Slight Ache* tries to impress the Matchseller with a sophisticated knowledge of mixed drinks (p. 85). He confesses to a black period in his life, during which he conducted a long struggle "against all kinds of usurpers, disreputables, lists, literally lists of people anxious to do [him] down, and [his] reputation down," but now, he insists, his "command [has been re-]established" (pp. 195–96). Miming a telescope, Edward imagines himself watching from a cliff "the progress of the three-masted schooner" (p. 196).

Women are often vital to such image building. Though his double Max, Richard asserts his ideal of the physical man, "his

whole body," in Sarah's word, "emanat[ing] love" (p. 172). Aware
of his loss of virility, Bates in *Silence* insists that he is still
"strong," although not "as strong as the bastards in the other
room," whose women he defensively brands as "tittering
bitches" (p. 204). Boasting about his own wife, who will ironically later be revealed as a whore, Max in *The Homecoming*
elevates himself above his brother when he asks Sam why he
never got married. As Max, Richard in *The Lover* prefers his
mistress to meet his own specifications, which favor plumpness
over thinness. Fearing that she will keep him from a bedroom
he claims as own, Walter in *Night School* tries to polish his
battered self-image by having Sally cross and uncross her legs at
his command. His need is that she be at once compliant and
innocent, and the photo of her he treasures is not the one taken
at a nightclub but rather of her at school, holding a net ball
surrounded by her female classmates. In *The Homecoming* the
men need Ruth to play whatever role meets their needs at the
moment—a wife, mother, whore, or business partner. Max's one
fear is that Ruth will not be "adaptable" (p. 97) to such needs.
What bonds Law and Stott, who are increasingly rivals for Jane
in *The Basement,* is that she has betrayed each of them in turn
(p. 166). Men also assert themselves, fashion their self image, by
sexual conquests, whether it be Goldberg who during his youth
"never took liberties" but does now with the youthful Lulu during Stanley's birthday party (p. 53), or Stanley himself who, at
the end of act 2, is seen bending over Lulu, who is spread-eagled
on the table.

   This need for conquest is at other times sublimated by men's
interest in sports. Gus and Ben in *The Dumb Waiter* argue over
soccer games, about a "disputed penalty" (p. 173), and about
which team was playing in its hometown. Max in *The Homecoming* defines boxing as "a gentleman's game" (p. 33); his redundant
advice to his son Joey, who is a boxer, is that "you've got to learn
how to defend yourself, and you've got to learn how to attack"
(p. 33). Disson and his rival Willy play a tense game of ping-
pong in *The Tea Party,* which is watched by Disson's twins. In
The Basement Stott and Law challenge each other's manhood in
a footrace, whose start is signaled when Jane waves a scarf.

   The mother, as a figure alternately comforting and threatening
the man, looms large in Pinter. Voice 2, the mother in *Family
Voices,* tries to impose her concept of a wife and a proper home
on Voice 1, her son, while Mrs. Withers becomes the surrogate

mother at the boarding house to her "pet" (p. 72). The mother in
A Night Out, who opposes Albert's leaving her house for the
"unclean life" outside the home (p. 207), is later physically
threatened by him when he returns after an abortive evening
spent a party where he was accused of making an improper sexual advance on one of the guests. On the way home, Albert had
stopped by at the apartment of a prostitute who tried to pass off
a girlhood picture of herself as that of her daughter. When Albert
returns repentant, his mother's "reproach turns to solicitude,"
and after taking a chair and sitting next to him, she "strokes his
head" comforting him with "It's not as if you're a bad boy . . .
you're a good boy . . . I know you are" (p. 247). At one moment
Max in *The Homecoming* sees Jessie, the mother of his three
sons, as a saint, at another moment as a "slutbitch of a wife" (p.
63). Now married to an American college professor, but soon to
return to her old life as a prostitute, this time financed by the
family, Ruth will take Jesse's place. At one point, her new "son"
Joe spends two hours upstairs in the bedroom with her, being
sexually teased but stopping short of actual intercourse. The two
aunts in *Night School* function as Walter's mothers, and he is,
fittingly, the "apple" of their eyes. Eager to get vengeance on the
doctor who hurt him, Aston in *The Caretaker* tells Davies that
he was hospitalized with his mother's permission. Meg clearly
wants to be Stanley's second mother in *The Birthday Party*, and
the drum she gives him as a present, though he will later put it
to violent uses, is a blatant attempt to buy his affection with a
childhood toy. Even as she challenges his manhood by her flirta-
tion with the Matchseller, Flora adopts a mothering attitude toward Edward.

The father figures in Pinter are alternately more distant or assertive. In *Family Voices* the father speaks from a "glassy grave"
(p. 87), and the Mother in *A Night Out* can do little more than
assure Albert that his dead father, who for her is still "living in"
the house, would turn in his grave if he knew of the son's plans
for the evening. Meg in *The Birthday Party* recalls that it was
her father who bought her first dress, and while the silent and
then mostly absent Petey in that same play appears to decline
the role of father in the first act, by act 3 he shows a fatherly-like
concern for Stanley, who enters the stage reduced to childlike
incoherence. Max in *The Homecoming*, who has troubles enough
as father to his three sons, recalls his own father, whose profession was that of a butcher, tossing him up in the air when he
was a small child, and catching him "coming down" (p. 35). In

Silence the older man, Rumsey, serves as both a lover and, later in life, a father to Beth, while even the younger, cruder Bates speaks of his own little girl. Sharing a cup of cocoa with him and tutoring him in religious matters, the sinister figure Riley in *Family Voices* is both a father figure to Voice 1, as well as a potential lover.

However fashioned by men, or seemingly fashioned by them, the women in Pinter often have an inner self, one of "wild sensuality" as Bill calls it in *The Collection*, that remains beyond the men's control, even as it intrigues them (p. 151). Classified as "all the same" by misogynists like Albert in *A Night Out*, sexually harassed by men, as is the secretary Wendy by her former boss in *The Tea Party*, the women can endure, even triumph. At the end of that play Wendy is an intimate with Disson's wife and brother in the office next door, while Disson, who had once sexually threatened Wendy but is now a defeated man, and moments away from total blindness, stands alone in an adjacent room. In *A Night Out* Eileen and Joyce take it upon themselves to "cheer up old Albert" (p. 223), whose problems with women pervade the play. Davies in *The Caretaker* recalls a woman who, incredulously (from his perspective), tried to seduce him. Compared to her bookish husband who is reluctant to step outside his living room, Flora is surely superior to Edward. Likewise, Beth is the stronger character in *Landscape* and her otherwise simplistic, romantic line that ends the play, "Oh my true love I said" (p. 198), reflects a depth of passion beyond the reach of her insensitive husband, Duff. Ellen in *Silence* floats free, at length, of the claims, sexual and fatherly, of Bates and Rumsey: "I walk in the wind to collide with them waiting" (p. 218). In *The Homecoming* Ruth is an intruder who not only survives but dictates to the men the precise terms of that survival.

These portraits of strong women are especially decisive, even comically so at the expense of the men, in Pinter's revue sketches. In *Special Offer* the Secretary tells of an old woman she met in the rest room who offers men for sale, with reduced rates for women employees of the BBC! The employer, Miss Piffs, in *The Applicant* directs a barrage of harsh questions to the applicant, Mr. Lamb, first attaching electrodes to his body, and then inquiring about his sexual life and his attitude toward women. "Do women frighten you?" she demands as she offers a list of potential female threats, ranging from their way of walking to their thighs. Lamb is dismissed with the noncomittal, "Thank you very much, Mr. Lamb. We'll let you know" (p. 234). Mr. Jakes, the pornographer in *The Interview*, is satirized as an amoral businessman who hypocritically despises his male clients, even as he caters to their lusts. Lamenting the fact that his trade takes "a bit of a bashing around Xmas time," he brands his clients as "all the same, every single one of them, COMMUNISTS" (p. 237).

Little wonder that sexuality in Pinter is so diverse. Flora, in *A Slight Ache*, recognizes the mutual nature of the act: "Sex is a very vital experience for other people" (p. 192). Sometimes this vital experience can be very romantic, as it is for Beth and her ideal lover in *Landscape*, or for the Man's Voice and Young Woman's Voice in *Mountain Landscape:* "I watch you sleep. And then your eyes open. You look up at me above you and smile. You smile. When my eyes open I see you above me and smile. We are on a lake. It is spring" (p. 39). At other times, it is displaced, or masturbatory, as in Bert's erotic description in *The Room* of driving his van through the snowstorm, or Duff's account in *Landscape* of how to brew beer: "The bung is on the vertical, in the bunghole. Spike the bung. Hammer the spike through the center of the bung. That lets the air through the bung, down the bunghole, lets the beer breathe" (p. 193). In *The Tea Party* there is even a suggestion of incest, when Willy hires his sister, Disson's wife Diana, as his secretary, and later in the play holds something of the prototypical "office party" with Diana and Disson's secretary, Wendy.

In a more general, nonsexual sense, the characters seek another, someone else, a human contact; there are few individuals in Pinter who can relax with, let alone take pleasure in isolation. The lonely woman in *Request Stop* tries, unsuccessfully, to engage others in conversation while they wait for a bus. Whatever his personal motives, Spooner in *No Man's Land* tells Hirst that he needs a friend: "You have a long hike, my lad, up which, presently, you slog unfriended. Let me perhaps be your boatman" (p. 33). Though he will later rue the words, Disson in *The Tea Party* speaks eloquently on the issue of our human "dependence": "To understand the meaning of the term dependence is to understand that one's powers are limited and that to live with others is not only sensible but the only way work can be done and dignity achieved. Nothing is more sterile or lamentable than the man content to live within himself" (p. 113).

At the same time, such dependence can obscure, even eradicate the individual's sense of self. Meg, who exists almost entirely for others, is told cruelly by her Stanley, "Tell me, Mrs. Boles, when you address yourself to me, do you ever ask yourself who exactly you are talking to?" (p. 31). Edward in *A Slight Ache* inquires plaintively of the Matchseller, "Who are you?," and in *The Dwarfs* Len makes the same demand of Mark (p. 111). Bill in *The Collection* finds his own identity threatened by the Voice on the phone claiming to know him: "This is ridiculous. Do I know you" (p. 126).

In *Silence* Ellen speaks of waking to a world that lacks people (p. 214), or any human against whom she might measure herself, and Rumsey admits that, having chosen to live by himself attended only by his farm animals, perhaps now he is not even needed by his horse. Jerry tries to hurt Emma in *The Betrayal* by telling her that now he does not "need to think of [her]" (p. 17). Spooner, in *No Man's Land*, at once boasts and laments his isolation when he tells Hirst that he elicits "indifference" from others.

The instability of names is another way to express this tension between the isolated self and the images of oneself fashioned by the perceiver. In *The Birthday Party* Goldberg is also known as Nat or Simey. In *The Caretaker* it is unclear whether the intruder is to be called Davies or Bernard Jenkins. The landlord in *The Room* is alternately Mr. Kidd or Mr. Hudd; Riley, claiming a special intimacy with Rose, calls her by the name of Sal. The Sally that Walter seeks in *Night School* goes by the name of Katins at the nightclub, and in *No Man's Land* Hirst first addresses Spooner by the name of Denson, while Foster, misunderstanding what Spooner has said about his friendship with Hirst, introduces him to Briggs as "Mr. Friend." Voice 1, the son in *Family Voices*, announces that his adopted family has given him a new name, Bobo.

At length, situated somewhere beyond or beneath all these dimensions of the generic Pinter play, beyond the rooms and intruders, the dialogue and that subtext waiting to be voiced, the relativity of perception and the past that, once refashioned, complicates the present, beyond the parents who both comfort and threaten, and the men and women seeking others while preserving a fragile self image, beyond all of this is silence, epitomized in the plays by Pinter's numerous and prototypical pauses and silences, and in *Old Times* enacted by the mime at the end which, in its own variation, reenacts the mime at the end of Sartre's *No Exit*. Sometimes this silence is that of the intruder, like the Matchseller in *A Slight Ache*, a silence doubly meaningful in the radio version of that work. At other times, it is the silence or near silence of a character onstage, such as Bert in *The Room* or Petey in *The Birthday Party*. The play whose title is itself *Silence*, and where the more customary pauses are replaced by cues for the far less frequent "silence," ends with the simple stage direction, "long silence," after which the lights themselves fade.

Considering these almost generic elements in Pinter's stage worlds, along with the theatrical history of *Old Times*, as well as the play's reception by critics and scholars constituted my own "homework," the preparation I would bring to the production. The next stage, the subject of chapter 3, is the actual preparation for the performance.

3

Preparing for Performance

Concept

THE sense of the play, what it is about, the larger statement it makes, its mood, atmosphere, style, how it might "look" and "sound" to an audience, whatever might be at its core, at its heart, and thereby colors, influences, even determines every other aspect of the production—the "director's concept" is in itself a paradox. The play's foundation, it is also the most perishable, subject to whatever happens during the rehearsal period, and to the minds, no less, the needs of the actors. Subject to the director, those actors are, in a very real sense, his or her collaborators.

Still, knowing that the wonderfully unexpected would happen—that a work like *Old Times*, coming as it does from a playwright who first made his mark as an actor, would more, than most plays, only be realized and shaped during rehearsals and would be *discovered* there; knowing, therefore, that my director's concept would be qualified, questioned, refined on its complex journey from the study to the stage—I nevertheless had a very clear idea of *Old Times*, and of what it might become. And so, deploring a vacuum, I had outlined a concept that, at the very least, would serve as a start, a "text" from which we might begin. For that concept, "dualities" and "triangles" were, perhaps, the most operative words.

Trite as it may be, the play's surface and events are perfectly clear and seemingly peaceful: this evening a sophisticated couple, living in the countryside outside of London, is visited by the wife's friend from her days as a young secretary in London. Here, the action and the dialogue are almost generic. The appropriate foods and refreshments are served: a casserole, coffee, brandy, and later—an addition in our production to underscore the references in act 2 to China and the Cultural Revolution—tea. The conversation, no less generic, embraces happy days of the past, old times, the husband's occupation, the absent husband, and the possibility that the husband has known the friend earlier. Even the evening itself, particularly the events of the first act, becomes a topic of discussion.

Yet pulling at this generic evening, this prototypical home entertainment of the guest, is Pinter's own "weasel underneath the whiskey cabinet," and while during the course of the evening nothing violent, let along sexual happens onstage, we realize that there is something special, momentous, unique, even—to use the two words that critics apply to Pinter—"menacing" and "sinister" going on. Still, this other side of the duality never surfaces, or if it does show itself, the manifestation is private, confined to the idiosyncratic responses of each and every member of the audience. The play, in this sense, is without a resolution, except on the verbal level when Kate in her final speech "kills off" her two rivals.

No less, there is a duality, and hence a tension, between the obvious social conflicts existing in *Old Times*—Deeley's efforts to win Kate from Anna, Anna's counter-strategy, Deeley's and Anna's efforts to possess Kate who in turn resists them—and those inner or psychological tensions that are no less ambiguous than the momentous tensions below the surface of the generic evening. Here the battle, the *psychomachia* in medieval literature, is within individual characters. On this level, *Old Times* approaches, but only approaches, the allegorical.

To some degree, for instance, Anna and Kate may be the twin projections of Deeley's ideal woman, someone at once potent and pliable, sexual and chaste, so that the visit, engineered by Deeley, becomes a wish-fulfillment of oedipal proportions. For Kate, as many have suggested, Anna may be seen as her other half, a self she abandoned in London, a role tried but now rejected. The evening then becomes Kate's dream, a revisiting of the past through Anna in order to reevaluate that past in light of what is a sterile, unfulfilled present with Deeley. Anna, conversely, would be the mother to Kate, trying to return the daughter to the house, the room, the past, and that idyllic period before men, before Deeley, from which Kate has escaped.

The texture of the play, the way it looks and sounds, is itself the product of, and reflects a tension in, the duality between its language and all that is nonverbal, physical, visual, and, in its way, counter to, even hostile to language. By the latter, I mean the numerous pauses and the less numerous but, for that very reason, even more potent silences.

For, on one hand, *Old Times* celebrates even as it abuses language, or stage dialogue. Deeley, in particular, is a self-conscious wordsmith, given to set speeches, to searching, in the midst of a sentence, for just the right word, even to correcting himself. The evening itself is nothing but talk, and hence a battle between its two chief talkers, Deeley and Anna. Deeley is the less subtle combatant, trying on not only language but dialects, from Irish brogues to the slang of American cowboys to the hip talk of the 1970s. Nevertheless, as she reveals in her description of the man who entered their room, or in her speech equating love and the effect of ripples on still water, Anna, too, is a poetess, a crafter of language, so intensely so that she is not above correcting herself when the wrong adverb intrudes in her narrative: "No, no I'm quite wrong . . . he didn't move quickly . . . that's quite wrong . . . he moved . . . very slowly." Language is the battleground, not only in the larger sense as characters offer competing scenarios of the past, which, by definition, can only be a recreation through language, but in seemingly smaller ways, as a weapon, as when Kate challenges Deeley's vague use of the word "friend" or Deeley questions Anna's use of such old-fashioned terms as "lest." Metadramatically, the atmosphere here is that of an audition, where Deeley and Anna tryout for Kate's approval, or or a party where rival playwrights have been thrust into the same room. Characters fight for the possession of words like "gaze" or "casserole" or phrases such as "best and only," coming to blows over the prepositions "in" or "out," as in the conversation about how and where one dries someone who has just bathed. Like a play by Oscar Wilde or a musical by Noel Coward, Old Times thrives on the word, the adroit phrase, the manipulations of style, even of grammar.

Yet, pulling against this is the play's subtext, and its moments—the pauses and silences—when language ceases or, brilliant as the characters' command of words may be, proves inadequate. In one way, the pauses reflect such moments, in any conversation, when someone hesitates before speaking, perhaps because he or she has been caught off-guard by a remark, or momentarily forgets what he or she was going to say, or, having heard something unexpected or that gave the conversation a new twist, needs time to rephrase, even to reevaluate an intended response. Likewise, the silences mark periods when conversation comes to a dead stop because a topic has been exhausted, or because somebody has just said something so devastating that fellow conversants become mute out of shock or anger.

Further, in Old Times these same pauses and silences often

resist such purely rational, normal, or "social" explanations. Some silences seem to indicate that time has passed, perhaps a half hour, even more, between the sections of conversation on either side. Such distortions of time, in a play that otherwise seems confined to a single evening, appear at one with the way in which the past itself—that of the young secretaries in London twenty years ago, and, increasingly, a potential past in which Deeley, who has known Anna and Kate, was the man in the room—is not a distinct entity, something that has "happened" and is no more. This same past threatens the "presence" of the stage action, of the play transpiring in time and space before the audience who simultaneously witness it with their eyes and ears, who occupy the same "room" (the house) as the actors.

Such distortion of time, or theatrical presence, is especially blatant when, once in each act, Kate and Anna revert to discussing topics—whether or not to go out to the park, what to do in the flat, what to wear, what man or men to invite over—that would only have been relevant in the past, as if they were actually still in London twenty years ago. At such moments when Deeley is present on stage but excluded from the conversation despite efforts on his part, *Old Times*, in its flashbacks, adopts the techniques of the cinema (such as *The French Lieutenant's Woman* for which Pinter wrote the script) rather than the stage.

Moreover, it is through silence, the mime at the end of act 2, that Kate's revised reading of an event, which in effect displaces Anna's or Anna's as interpreted by Deeley, so usurps the present that dialogue itself gives way to tableau. The mime itself is reminiscent of the concluding action without dialogue from one of Pinter's "sources," Sartre's *No Exit* that predates *Old Times* by some fifteen years.

Deeley's own "Now what the hell does she mean by that?" itself signals the other force joining with pauses and silences and thereby pulling against the dialogue. For in *Old Times* there looms a subtext, all the things a character is thinking or feeling, consciously and unconsciously, that remain unheard but, nevertheless, influence what he or she does say, and the way in which the actor delivers the text or dialogue as written. This subtext is itself an intruder, a kind of dialogue not fully under the control of the character, that lends depth to, and, at certain moments, threatens to break the surface of what the character is actually saying. More than with most plays, this subtext needs to be rehearsed, to be voiced in rehearsal and then, properly, to be restored to its proper place, out of sight, but hardly out of mind.

In this way, *Old Times* is simultaneously charitable and stingy, giving us, whether actor, director, or audience, all that we need to know, or can know, and at the same time holding back on us, suppressing most of the facts, most of the feelings. The play does this in the same way that real people, under the restraints of a social occasion, such as the visit by an old friend, hide their feelings, consciously or unconsciously hold back things that need to be said, or disguise emotions under the euphemisms and jargon of the cocktail party.

Sandra Langsner, the actress who played Anna, suggested that we "might as well stage the production in someone's living room," that the play was intimate, "real" in the sense that it perfectly duplicated the talk and, through its pauses and silences, the rhythms of social entertainment. Hence the mood would be that of the audience as fellow guests in the country house of Deeley and Kate, gathered on the peripheries of a handsome, well-appointed living room where, toward the center of that room, Pinter's three characters, overheard by the other "guests," conducted their conversations. At one with this sense of realism and intimacy is the fact that I very much wanted the audience to play a "role," to struggle, as the characters themselves struggle, both between (as well as among) themselves, and, in the case of Deeley and Anna, within themselves. We, too, would have to ask with Deeley, "What the hell does she mean by that?"

I think this sense of tension, born of dualities whose competing halves exist not on parallel (as would normally be the case) but incompatible levels, is something beyond what we usually mean by conflict in the theater. Conflict implies the clash of radically different world views, or political or social principles, or a clash of perspectives and reactions to a single event or (in the case of, say, Ibsen) an event that has occurred before the play proper. Nor do I think it is enough to say that the tension here is artificial, a mere strategy on Pinter's part, as has been charged, to engender "an evening of theater," or "provide an excuse for" the playwright's admittedly clever dialogue. Rather, the tension in *Old Times* is justified by the larger issues it alludes to or *seems* to invoke; that is, the conflict of genders, of memory, of past with present, of the self (as vested in Kate) with the demands made, the feeling of possession generated by the world outside that self. But take such "issues" too far and, I think, *Old Times* acquires a philosophic weight that will prove reductive. While he can be alternately coy or irritable during interviews, sometimes with just cause, perhaps at other times without, Pinter speaks revealingly about this obscure "heart" of *Old Times* when he says, "It happens. It just happens."

Given my own concept, I wanted our production likewise "to happen," to be as close as possible to a real-life social evening, at once as shallow and as profound, even beyond the conscious intent of the participants, as such an evening can be. And if that evening with Deeley and Kate was to work, everything needed to be done with restraint: no heavy breathing on the word "gaze" (even when it occurs seven times within a single speech), no dramatic pauses when Anna informs Deeley she lives on a "volcano." We simply overhear them talking, and they are all "on," the way all of us, at a cocktail party, put on our "party selves." Yet even though the evening should be merely social, an entertainment, the needs of the characters, resting just below the banter, the songs, and the routines (such as lighting the guest's cigarette or serving coffee), would intrude, providing ripples for the dialogue and clinging to words otherwise more innocent, even banal. Listening intently to each other's conversation, aware of their competition through memory and its midwife language, both Deeley and Anna know that their success—against each other end, as they foolishly imagine, with Kate—depends on their ability to "read" the other better, more quickly than he or she can.

Still, if they hang on Kate's every word, it is nevertheless Kate who proves most difficult, for her rivals as well as the audience. For until her "bath" speech in act 2, she hardly says a word, and what words she does say are, apparently, trite, simple, or so diffuse that interpreting them seems futile. However, I think that ultimately Kate represents this more complex half, the hidden or ambiguous half of the various dualities discussed so far—all that remains unsaid, silent, or said in a way that suggests a subtext, something only partially formed or literate, rather than a text, or such social conversation as invites dialogue. In Kate's final, extraordinary speech, a speech that literally ends the verbal, though not the visual part of the play, this other half emerges, brilliantly. Then, and only then, *Old Times* can complete itself, can cease to happen.

All these dualities, and more that for the present go unvoiced, are contained within two triangles: one of the set (to be discussed in a subsequent section of this chapter); the other anticipated in the title of the movie, *Odd Man Out*, thrice invoked in the play, at which Deeley claims to have picked up Kate and to which

Anna claims to have taken her. The title itself implies an odd number—in the movie James Mason is the fifth man, who falls out of the car. An odd number exists in tension, and thereby constitutes a dualism with even numbers such as two. More immediately, that number is here three, the very three characters who comprise the cast of *Old Times*, who, like the three angles of a triangle, define the play as the boundaries of its world. From the perspective of Deeley and Anna, only one of them can, and will, win; only one can have Kate, even if Deeley, momentarily at the beginning of act 2, appears to propose a *menage à trois*. Two will form a couple, so each reasons, and the third will be excluded and will become the odd man. But the numbers and even the phrase "odd man" work in a way Deeley and Anna never imagine, and this, in the old-fashioned sense of the word, is the basis of the "suspense" (or surprise, or shock) of *Old Times*. For instead of collapsing from a trinity to a couple, from three to two, the play at its end becomes Kate's when she emerges as the "odd man out," the single soul, free of her rivals, on her own, having established her own identity now independent of friend or husband.

These three operative numbers—one, two three—were at the heart of my concept of the three characters. In one way, the sum of each personality reflects a single, unique individual, someone seeing himself or herself in league with, as a partner of, as a rival to, or in light of, even as defined or validated by a second person. In another way, each character is part of an evening, both social and theatraical, bounded by that self and two others. I should add that my concept of each character, which I shared at once with my actors, drew from what I took to be their own emerging conception of their role. Developed with them during the period of rehearsals, this sense of the characters reflected the tension between dependence and independence in Anna, Deeley, and Kate. Late in the rehearsal period I tried to sum up these concepts of the three characters in a note to each of the actors, and here I, essentially, transcribe and at times refine what I said there.

Anna is the dominating woman, but in the best-intentioned, most nurturing, "motherly" sense of the word. She is the one who goes outside to experience the world and then bring that experience home to what she takes to be a more innocent daughter. In a play without villains, Anna is possessive to a fault, yet her dominance is inseparable from her strength and hence her appeal. Thus, she has a deep attraction to her "other," her opposite or—perhaps to be more accurate—her "complement" in

Kate. She envies in Kate what she does not find, or has erased in herself: shyness and, no less, what she assumes in a pleasure in being dependent. If Anna misreads Kate, she does so inevitably because she fashions someone who cannot be or cannot exist for long, someone representing not a real person but Anna's own ideal. If there was, if there is a bond between the two women, it is predicated, therefore, as much on difference as any similarities.

In a cruel sense, Anna, while a sophisticated, liberated woman of the world, who, instead of retreating to the country, stayed longer in London and then married a cultured European, is also "arrested" in her developoment. She longs to go back to an earlier time, an earlier stage that, she will realize at the end, is infantile, a transition or prerequisite to those subsequent stages of adulthood and independence. This sense of being arrested is at one with the pleasure Anna takes in the room, in its confines, for as much as she likes to go outdoors, enjoys all the attractions of a city like London, and even takes pride in having introduced Kate to the world of museums, concerts, and cafes, ultimately she most enjoys going back into the room, shutting out the world, being there alone with Kate, her ideal, her daughter. (All this, of course, from a playwright whose first major work for the stage was titled The Room.) This pleasure in the room is related to the sense we have that Anna is an "internal" person, one for whom "essence" is more important than existence. She is all that is below the surface, deep, all that is hidden from the public world in the nice warm room that she cherishes. For her, London, the public world of the city, is a foil for this internal self.

If the stereotype holds that the male goes out, while the woman stays in—this is clearly Deeley's bias—then Anna, unwittingly, sustains or refashions this bias. She prefers women to men, the world of women to that of men. Yet to speak of this preference as evidence of any lesbianism is, I think, to reduce the play, to impoverish it, and Pinter's own objection to this label for the relationship between Anne and Kate needs to be considered seriously. Rather, Anna's attraction to Kate, to the world of women, stems from her arrested state, from wanting to remain in, or return to that time in a young girl's development when her attraction is more to her own sex. This is something going far beyond an issue of sexuality. Anna is married, to be sure, and while Deeley's curiosity about her husband and his absence probably reveal more about him than Anna's marital status, the fact is that Anna's husband is absent, is not a character in the play, and that Anna arrives not with her husband, as would normally be the case, but alone. Her expressed purpose is seeing her friend Kate, "to celebrate a very old and treasured friendship," something that was forged between the two women "long before" Deeley "knew of [their] existence."

Yet, Anna is not unlike Deeley; indeed, they may even have been lovers in the past. Like Deeley, she builds scenarios, though in her case these scenarios are based on actual, albeit past events, or—at the very least—from Anna's own intensely private interpretations of those events. For her, as for Deeley, words, language, and dialogue are avenues to the past, to her essence, to what is internal. As a result, Anna is not especially interested in words as they serve, or refer to the external reality, or to the present world actually before us. Thus, even when she speaks with a sense of detail worthy of a tourist book of the various attractions of London, she refers less to the actual events or structures, to concert or the musuem, than to the essence, the meaning of the thing. Also like Deeley, she is the actress, aware of her performance, as in the present she tries to shape the past and thereby allow it to usurp that present, literally, Kate's marriage to Deeley. Like the hero of some Elizabethan revenge play, she is a playwright and an actor, attempting to nullify what she takes as a present insult—Deeley's marriage to, his possession of Kate—by recreating it, and in that theatrical recreation rearranging the role: by marriage to Kate, Deeley made Anna the odd man out, and so now Anna will recast that performance by changing roles with Deeley. In a sense, she can see part of herself in Deeley, for he, too (although with a different style and for different reasons) is also an actor, or a shaper of the past. "It takes one to know one," as the old saying has it, and as much as Anna opposes Deeley, even despises him, she is "attracted" to him in the way that a rival actor respects the skills of, the choice in career of someone competing for the same part.

For his part, Deeley senses, and does his best to deny, a feeling of inadequacy. If his boasts of sexual conquests are patently defensive, this inadequacy is not fully, or even ultimately sexual. Rather, it has something to do with his professed occupation, although it is also not fully explained in light of it. What Deeley claims to do and what he actually does may be at odds: we suspect, possibly, that he is a director of B-grade documentaries, or, in our day, made-for-television films. Perhaps his inadequacy has a less definite source, or sources. Like Anna, Deeley may be arrested, caught at the stage of being a little boy in his father's company, or in that all-male, nonsexual world "before women." Or his neurosis may stem from the fact that he is unlike others, unlike other men, and thus encompasses both a sense of superiority and inferiority. More immediately, Deeley, like the audience, may sense that something is wrong in his marriage, that Kate holds an opinion of him that varies from his own self-image, and this fact, unnerving Deeley, drives him to assert a wounded male ego.

Deeley is not a villain; what he does, to both Kate and their guest, not to mention his desperate attempts to flaunt a positive self image, all stems from a sense of being different or rejected, or incompetent: feelings real or imagined or (more likely) both. These are very human emotions. Indeed, perhaps it was this lack of confidence, this "male weakness" as Deeley might presently define it in other men, that once appealed to Kate, that is the "sensitive" quality she once found attractive in him. Thus, Deeley's self-posturing during the evening, his self-portrait as a confident, sexually active, important man-of-the-world is especially grating to his wife. And yet when this same posturing is exposed at the end of the play by Kate's monologue, Deeley, in a curious way, is allowed to "return" to his wife, like a child chastised and returning to his mother.

There is a split, therefore, between the well-spoken, polite host, and the passionate, frustrated man inside. Deeley wrestles with this second half of his character, alternately aware and unaware of it, trying to keep it under wraps, but being less successful in doing so than he imagines. In a way, Deeley embodies a strange combination of Anna's London sophistication and Kate's private side.

As with Anna, he also has a problem with genders, and if he did not "need" a woman to bolster his sense of self, he would— beyond his conscious recognition—prefer to be without women and among men who "spoke their mind." He longs for that even earlier world he knew with his father, when they bought a tricycle, in fact, the "only tricycle [Deeley] ever possessed," on the same street where the theater showing Odd Man Out was located. Perhaps Deeley's lashing out at men "with stinking breath" is a defensive posture against this very desire to free himself of women, to be again with "old [male] friends." As with Anna, the issue is not homosexuality.

Also, like Anna, Deeley takes pleasure in being confined in a room with Kate, for despite his claim that he goes about the globe, he delights in the home, in its security, its removal from the very people who have perhaps not given him the approval he has sought. Anyone's entrance into that home, Anna's especially, is therefore threatening, for Deeley needs a private world that he can control.

And if that private world is threatened, as it is this evening in the form of a cosmopolitan woman married to a cultured Sicilian, Deeley resorts to even more private scenarios, to wish-fulfillments—cafés and parties where, despite the crowd, he tries to be alone with a woman, or a cinema which, except for Kate and two anonymous usherettes, is otherwise deserted. Like the filmmaker he claims to be, he tries to seduce others into these private scenarios; the problem is that others are not always willing.

If he proves no match for Anna in her powers of narration, in the reconstruction of the past, Deeley is, nevertheless, very potent: his tale about seeing *Odd Man Out* surely equals Anna's account of the man in the secretaries' room. For Deeley, then, life, the present is a film script, a matter of perception, something to be fashioned as one sees fit or—to be more accurate—as one thinks if "fit" for all others. As a consequence, Deeley, almost tragically, confuses such self-perception for the facts, even for the *truth*.

As opposed to Anna, however, he does trade more in the present, the world of facts, valuing what is definite, clear, logical. In the simplest of equations, and reflecting his own chauvinism, he is a male, a left-brain person; Anna, a female, is a right-brain person—even though this chauvinistic dichotomy, like all dichotomies, oversimplifies the issue. Defending what he sees as reality, a world that accommodates woman but is not governed by them, this warrior, this male, uses language as a weapon. Words are pens, surrogate penises, and, while abusing and distorting language himself, he jealously guards his preserve: Anna is chastised for using words out of date. Yet like Anna, Deeley is an artist; like her, and until Kate's final speech, he imagines that these two rival artists, these two performers, play and compete for their audience of one. There is a bond, therefore, between Deeley and Anna; they can appreciate each other's talents.

During rehearsals I would raise the possibility that Kate's mission in the play, or what actors call her "object," is to find herself, a self that, while indebted to those offered by Anna and Deeley, is still her own. When she finds this self, whatever the cost, then she can be free. This does not mean that she will divorce Deeley, or even forget Anna, but rather, in becoming her own person—

in the fullest sense of the abused phrase—she will radically alter her relationship with them, finding her deepest self, one that has been there all the time, that is present from the very start of the play, a subtextual person, in a way, making its way to the surface. Kate is Pinter's "surprise" that, upon reflection, is no surprise at all. This means that for most of the play Kate speaks in her silence, with a paucity of words, even through clichés.

The evening, the play itself, even the conversations between Anna and Deeley, may be construed as Kate's dream. Rather than being a passive audience to their verbal battles, Kate is their creator, staging a play in which one man and one woman battle for her affection, whereas all the time Kate is observing her creations, testing them, weighing the competing claims of husband and friend, of these two lovers. Just as Beckett is reported to have said, "If I knew who Godot was, I wouldn't have had to write the play," so Kate stages *Old Times* to find herself, to find what she suspects is there and knows must, at the end, come to the surface. She thereby "entertains" Anna and Deeley only to silence them, to kill them off.

A playwright, Kate, as Pinter himself has done in *Old Times*, is also a playwright acting in her own play. And in the sense that an actor knows the end of the play, even as he or she convinces the audience, by the exercise of a craft, that the character, like the audience, is experiencing the play, its events, "fresh," innocently, from moment to moment, so Kate, the actor, knows that the play will end when, the time auspicious, she delivers her final (the play's final) speech. Along with the "madonna" look that many actors and audiences have ascribed to Kate, there is about her a feeling of omniscience: in this regard, she is like Shakespeare's Prospero. Like an actor—and all three characters, therefore, are conscious of being actors—Kate, beyond Deeley and Anna, can empathize with others. Whatever anger and resentment she feels toward Anna and Deeley, she can also empathize with them, can *feel* for them, can, like a good actress, put herself in their shoes.

Her silence is at one with this ability to empathize; indeed, it is her strength. Such silence, of the playwright overseeing her drama, of the actor empathizing with others, is not the "shyness" on which Anna discourses and embarrasses Kate, nor is it the "admirable" quality in women that Deeley praises. Kate's is the silence of a judge, an observer who, at some point, will be called to action. Kate's silence is the real, ultimate text of *Old Times*, the signal for the emergence of her true self, for which words, her words, few as they may be, are essentially signs to alert the audience yet, like all signs, only that, imperfect representations of the real thing. Anna inadvertently defines this stance when she speaks about Kate as waiting for the ripples to pervade the depths, as not jumping carelessly, or too quickly into things.

There is an "act 3" implied in *Old Times*, with only one character, Kate, walking along a deserted beach, "hands in pockets, that sort of thing," or lying in her tent, looking out through mosquito netting at the sand—"that sort of thing." Set not in London, or in the English countryside, this third act is "somewhere in the east," without Deeley, without Anna.

There is an innocence about Kate, an otherworldliness that is in reverse proportion to Anna's maturity, sexual and otherwise, or her own commitment to this world, its culture, its music, and its social gatherings. Hers is an innocence, an otherworldliness that is Christlike—and hence it is Christy of all the suitors whom she would invite to the flat. Like Christ—though *Old Times* is at the opposite end from any religious allegory—Kate is at once admirable and disconcerting. We are to some degree uncomfortable with this sort of character, so superior, so given to the self, so perfect, wanting at length to be free of us fellow mortals. In contrast, Anna and Deeley, however possessive, however flawed, are that much more attractive in their pathetic, understandable "humanity." To be sure, Kate's action, her decision at the end of the play is "right," inevitable; still, it makes us uncomfortable— we may wish the situation could be otherwise.

This is not to say that Kate is inhuman, or not a psychologial being. In fact, she resembles Anna and Deeley in certain respects. They might even be thought of as projections of elements in Kate's own personality. Kate remains deeply attached to Anna, her "other." Not only has Anna been a formative power in her life, a sister with whom she has "bonded," a fellow woman, but she also expresses Kate's own sexuality, her passions, and her pleasure in the world outside the room. But to excess. Kate is passing through a stage rather than being arrested as Anna is.

Like Deeley, but for vastly different reasons, Kate likes to distance herself from others. She too likes the home secluded by the sea, although, as we learn from her "bath" speech, she would want to go further, somewhere "east." Like Deeley and Anna, Kate is attracted to rooms; in this regard, there is a kinship among all three. Kate, however, insists on defining her own room.

"What do you want in this scene?" the director will often ask the actor. "What is your object?" The answer is usually brief, a sort of shorthand or rationalization for the character to be spelled out at greater length, to be enacted in the actual dialogue, and movement of the scene in question. If such a question could be asked of each of the three characters in *Old Times*, but in terms of the entire play, of both acts, a potential answer for each would be: Anna wants the past to be reborn; Deeley, the present, as he perceives it, to remain unchanged; and Kate wants a future of her own making. Kate "wins" in *Old Times*, albeit at a heavy cost, for at the end the play is delivered to its own future, the audience, who, leaving the theater, will take what they have witnessed into their own rooms, the idiosyncratic privacy of their hearts and mind. We have, in effect, been the fourth "character" of Pinter's play, the totally silent guest observing Kate observe Anna and Deeley. And our presence is signaled by the mime at the end of act 2, for here even Kate ceases to be, is frozen in the photographlike tableau created when the lights, that had been dim for the mime, suddenly come up "full sharply. Very bright."

"It happens. It just happens." Of course, what happens, literally, is that nothing happens, for *Old Times* does not have the events, the incidents that constitute plot as we normally define that term. Characters enter the set of *The Birthday Party*, and Goldberg and McCann thus alter the life Stanley has been leading. An event, like the boss's goosing the secretary, happens in Pinter's *A Night Out*, and when Albert is falsely accused of the indiscretion, the plot itself is altered. In contrast, *Old Times* has nothing but its dialogue; Deeley does not seduce Anna while Kate is taking a bath, nor do Anna and Kate, after Deeley refuses to go to China or Sicily, leave the set. *Old Times* is propelled forward by its dialogue, by what is said, rather than what is done. Indeed, the play seems to parody the actions—the battle with marbles conducted by Stott and Law in *The Basement*, the father's groveling onstage in *The Homecoming*—of other Pinter works. Here nothing happens beyond coffee being poured, or the lighting of a cigarette. Rather, its structure is determined by the flow of the conversation, by distinct segment of dialogue that, taken as a whole, establish the evening, the play itself.

Along with the terms "dualities" and "trinities" in my director's concept, then, I would add a third, "conversation," to designate the world of *Old Times*. In this light, I divided the play into fourteen sections, or "stages" of that dialogue, giving each a title as a way of defining the mood of a particular section. In a play without plot, these sections, in sequence and taken as a whole, substituted for plot, provided a way of assessing "what happens" in a work where literally nothing happens. *Old Times* is therefore about "what happens" when people talk, To reinforce this dimension of the director's concept, we used the fourteen sections below, and their titles, to indicate what part of the play we would be working on at any given point during the rehearsal schedule.

ACT 1

1. *The Questioning and the Questioner* (from the start to Deeley's line, "Well, anyway, none of this matters," just before Anna's first speech):

His questions, whatever their object, reveal as much, or more, about Deeley himself, the questioner, as the object. The initial subject, Anna, broadens to that of what a "friend" means. As Kate becomes increasingly aggressive, frustrated by the real, albeit, unconscious issue behind Deeley's questions, she complicates the conversation by introducing the "fact" that Anna was a thief who stole her underwear. Put on the defensive, Deeley counters by insisting he will uncover the real Kate through Anna. When Deeley attempts to learn more about Anna—and, by implication, about Kate—through speculations about Anna's husband, Kate counters again with a second fact: she and Anna lived together. Reeling, Deeley desperately attempts to dismiss all that they have said with "none of this matters."

2. *Anna's Presence/Present* (Anna's opening speech to Kate's pouring of the coffee):

Anna's speech is designed for both Kate and Deeley as she invokes the past in luxuriant detail, so as to seduce her friend from Deeley's presence. In effect, she offers a gift or present for the hostess, and establishes her world in opposition to the interrogationlike atmosphere of Deeley's time alone with Kate. Kate's pouring the coffee, where she remembers, after twenty years, that Anna takes cream and sugar, and her "Yes, I remember," acknowledge Anna's gift and unsettles Deeley.

3. *Deeley/Anna—the First Combat* (Deeley's "Do you drink brandy?" to his "I've been there" when Anna mentions she lives on a volcanic island):

Offering Anna a brandy, Deeley counters Kate's offer of coffee and, in effect, "shakes hands" with his opponent before the opening round. In order, Anna and Deeley now offer different perspectives—and hence clash verbally—on three topics: silence, the casserole, and the sea.

4. *Kate as Object* (from Anna's "I'm so delighted to be here" to Deeley's "They don't make them like that anymore," after the songs):

Breaking the tension after their first battle, Anna introduces Kate as a subject, and the rivals proceed to offer very different perspectives on her. Agreeing only that she is or was a "charming companion," and thereby calling a temporary halt to the second skirmish, they soon renew the fight as each uses lyrics from popular songs to court Kate, the courtship halted by Deeley's simultaneous acknowledgment and dismissal of the past, the golden era of songs.

5. *Two Movie Scenarios: "Odd Man Out" and "The Sobbing Man"* (from Deeley's "What happened to me was this" to Deeley's "Stop that" as he observes Kate lean over Anna to light her cigarette):

Music gives way to competing "plays" or scenarios as a battlefield for the rivals. Deeley's story of picking up Kate at the showing of *Odd Man Out*, intended both to belittle Kate and confirm the start of his relationship with her, is met by Anna's account of the man in their room, designed to belittle Deeley and to underscore the fact that the two women were once intimate. Kate asserts herself by interrupting the dialogue when she rises and goes to the table to light her cigarette. But the break itself becomes an object of contention when her lighting Anna's cigarette recreates a similar moment from their past. This time Deeley provides the interruption with his petulant, aggressive "Stop that."

6. *Deeley/The Husband as Object* (from Deeley's "Myself I was a student" to Deeley's "Per Paulo"):

The subject changes from women to men. The change, initiated by Deeley's self-serving account of his student days, as he tries to reestablish his primacy in the evening, is used by Anna to her advantage as she, daring her rival by acknowledging the marriage, then excludes Deeley by recounting the life of museum exhibits and concerts she once shared with Kate. Anna's coda to that story, going with her friend to see *Odd Man Out*, her first direct challenge to Deeley's scenario of the past, infuriates him.

Deeley then tries to discredit Anna's husband, and their life in Sicily.

7. *Innocent Secretaries* (from Kate's "Do you have marble floors?" to Kate's final line, "I'll think about it" as she exits to take her bath):

Deeley's crude efforts to discredit Anna's husband drive Kate toward Anna, and in the cinematic-like flashback Kate recreates, with a willing Anna, a moment from their days in London. Deeley is excluded as the past is resurrected, but Anna, the "mother" in their relationship, goes one step too far in asking if she should draw Kate's bath. Poised between a possessive, self-inflated husband and a loving, but no less possessive friend, Kate asserts her independence by saying she will run her bath herself "tonight." The fight has tipped, or so she mistakenly believes, in Anna's favor, but after Kate's exist, Deeley, raising his glass in a toast to the evening so far, concedes the first act while reminding Anna that the evening is not over.

ACT 2

8. *Deeley (Mostly) the Aggressor Alone with Anna* (from the start of act 2 to Deeley's "I wouldn't recognize you" as Kate enters):

Refreshed between acts, Deeley enters with renewed confidence, even making some efforts to seduce Anna while Kate is offstage. In his story of Anna at the Wayfarers Tavern he appears to gain the upper hand. However, the victory is just as suddenly qualified when Anna more than holds her own on the issue of drying and powdering Kate after her bath. Stung by what he perhaps takes as a "draw" after an apparent victory, Deeley hits below the belt with his slur on Anna's age. Kate enters during the final moments of this section, reacts silently upstage to the quarrel. Aware of her presence, of the fact that she may have overheard them, Anna and Deeley are suddenly pulled back into the battle, both against each other and (now) to regain favor with Kate.

9. *The (New) Kate, after the Bath* (from the song sung by Anna and Deeley on Kate's entrance to Kate's "Oh what a pity"):

The song both revives the musical competition from act 1 and serves as a fanfare for Kate as she enters. She is changed outwardly (by the bath and the play's one costume change) and inwardly, as her first major speech suggests. The implications of that speech, in part rejecting the "worlds" offered by the rivals, in part signaling Kate's dream of a new existence, are not fully understood by Anna and Deeley. Upon Kate's dismissal of London, Deeley, for a moment, has his confidence renewed, as with sexual innuendoes he questions Kate on her bath. Yet his hopes are dashed as, once more, Kate decides, as if it were a final test, to revisit the past with Anna, though this time the daughter is dominant, the mother overeager and compliant.

10. *A Question Turned against the Questioner* (from the silence after "Oh, what a pity" to Anna's "no one except Kate"):

Deeley exposes himself in asking Anna if she plans to visit anyone else while in England; Anna's response only underscores Kate's remark in act 1 that Anna was Kate's "one and only friend."

11. *Shy Kate/Passionate Anna: Anna's Power and Her Mistake* (from Deeley's "Do you find her changed?" to Anna's "be my guests"):

Deeley's not-so-innocent question, "Do you find her changed?," drives Anna to her most blatant error of the evening, precipitating her own downfall (Deeley is already "down" and almost "out," in the lingo of prize-fights). For the shy, voyeuristic, dominated Kate she describes, in part because Anna becomes too absorbed in her own narration and hence her own reliving of the past as she imagines it, is at variance with the Kate of the present play, and the Kate who, in her bath speech, has given off very different signals as to her notion of herself. Deeley fares no better, for his crude reaction to what he takes as a new bond between the women drives Kate to her most glaring rejection of him, as she suggests that he leave the set. Overreacting, misinterpreting, Anna offers a shallow invitation for the couple to visit her in Sicily.

12. *Two Final (Self-Revealing) Statements* (from Anna's "I would like you to understand" to Deeley's "so little"):

Misreading the new Kate, Anna tries to establish her power over her friend's life, even while professing that all she wants is Kate's "happiness." Desperate, Deeley plays his final card, revealing his past intimacy with Anna, and, in the process, revealing much more about himself, so much so that he ends the speech confused as to the separate identities of the two women. In effect, halfway through the speech he loses focus on its original object.

13. *Kate Takes Charge* (from Kate's "What do you think attracted her to you?" to her final line, "No one at all"):

Kate's questioning of Deeley, a humane counterpart to his self-centered questioning of her in act 1, balances the picture of the (present) fool with a Deeley from the past, more sensitive, more appealing. When Anna in turn confirms Deeley's story of their relationship, thereby linking the rivals in ways she cannot comprehend, Kate provides in her final speech the ultimate reason for linking them: both want to possess her, for reasons ranging from the deliberate to the unconscious. Both Anna and Deeley, and in that order, must be "killed off." And this Kate does, with pain, and anguish, but also deliberately and clinically.

14. *The Play Delivered to Its Audience* (the mime to the end):

In this play whose "plot" is the dialogue, the evening, as far as the characters themselves are concerned, is finished. The mime, where Anna and Deeley in turn try to escape, only to take their places on either side of Kate, allows the audience, without the complexities introduced by the characters and by dialogue, to witness a simple visual tableau asserting the emergency and primacy of Kate's vision. The brief flash of light at the end, illuminating the three figures in the fashion of a photographer's camera, underscores the deeper, silent half of *Old Times*, even while providing a image for us to take upon leaving the theater.

Set

Pinter's directions for the set, for both acts, are at once sparse and yet, properly, prescriptive. For the sitting-room set of act 1 he asks for two sofas and an armchair, and for the bedroom set of act 2, two divans and a chair. In both sets there is a window upstage. Further, act 1 requires a door through which Kate exits for her bath; act 2, a door leading back into the sitting-room, and a door stage-right leading to the bath, from which Kate enters.

The wonderfully prescriptive part, of course, is that the arrangement of the furniture for the second act at once duplicates and reverses that of act 1: The divans and the armchair "are disposed in precisely the same relation to each other as the furniture in the first act, but in reversed position." Pinter's "text" here is, typically, both suggestive and irresolute. Act 2 should be more of the same, but with a variation. In a play about the odd man out, Deeley is first seen slumped in an armchair on one side of the stage, and at the end he is slumped in a second armchair but on the opposite side. Anna "moves" from the window of act 1 to a divan opposite the side occupied by Deeley, in effect on the side he occupied in act 1. First seen on the sofa opposite the armchair on which Deeley sits, Kate winds up in the center, equipoised between her rivals.

But in light of the dualities mentioned earlier, there is also a countermovement to any pattern, any sense of symmetry. Act 1 opens with two seated characters, and one standing, with her back to us, and hence not fully within the play. Act 2 opens with Anna alone onstage. Act 1 ends with two characters alone on stage—in our production with Anna sitting, Deeley standing. Act 2 ends with all three characters present, but "frozen" the way Anna herself was for the opening segment of the previous act.

The arrangement of the furniture in both acts is parallel and different. Sofas metamorphose into divans, even as the divan, as an article of furniture, is halfway between a sofa and a bed. Old Times moves from the sitting-room, the appropriate place in which to entertain a guest, to the bedroom, a most inappropriate place under normal social etiquette. Tremendously significant in act 1—Anna is first seen there, and later she returns to spot a light along the coast—the window is unused in act 2, unless the director wants to locate some of the action there.

Is act 2 therefore a repetition of act 1, but with its own variation, the "child" of the previous act that, in the course of its enactment, has acquired signs of its own identity? Kate takes a bath somewhere between acts, during the single intermission. Has the play itself somehow changed, or grown at the same time? The sole "woman" seated onstage in act 1 changes in act 2 from Kate to Anna, here in a play where scholars as well as theatre people have raised the possibility of Kate's and Anna's being aspects of the same composite person.

While he describes the home as a converted farmhouse, Pinter does not specify the style of its furniture, although Deeley does speak of the divans in act 2 as having castors and hence as mobile so that they can be arranged at various angles to each other. Pinter, of course, does not dictate the exact arrangement of the furniture in act 1, although whatever arrangement the set designer with the director's advice chooses determines that of act 2, again "in reverse positions." Other furniture seems optional, or required by the action, namely, a table on which to put the coffee, brandy, cups, glasses, and containers for cream and sugar in act 1, and for the tray carried onstage by Deeley in act 2, bearing the pot of tea and the various dishes it requires. We also decided to use a small table in act 1, located to the right of the stage-right sofa in which Kate sits, to hold a box of cigarettes, a lighter, and an ashtray.

Given the notion of triangles, and the tension between dualities in the play, I decided to place the two sofas at a forty-five degree angle to each other, two-thirds of the way upstage, at either side of the stage, with some three feet between them at the apex of the triangle they formed. Way downstage, and perpendicular with that space was a round-table for the drinks. Deeley's armchair was to the left, and slightly downstage of the stage-left sofa. Slightly to the right, and parallel to the stage-right sofa stood a small table. The "window" was on the upstage wall, in a line with the downstage table. Further, the act 1 furniture rested on a medium-sized carpet, just large enough to contain it, so that underneath that carpet was the wall-to-wall studio carpet—or, in the stage production, a similar wall-to-wall carpet extending from the "stage" side of the theater through the house. In act 2 that same medium-sized carpet was removed. The two divans occupied precisely the same space occupied earlier by the sofas; this time, the armchair—or rather, a chair, without arms—was beside the stage-right divan. The same downstage table used in act 1 for the coffee and brandy "miraculously" reappeared, and in precisely the same location, in act 2. This time, however, there was no small table upstage.

The set is sparse but, of course, suggestive in its arrangement. Most certainly it is not a cluttered set, like that required by, say, Pinter's *The Caretaker*. And while I wanted all the focus to be on the three characters, and the dialogue, the set would be something more than a "playing area," and would, in its own spare, understated way, complement as well as support the dialogue. For the very fact that it was so minimal would only lead the audience, their threshold for details lowered, to focus on what there was to see onstage. Further, in the stage production we used no curtain, and hence the act 1 set stood as an object of contemplation as the audience waited for the play proper to start.

I wanted the set, in both acts, to reflect both the sterility, the dryness of the marriage and the lush, seductive past of Kate's London days. Therefore, for act 1 the two sofas, both two-seaters, were nondescript and conventional. The stage-right sofa was a sickly tan, the stage-left one, an equally anemic red. No less unremarkable was the armchair on stage left or the entirely functional end table for the sofa on stage right. However, this generic furniture rested on a complex, multicolored Persian rug, rich and suggestive in graphic contrast. And downstage was an ornate, curved, drum-table, a stunning piece, an antique, of nineteenth century origins, with tripod feet and brass inlays around the edges.

That drum-table was divided into what we called "Kate's and Deeley's halves," his on the stage-left side—that is, the side on which his armchair was located—containing a large, almost bulky decanter of brandy (a thick, somewhat gawdy piece of crystal) and three almost oversized brandy snifters. On Kate's side were three delicate tea cups and saucers. Two rather ordinary containers for sugar and cream, and an ornate but tasteful sterling silver pourer for the coffee. At the start of each performance, these props would be intermixed, the otherwise separate "equipment" for husband and wife having strayed to the wrong side. Early in the act Kate would come down to the drum-table and meticulously rearrange the various pieces on their proper halves.

The drum-table and the area immediately around it became something of a "safe place" to which a character could retreat to refortify himself or herself for the next round in the battle, or to escape from an embarrassing or threatening conversation, to "clear some space" for himself or herself or, as was often the case with Deeley who would consume four glasses of brandy in the first act, to refill a empty glass. The end-table held an inexpensive plastic ashtray and a silver lighter and cigarette box.

The divans for act 2 were, essentially, longish benches, identical in shape and color (an unimposing gray), yet across each was thrown a single long pillow, deep reddish-purple in color. A chair, without arms, was placed on the downstage-right side of the stage-right divan. The Persian carpet was removed for act 2, exposing, both in the television and stage productions, a rather ordinary carpet, without design and of a single, equally ordinary color.

As if it had traveled between acts, the drum-table from act 1 reappeared in precisely the same position—far downstage center, at the bottom of the screen for long-shots in the television production, for the stage production a mere two feet before the first row of the audience. Thus forming with the two sofas or the two divans the upside-down top of a triangle, the drum-table, whatever its function for the characters and in the blocking, also seemed to reach out to the audience, or, conversely, having "emerged" from the house, to have barely made it to the stage.

In act 2 Deeley brought onstage a small black tray, containing three Chinese tea cups, along with the prerequisite containers of sugar and cream. Pinter's script calls for more coffee in act 2, and the change to tea was in part an act of sentimental indulgence on my part—I had spent the previous summer teaching and directing in China, and the cups had been purchased in Shanghai— and in part to underscore the reference Kate makes to China when she suggests her husband leave the house. Earlier denying he owns a white dinner jacket, as he imagines Anna's husband does, Deeley inexplicably reverses himself when he reminds Kate what the Red Guard would do to him if they saw him wearing one.

If the furniture, alternately prosaic and lavish, was real, the sitting-room and bedroom themselves were not. In the television production, the studio walls, seen upstage and halfway down on the stage-right and stage-left sides, were masked in black paper, so that the furniture and its occupants appeared to float in the blackness of space, or as if the house, without discernible walls, stretched out to infinity once one left the realistic, solid confines of the rug. Hence, the upstage window, which Anna, her back to the camera, faces at the start of act 1, was purely imaginary. Later, when Anna crosses upstage to ask if Deeley or Kate can see "that tiny ribbon of light," "the sea," or "the horizon," she would "mime" a window as she stared into the darkness.

In the stage production, the room was, in one sense, more real, for upstage was a floor-to-ceiling pane of glass, stretching the length of the room, covered by porous drapes. Part of the spacious lounge in which the production was staged, this wall of glass, because it could not be concealed, by necessity became the sitting-room window facing the sea in Old Times. To spot the ribbon of light Anna would simply part the curtain and look, at once literally and imaginatively, at the horizon. Conversely, since the audience was grouped in a semicircle encompassing three sides of the set, the rest of the large room seemed patently unreal, part of the theater. For both television and the stage, the doors through which Kate departs for her bath and through which Deeley enters with tea were imaginary. Likewise, the lamp that Anna switches off in the mime was, in both productions, an imaginary switch, beside a no less imaginary door located upstage-right.

When seen in sequence, the two sets suggested a paradox. Moving from the sitting-room to the bedroom was to go from the public to the intimate. Yet the bedroom seemed colder, for the divans were even more sparse than the sofas, and the pillows draped on them, rather than mitigating that impression, only accented just how functional, how unadorned the divans were, despite Deeley's encomium to the place where he and Kate sleep and to the castors that make "all this possible." If the sitting-room suggested that the couple rarely entertained, the bedroom looked like a place where there was very little love, or lovemaking—a room in which one slept, to be sure, but did little more. The house, curiously, gave very little clue to its owner—no pictures on the wall, no objects of art, family heirlooms, furniture, or accessories that would indicate something of the tastes, the idiosyncracies, the histories, even the personalities of their owners. On the other hand, both rooms, and particularly the bedroom, might have shown Anna that the marriage is ripe for exploitation. Thus, such conflicting, contradictory signals given off by both rooms seem at one with the dualities and the concomitant tension that had informed my director's concept as it was derived from the script itself, from the verbal half of *Old Times*.

My feeling for the time setting for each act was that act 1 takes places during "early twilight," or that point in the day when the sun has set although the sky is still light enough that turning on the lights would seem unnecessary, wasteful. Nevertheless, one could sense that full twilight, then night itself, were approaching. The time, therefore, for the sitting-room would be the cocktail hour, at the close of the day, just before the onset of those shadows and darkness that Anna fears. Actually, on this issue of time, the play itself offers confusing evidence: even though coffee and brandy would normally be served after supper, Deeley talks as if the casserole were yet to be eaten. Act 2, preceded by Kate's bath during the intermission, takes place at night.

Lighting

Because of the demands of the medium—more wattage is required to produce the same effect as that of a stage production—and limited equipment, for the television production we used a neutral white lighting for both acts. However, by using spots that lighting was increased around the area of the two sofas (and Deeley's armchair), the drum-table, centerstage (halfway between the sofas and the drum-table), and the upstage "window." In like fashion, the divans in act 2 were given increased lighting. The same held true for the stage production, with one significant, and, I think, wonderful addition. Since those performances took-place in the evenings, two floodlights were placed outside that long, full-length upstage window (that is, the "real" window), at either side and at oblique angles to each other. For act 1, two warm amber lights, shining out of the real-life darkness, shown through the porous, floor-to-ceiling curtain, spilling onto the upstage area. Blue gels were substituted during intermission, so that in act 2 that light from outside was cold, "blue-ish," as if the superficial conviviality of the first act had given way to the austere, sterile atmosphere of the bedroom to which the evening's entertainment had moved, however inexplicably. Somehow, the evening had become more serious; or, rather, those darker elements, always present, had made their way closer to the surface, most noticeably in Kate's angry charge to Deeley that he "go" and, even more, in her final speech.

As Pinter's stage directions instruct, both acts began in dim light, with the stage reduced to roughly one-half its normal illumination. In the television version Kate and Deeley, seated, appeared in this darkness for seven seconds, with Anna standing, her back to the audience, at the upstage window. In the stage version, during that same darkness, Kate entered smoking a cigarette, examined the room, and then took her seat on the stage-right sofa, followed by Deeley who, after similarly examining his "half" (stage-left) of the room and glancing briefly at Kate, sat down in the armchair. When both were in position, Anna entered and went straight to the window. In both productions full stage lighting came a split second—deliberately and ironically so—after Kate's opening line, or rather word "dark." In effect, in the television version the viewer first contemplated the darkened tableau of husband and wife, with that tableau both activated and illuminated by a character, ostensibly responding to Deeley's question about the color of Anna's hair, or perhaps her complexion. In the stage version, the audience, once seated, saw the characters, in the fashion of a Pirandello play, enter and examine the set and, in the case of Kate and Deeley, give some evidence of their personalities before dialogue began and lights were raised. Kate was very much the proper hostess, checking out the preparations, her focus seemingly on the arrival of their guest. Deeley, in contrast, strode into the room as if it were his preserve. His manner suggested that, since they had been discussing, perhaps even arguing about Anna's arrival earlier in the day, he was now assessing Kate's mood—in a phrase, "examining her" as he prepared his own strategy for dealing with the intruder.

Again, at the start of act 2, lights were at half strength. Whereas the television viewer discovered Anna in the darkness seated in the exact place Kate had occupied in act 1, in the stage version she entered from upstage-right (the door supposedly leading to the sitting-room), somewhat apprehensive, perhaps contemplating what had already happened so far, knowing that Kate would take a long time with her bath and that Deeley was about to enter with tea.

Also in both productions, lights came to full strength when Deeley, entering with the tea, made a righthand turn by the window as he crossed downstage to place the tray on the downstage drum-table. In both productions act 1 ended in a slow fade of the lights to a blackout as Deeley raised his brandy glass in that toast complimenting yet also challenging Anna. In act 2, lights went to dim, as Pinter specifies, when Anna, the character initiating the mime, crossed to upstage-right, thought about making her exit, and suddenly realized this was impossible. She was locked in with these two characters, assigned by her playwright to challenge Deeley forever, to challenge him at the next performance, and—no less—even after being rejected by Kate to try one more time to capture her from Deeley. Anna would flick an imaginary light switch, located to the door's stage-left side, that movement serving as a cue to dim the television or stage lights. In the stage version, it was at this very moment that the two outside floods, with their blue lights, became especially effective. Indeed, on opening night the inside lights, having short-circuited, suddenly went out, and we were forced to play the mime using only the floods. The effect was that of the outside world taking over, silhouetting the three characters as they act out, in silence, Kate's ultimate and victorious version of that night a man came to the secretaries' apartment and was rejected by both women.

Once Deeley, after being "mothered" by Kate on the stage-right sofa, returns to his chair, the characters held their poses in the darkness—"Deeley [slumped] in armchair. Anna lying on the [stage-left] divan. Kate sitting [erect] on [the stage-right] divan." The stage lights came up "full sharply. Very bright," as the tableau is impressed for roughly two seconds on the audience's eyes in the fashion of a photographer's flash: the humiliated, and perhaps now wiser husband; the friend dormant until she is once more activated when Kate revisits her past or, more literally, when Anna pays another visit. Saddened by, but resolute in her decision to dismiss her past, even acknowledging its poverty,

Kate elects to remain married to the *man*—unlike Kate and Anna, Deeley is never called by name in the play—at her right.

Music

Since *Old Times* is full of popular songs—"Lovely to Look At," "Blue Moon," "They Can't Take That Away from Me" (which is repeated when Kate enters in act 2), "I've Got a Woman Crazy for Me," "I Get a Kick Out of You," "These Foolish Things," and "All the Things You Are"—I decided to use the final song, "All the Things You Are" (without lyrics) at the start of both acts and, briefly, at the end of act 1. In the television version, it played as the title came on-screen, continued during the dim tableau at the start of the act, and faded at length with Kate's "Dark" that brought up the lights. The melody returned at the end of act 1 as Kate began her exit and played straight through the break (during which an "Act 2" appeared on-screen), and through the start of the second act until Deeley made his right-turn, as he headed toward the drum-table and thereby gave the cue for full-studio lighting. The melody returned a third time for the credits at the end, after the screen went dark following the "photographer's flash" that ended the mime.

For the stage version the music covered the entrances of the three characters in act 1, with four bars separating Kate's and Deeley's entrances—so that each appeared on the first note of the melody—with Anna's entering during the song's final two measures. In the stage version we also held back the music until Deeley made his toast—in effect, two seconds before the blackout. When the stage and house lights returned and the audience rose and went into the lobby for intermission, they encountered a (live) musician at the piano, who brought the song to its conclusion before segueing into a reprise of the other songs employed by the rivals for Kate's hand.

This use of "All the Things You Are" was not incidental, or merely decorative. In the production the song is initiated by Anna who, having sung lines from two other songs (Deeley sings three songs), rises from the stage-left sofa and moves toward Kate. In effect, the song signals Anna's physical challenge to Deeley's space. Having been content so far to trade songs with his rival, Deeley now meets the challenge by jumping to the final two lines of "All the Things You Are," as if by doing so he could remove the song from the competition.

The song itself consists of a series of metaphors used by the singer to define his or her loved one—"the promised kiss of springtime," "the quiet hush of evening," "the angel's glow," "the dearest things"—and it is only in its final third that such metaphors are abandoned as the singer makes a more direct statement of passion: "Someday my happy arms will hold you, / And someday I'll know that moment divine, / When all the things you are, are mine!" From my reading, the song moves from poetry and indirection to a blunt, albeit loving wish for that day to come when the singer will possess the loved one, when "all the things you are [those metaphors enumerated earlier], are mine!" Whatever her other motives, and despite the possessive mother that characterizes her as she relates to Kate, Anna remains content here to describe her friend, whereas Deeley is more raw. He wants to possess her; she, after all, is his wife, not Anna's. I also decided on "All the Things You Are" because, like the other songs, as well as the movie *Odd Man Out*, it represents something from the real world, a creation outside Pinter's own present play, something from the actual past that intrudes on the otherwise aesthetically sealed play being enacted before us.

Costumes

I asked my three actors to wear clothes already in their possession but that would, of course, fit the concept of their characters as they evolved in rehearsal. Accordingly, Kate, for act 1, dressed in a comfortable, rather plain long dress, with large pockets, not fancy but rather the type of dress one would wear when entertaining an old friend, as opposed to strangers—special for the occasion but comfortable. Anna, in contrast, wore a traveling suit, its colors noticeably brighter than the restrained colors (and design) of Kate's housedress, with a jacket, blouse, and knee-length skirt. The guest's costume, in effect, was what one would expect of a sophisticated woman from London and, no less, from a visitor, the sort of outfit Kate herself might have worn if she had visited Anna and her husband in Sicily. Deeley dressed more casually, in rather nondescript pants and a shirt, with a blue sweater—in essence, the sort of clothes he would wear when alone at home with his wife. It is as if Deeley purposely decided not to go out of his way for Anna's arrival.

For the stage production, Anna changed to an outfit with even brighter, contrasting colors, although still refined, not gaudy. We also abandoned the idea of a sweater for Deeley. Indeed, in act 2 he rolled up his sleeves, as if getting ready for another battle with Anna, or as if, now in the bedroom, he had become even more casual. Both women wore makeup, at the level one would use for a special occasion, for the roles of hostess and guest. For Deeley we used only a minimal amount, just enough to soften the effect of television or stage lights; the effect here was that, as with the clothes, Deeley had not gone out of his way in the slightest for the visit. Likewise, Deeley's hair was combed but hardly styled like Anna's, which showed the hand of a beautician. Kate's hair was also styled, but at the level she herself might have performed at home.

I rejected our initial impulse to have Kate appear after her bath in a basic, long terry-cloth bathrobe. Rather, to underscore the "new" Kate, refreshed after the bath and now offering more blatantly to Anna and Deeley a signal that her real self had emerged, one that could no longer be shaped or possessed by them, she wore a floor-length black, silk dressing robe, made in China (and hence at one with the Chinese tea cups and saucers). On the back in several colors of dyed silk thread was an intricate floral pattern. The robe glistened as it caught the overhead lighting, especially in the television version. It further lent a visual texture to the song that the rivals sing to Kate on her entrance, as well as to their shared announcement: Anna's "Doesn't she look beautiful?" and Deeley's "Doesn't she?" This same black gown seemed even more formal during Kate's final speech, as if it were a costume she had chosen to mourn the death of the rivals. When the lights went to dim for the mime, the gown looked almost funereal.

Blocking

As with almost any other play, much of the blocking and movement for *Old Times* functions as a psychological, visual complement to the dialogue, to the intention of the character speaking or responding to what is said. In one sense, the set is simple, two sofas and an armchair, or two divans and a chair, and since nothing really happens this evening, since the "plot" is structured by conversation rather than events, let alone physical actions, the characters have little reason to move about. Indeed, in one London production they remained seated as much as possible, except for, say, the serving of refreshments or Kate's exit for her bath.

Still, in terms of such movement *Old Times* is not, indeed, cannot be static. After all, movement onstage is never natural in the sense of being real, any more than the dialogue is: the cliché that a stage play can offer a "slice of live" is an inherent contradiction. Everything, even in the most "realistic" of works, is heightened, compressed, unnatural in that the design is already in place, the lines and movements rehearsed. Like dialogue, then, blocking is not a facsimile for real-life movement. Like dialogue, it is part of the "text" of a imaginative creation that, more than merely duplicating reality, tries to get at its essence. In a word, I moved the characters about the otherwise simple set to underscore their feelings, their sense of the changing relationships among them, the closeness or distance each of them feels, at any given moment, to their object.

In this latter regard, Deeley and Anna move more than Kate, although Kate herself is not stationary. When Anna embarrasses her by the comment on her shyness—Pinter notes that Kate "stares at her"—Kate moves from the stage-right divan she had been occupying with Anna to the empty one on stage-left, distancing herself from this woman who, perhaps unconsciously, persists in believing a false image of her friend.

Realizing that she has rendered Deeley helpless as he struggles with her concept of "ripples," that her account of Kate's conservative approach to experience is a revelation to him, Anna leaves the couple at stage-right and, crossing to stage-left, sits alone on the sofa. The move here underscores her confidence: Deeley has been so disarmed by her account that she can "afford" to leave him alone with Kate. Even though now isolated on the stage-left divan, Anna has never been—so she imagines—spiritually closer to Kate. Conversely, believing that he has put Kate in her place by quizzing her, as a teacher would, on the day of the week—this in response to Anna's tale about Kate's confusion of Saturday with Friday—Deeley crosses to Anna, momentarily identifying himself with her. He is convinced that, whatever tensions exist between them, they are both alike in being superior to Kate when it comes to the basics of life, such as knowing the correct time and day. Near now to Anna, Deeley, who will later object to her visit, pronounces his rival a "healthy influence," and wishes she would come more often.

Kate remains on her sofa for much of the opening conversation with Deeley; indeed, Pinter indicates no movement for her until, later in the scene, after Anna's speech, she "goes to a small table and pours coffee from a pot." Nevertheless, I decided to move Kate before then: she rises and crosses to the table stage-right to extinguish her cigarette as a way of showing her frustration with Deeley. His incessant questions about Anna, about her husband, about Kate's feeling for Anna, are stifling her, so that, feeling she is some witness or accused person sitting while a lawyer moves about her in his interrogation, she asserts her own independence by leaving the witness stand. Later, his question about whether Anna is married intrigues her—Kate believes that if Anna is married her effort to separate herself from her girlhood friend will be easier—so that while she has otherwise tried to avoid Deeley, she now crosses to him, "seduced" to his side of the stage by the question and exposing to her husband a slight weakening in her reserve, her practiced indifference to his cross-examination. When Deeley once again annoys his wife on the issue of Anna's friends, she, spotting the items in disarray on the drum-table, eagerly crosses downstage, getting away from him. There, her back to him, recovering from his lawyer-like dialogue, Kate drops her "bombshell": she and Anna have lived together. She does this without facing him, taking pleasure in imagining the reactions of a husband who, upstage of her, is now getting more than he bargained for from his questioning.

Almost every moment in the work is marked by this sort of interrelation between what we might call the verbal and the physical "psychology" of its characters. This applies as much to the set speeches as it does to the dialogue. For example, Anna and Kate sit on the stage-right sofa as Deeley's unwilling but curious audience when he recounts his experience at the showing of *Odd Man Out*. Deeley's movement here is very deliberate for he is the self-conscious performer trying to control the women, even as, unconsciously, he is defensively rebuilding a self-image battered by Anna's presence. All his movements, therefore, are determined by the text. In itself it is a powerful speech and, as such, might have been delivered by Deeley seated, say, in the very armchair he occupied at the start of the act. I opted instead to move him about the stage, to choreograph what I took to be the various sections or stages in the speech. He starts at the drum-table, casually pouring himself another glass of brandy, but then begins a cross toward the two seated women on the mention of the two usherettes, as if he were trying to make sure that they will see the connection between themselves and these characters from the past. Believing that he is now humiliating them with this account of lesbian passion, Deeley allows them to "stew" as he crosses upstage of their sofa, delighting in imagining, if not seeing their reactions. Now himself making the connection between the woman he picked up and Kate—"there she is. And there she was"—he moves between the two sofas and stands before the two women, sure that his story has had the intended effect. As he returns to the subject of the lesbian usher-ettes—the fate from which he has rescued Kate—he again confi-dently turns his back on the women, crossing to the upstage side of "his" sofa on stage-left. Relishing the part of the story where he picks-up Kate and takes her to a cafe, and asserting the pri-macy of heterosexual over homosexual passion, perhaps even remembering Anna's own earlier rival account of intimate times in London cafés with Kate, Deeley casually, almost playfully, moves about the back of the sofa, taking a seat on his declaration that it was Robert Newton who brought them together and it is only that actor "who could tear [them] apart." In sum, Deeley moves from the drum-table, circles the upper half of the stage and, his story over, his point, as he imagines, made, returns to his side of the stage, believing that he can safely leave Kate sitting close to the visitor.

When Anna rattles Deeley by daring to suggest that F. J. McCor-mick "was good too" and Kate then unsettles him further with her ambiguous response to his asking if she remembers the film, Deeley, disturbed, must leave his sofa, this time crossing to a position in front of the women as he reminds both of his subse-quent physical intimacy with Kate—"our naked bodies met." He even goes so far as to squat down before his wife, brushing her knee on the phrase "touched her profoundly all over." After this, he rises, crossing confidently once more to his sofa as, reas-serting the name of his favorite actor, he challenges Anna with the question "What do you think he'd think?"

The numerous pauses and silences are as much a part of this physical text as is the dialogue. Sometimes characters move at the start of a pause so that the move indicates the character's using that pause to back away from another character, to reflect on what was just said, or to take time to prepare an answer. In this fashion, the pause serves as a break in which to assume another position, or as a silent overture to the phrase that the character plans at the end of the pause. At other times, a charac-ter will move after a pause, having, say, used the pause to observe the effect of something just said, as Kate does increasingly with both Deeley and Anna. She thereby allows someone time to respond without being seen by her, sure that she has created the desired effect with her own line.

Movement can even occur in the middle of a pause, so that the character, having moved, or even adjusted a position on the sofa in regard to another character, then employs the pause's second half as a prelude for his or her next line. Deeley, for instance, uses the pause in this way during his account of the Wayfarer's Tavern in his conversation with Anna at the start of act 2.

By definition, pauses are punctuations in the dialogue, a so-called "pregnant moment" when a statement or even a phrase is given emphasis by silence. No less, they are punctuations for movement, either as a prelude to movement, or its accompaniment. Movement, so distinguished, is very different from that complementing lines, such as Deeley's neurotic pacing back and forth as he complains to Anna about the pathetic state of her husband all alone "lurching up and down the terrace, waiting for a speedboat" in their Sicilian home. When the same character, with lines before and after the pause, moves halfway through the pause, then movement, dialogue, and silence form a trinity of signification.

Pinter has, generously, suggested that actors and their director will find places to pause beyond those he had indicated. Kate's bath speech provides a good example of where such options can be taken. In this case, the pauses not only demark the three sections of the speech—her separate warnings to Deeley and Anna, followed by her "announcement" of the life she prefers to lead without them—but also allow for slight movement on Kate's part to block off those sections. Essentially, Kate is stationed between Deeley seated on the stage-left divan and Anna on the stage-right divan. The first slight pause comes between her reference to the water's being softer in the country than in London and her more direct charge that the water is "very hard" in the city. Kate remains in position on this first pause, but on the second pause, just before the line "There aren't such edges here," she moves a step toward Anna while turning her face toward Deeley. Though she prefers the country to London, she still detests "harsh edges" (that is, Deeley) no matter where they may be. With the third pause just before "I don't care for harsh lines," Kate moves back to her original position, as if to put a double stress on the harsh edges of men who try to dominate women. The word "urgency" only reemphasizes her point, and in the pause after that word, she sits, ironically, next to Deeley who is now flattered that she has "chosen" him, even though he does not fully understand, or perhaps want to understand her reference in "harsh lines" and "urgency." A fourth pause comes after the reference to the rain's blurring the lights of cars, as if to give Deeley time to think about this, while a slight pause after the comment that the rain "blurs your eyes," delivered to Anna, similarly provides her a chance to respond.

In the television production we took a pause before Anna's response, so that, threatened by Kate's apparent denouncement of the city, and using the pause to collect her thoughts, she rises on the end of the pause, moving slowly to the drum-table as she enumerates the charms of the city. As if reliving their days in London, Anna pours her a cup of tea, thereby anticipating Deeley's role as host with the refreshments in the second act. In the stage version we kept Anna seated during her response, and took out the pause so that, already thinking about her reply during the final lines of Kate's speech, she speaks, without a pause, almost on top of Kate's "That's the only nice thing about a big city." The deleted pause was reinserted, however, after Kate's announcement a few lines later that she has decided to stay in tonight "anyway." With the change of plans, Anna, her spirits raised, thinks for a few seconds and then heads for the drum-table, there to prepare Kate's cup. By not having Anna pause, or move, after Kate's speech, but instead deliver her line from the divan, focus was kept on Anna's facial reaction, just as restoring the pause a few lines later frames her pouring an actual cup of tea when, moments before, her image of "a nice hot drink" had brought no response from Kate, indeed had led only to a pause in the dialogue (this time indicated by Pinter himself).

Even blocking indicated by the text is never automatic, or mechanical. Indeed, since this movement is required by what a character says or proposes to do, it has a psychological basis, and is, in a word, meaningful. Kate's pouring of the coffee, followed by Deeley's pouring of the brandy, is such an instance. To be sure, coffee and brandy are called for in the dialogue, or rather, the stage directions indicate that Kate pours coffee, whereas Deeley asks if Anna drinks brandy. On Anna's courteous "I would love some brandy," Deeley rises and crosses to the drum-table. For me, his suggesting brandy just after Kate has delivered cups of coffee to Anna and himself is a form of rivalry. The couple has been on edge all day about Anna's visit; that tension has only been aggravated by their conversation so far, and aggravated further by Kate's response to Anna's opening speech. (In our production, Anna delivers a large portion of that speech directly to

Kate, leaning seductively on the arm of her sofa, staring into her eyes on the passage about their cooking scrambled eggs together.) Angry at Kate, therefore, Deeley challenges what he takes to be a "feminine" coffee ceremony with a man's drink. Anna is caught in the middle of the quarrel. In fact, in the stage production we took out Anna's placing her coffee cup on the table to prepare for Deeley's brandy and, instead, had her balance, skillfully, both coffee cup and brandy glass in her hand. Hence the blocking for this textually "necessary" or required social routine also underscored the quarrel between husband and wife over the latter's acceptance of her friend's account of the past, that acceptance signaled verbally by Kate's "Yes, I remember."

Kate's rise just after Deeley's blunt "We rarely get to London" (her response to Anna's more expansive question about whether the London she remembers still exists) is her way of drawing attention from her husband's curt remark. While Kate prepares the coffee, Deeley divides his attention between that ceremony—noting that Kate has also remembered just how Anna takes her coffee (with cream followed by two teaspoons of sugar)—and Anna, as he watches her watch Kate fondly and intensely. When Kate offers Deeley his coffee, he not only doesn't meet her outstretched hand halfway with his own but in fact moves his hand slightly away from her, so that she must expend an extra effort in delivering his cup. Seconds after she returns to the drumtable to prepare her own cup, Deeley makes his proposal for brandy. Recognizing the tactic, used to, even anticipating it, Kate still registers her annoyance. Deeley then crosses to the downstage table, deliberately hands his coffee, untouched, to Kate for her—not him—to replace on "her" side. While she crosses upstage to sit beside Anna, he pours two glasses of brandy and crosses to the women. Anna takes hers graciously, while Kate, returning Deeley's insult, indicates by a slight nod of her head that he is to place it on the table to her right. She never touches the brandy. Though required by the text, this same investment of movement with meaning characterizes every such instance in *Old Times*. The routine where all three light cigarettes, to be discussed at some length under the section on the rehearsals, is a case in point. But it is not isolated, by any means.

The rationale for other blocking is not so much psychological, and hence not "realistic," as I have qualified that word when it applies to the theatre. In a sense, such blocking is more "honest" or even obvious since, theatrical or thematic in origin, it only reminds us that we are witnessing not life but, at best, a play about life. Pinter himself has said that his works are "realistic, but only to a point." Deeley's final speech, where in three fairly distinct segments he reveals his alleged affair with Anna, reminisces about the men of his youth, and then, as if forgetting his initial object, confesses that now he cannot not be sure just which woman he took to the party, is not only isolated from any demand for conversation with the women but seems, beyond its immediate origins, to be a moment of an atypical self-confession. Here Deeley is no longer the host but a man alone with himself, seeing himself, even wishing to retreat to the past. In fact, the speech resembles a movie flashback, not unlike that in which the two women engage earlier. Hence, in "Deeley's clock speech," as we called it in rehearsal, the character leaves the two women upstage, makes a half-circle clockwise to the drum-table, during which time he pursues his object, directing most of his comments toward the women. But once he reaches the drum-table and there, most uncharacteristically, does not refresh his drink or pour himself a new one, he begins to recall his old buddies, so that the second half-circle, as he moves stage-right and toward the women, has a very different tone. Now Deeley is lost in his own thoughts, desperate, as if in his later years—the times on the clock after the "6" represented by the downstage drum-table—he has mellowed, and grown introspective. The blocking here, then, suggests the span of a man's life, from his youth where he was "slim-hipped" and "kinky" (by his own admission), to middle-age, to the start of old age where memories usurp any present activities. But those memories also become cloudy: Deeley is unsure now whether it was Anna or Kate in the pub.

This "unrealistic blocking" was also used to signal turning points in the play. Telling Deeley to go to China, Kate stalks away from him, crossing upstage, and then, as if on cue from her, Anna similarly rises, moving quickly to stage-right. It is as if she were completing a pattern. Similarly, when Kate crosses to the drum-table to return her cup of cold tea, she goes to the table's downstage side, looks at Deeley sitting on the stage-left divan, then at Anna on the stage-right divan, as if she were weighing husband against friend, the present against the past, before crossing up to Anna, there to initiate the second of the play's two cinematic flashbacks to the secretaries in their London flat. Motivated by the flashback—in effect, Kate decides to visit the past one more time—this moment was clearly distinguished from that at the end of act 1. There Kate stands halfway between Anna who, sitting on the stage-left sofa, had grasped her hand tenderly as she asked if Kate would like her to run the bath, and Deeley, standing by the stage-right sofa. Feeling Anna's hand on hers, Kate looks at Deeley. Unwilling to dismiss him at this point, and yet both touched and annoyed by Anna's bold gesture, Kate postpones a decision. Announcing that she will run her own bath tonight, she exits gracefully, but quickly.

I should add that given the fact that the audience surrounded the actors on three sides in the stage production, some of the blocking was influenced by the practical consideration of not obscuring for too long the sight lines of any given section of the audience. For example, it was necessary to move Deeley about slightly as he stood on stage-right listening to the women during the flashbacks.

Furthermore, in a play where, technically, the characters could have remained sitting most of the time, much of the blocking stressed the significance of the furniture. The issue was one of who sits alone, or who sits alongside of whom, who is standing and who sitting, who gets up from sitting, or—especially—who, leaving one character on a sofa or divan, takes a seat with the other character on the opposite sofa or divan. In act 1, the stage-right sofa was, essentially, "Kate's"—in the television production she is discovered sitting there, while in the stage production, entering first, she "instinctively" takes that same sofa—while the armchair and the stage-left sofa were "Deeley's." When she talks about Anna's stealing her underwear, Kate lures Deeley up there—he had been centerstage, abandoned there by his wife— but he does not sit with her. Instead, he takes a seat on "his" sofa, and, along with Kate, is "frozen" there for the first part of Anna's speech, which she delivers with her back to her hosts and the audience. When Anna turns to confront the couple, she turns, almost automatically, to Kate on the stage-right sofa.

Often, when Anna is confident that she has scored a victory over Deeley, she leaves stage-right and takes a seat on Deeley's sofa or, in act 2, "his" divan. At one point, when Deeley, sitting with Kate on her sofa, is especially flustered by insinuations that he leaves his wife at home too often, Anna, on the stage-left sofa, beckons Kate to come over, patting the cushion next to her on the line "I think I must come and keep you company when he's away." Early in rehearsals, Kate would get up a few lines later and join Anna, leaving Deeley alone on the stage-right sofa. How- ever, we discovered it was more effective for Kate not to succumb to Anna's offer, but, instead, have Deeley rise and cross to Anna on his line "Won't your husband miss you?" In effect, Deeley changes the topic from his absence from home to that of Anna's.

As he questions her about her husband's dietary habits and, then, about the precise location of their home, Deeley like an inquisitor circles Anna seated on the upstage side of the sofa. However, once she proves more than equal to his tactics, he resorts to a parody of what he imagines is the conversation of the international set—"Captain steer a straight course" and "Don't you find England damp, returning." Now unwilling to join his rival who has usurped his sofa, he is forced to sit in the armchair. On Deeley's peevish insult of the nationality of Anna's husband—"What's his name? Gian Carlo or Per Paulo"—Kate suddenly interrupts from her sofa, as she questions Anna about the nature of the very same Italian villa that had aroused Deeley's jealousy. As if to defy Deeley by invading his space, Kate rises and crosses stage-left, joining Anna on Deeley's sofa, so that for one of the rare times in the play the two rivals and their object are clustered on one side of the stage. The women are seated close together—it will be only a few moments until their first flashback—while Deeley is in the armchair, inches away, but still occupying a separate piece of furniture. Soon he will be separated from them by a decade when Anna invokes the past with "Don't let's go out tonight."

In a similar fashion, Deeley is pleased that Kate sits on his stage-left divan halfway through her bath speech. Disturbed that she has slandered the city, and trying to win Kate back by handing her a "nice hot drink" as a reminder of the pleasures of their once living together, Anna stands, expectantly, just to Kate's right. Yet when Deeley starts playing the loving husband with his sexual innuendoes about Kate's drying herself properly, Anna, rejected from the conversation, is forced to take a seat on the stage-right divan, embarrassed that she has been standing during the couple's intimate conversation, and perhaps now glad for this refuge. Confident he has won, Deeley rises and crosses over to Anna as he discusses Kate's smile, even sitting close to her as if they were intimate colleagues analyzing an object together. But Deeley is soon stung by Kate's cold "I'm not smiling," and when she rises to return her teacup to the downstage drum-table, Deeley also rises and returns to his side of the stage.

As mentioned earlier, that drum-table functioned as something of a "safe-spot," a place where a character could go to extricate himself or herself from a particularly intense part of the conversation, to "refuel" as Deeley literally does when he refills his brandy or as Anna does figuratively in preparing to retaliate against Deeley's story of the usherettes with her own about the man entering their room. On this latter occasion, Deeley is sitting on the stage-left sofa as Anna, leaving Kate on the stage-right sofa, goes to the drum-table, which she completes by crossing over to Deeley and boldly sitting down beside him. He struggles to remain clinical or indifferent to an episode in which he himself may have been the man in question.

For Kate on her infrequent trips downstage, the table is clearly a place to escape from Deeley, as in their opening conversation. During Kate's final speech, that table is reserved for her announcement about "last rites"—or the absence of them—for Anna. Once the picture of Anna's "dying alone and dirty" is complete, Kate leaves the table when she turns to the new issue of her bath, itself a prelude to her dismissal of Deeley.

Centerstage, the area bounded by the two upstage sofas (or divans) and the drum-table, doubled as both a performance area—as in the opening part of Deeley's speech about the two usherettes—and an arena of combat, as when Deeley and Anna clash on the issue of Kate's being friendless or on Anna's metaphor of the ripples. Upstage, particularly near the window, is, of course, the area where Anna waits until being activated by Deeley's "Well, anyway, none of this matters," as well as where the two women gather during Deeley's "clock speech." Anna uses that location when she breaks an awkward silence with her inquiring about the lights on the horizon, and Kate goes there when she loses patience with Deeley.

The bulk of the *Old Times*, however, was performed within the area bounded by the furniture and the drum-table, and this convention thereby established the interior nature of the work, its being about conversation between and among the three characters. With the upstage darkness in the television production and the generic, real curtains and floor-to-ceiling neutral glass of the stage production, the scenic "poverty" of the upstage area suggested that surrounding the circle of conversation was a no man's land, a no exit. To be sure, there was an exterior, an outside, such as is referred to at times in the dialogue, but it was dwarfed by the intimate, psychological dimensions of the interior play enacted before us. Kate alone makes an exit, for her bath. Perhaps the world outside the play is no more certain than that envisioned in her speech upon entering in act 2—the east, "somewhere like that." Anna enters, in effect, from the upstage window, but she never makes another exit or entrance in the play proper. Otherwise, the upstage area is off-limits, and when Anna and then Deeley try to walk through the imaginary door upstage-right, their exits are barred.

In the stage production and also, by implication, in the presence of the viewer on the other side of the television screen, the real-life audience is a major, if not the major, factor in any decision about blocking. Onstage, of course, the action is arranged for a stationary viewer, and is one way in which the director exercises some, though hardly complete control as to what the viewer sees or, to be more accurate, what is allowed to stand out, be rendered important in the movement onstage. In television that directorial control is surely even greater, for while in our production roughly 80 percent of the stage blocking duplicated that devised for the stage, still, with the use of the close-up or medium-range shots the action can be further isolated. More than in the theater, therefore, the director in television selects the moment-by-moment stage picture for the viewer's contemplation.

Yet though in each media its role may be different, the audience, the recipient of whatever stage picture emerges, is the object, the witness, and the final arbiter of blocking. Hence, while a psychological sign for the characters, the blocking is a thematic, even a symbolic one for the audience. Pinter himself seems to announce this double function and hence the concomitant primacy of the audience when Deeley's italicized *"What,"* unheard by Anna and unacknowledged by Kate, intervenes between Anna's philosophical point about events in the memory gaining the status of reality and the opening lines of Anna's story about the man in the room. While not a direct address to the audience, Deeley's single word, not part of the dialogue proper, can only be heard by us. It may be a rare moment in *Old Times* when a character appeals for explanation to the silence, or the silent auditors surrounding him. Later, Deeley's "Some people do *what*? (to KATE.) What did she say?" seems split between those auditors and a wife who does not, perhaps will not respond to a husband's plea for some clarification. When Pinter labels Deeley's "What the hell does she mean by that?" as being delivered "to himself," the line is, in a way, an aside; like a Shakespearean aside, it may focus on the audience offstage. Pinter's work, here and elsewhere, is certainly not Brechtian, but it does seem to *allude*—perhaps that is the most accurate word for the situation—to the area and the people, the other guests of the evening, just offstage.

And this seems appropriate for a play where the image of the offstage audience is so pervasive, most noticeably in the word "gaze" bandied about by Deeley and Anna with full Sartrean/ existential implications. Or consider Kate's annoyance at being the object of the onstage audience of two, who look at her constantly, speaking of her as if she were an object of contemplation. Complaining that they treat her as if she were "dead," in her final speech Kate reduces her friend and then her husband to mere objects. Deeley's "I'll be watching you" may be ironic if we read *Old Times* as Kate's dream, in which she watches characters of her own creation perform. It also appears to set the metadramatic boundaries of the work.

Pinter, to be sure, offers his own directions for blocking and movement, whether it be that moment when "Anna stands, and walks to the window," or her being "discovered sitting on the divan" at the start of act 2. Such moments themselves cover the range of blocking, as it involves playing space, furniture, and areas of the stage. In this way, the playwright himself points to the pervasive, vital visual "text" by which the stage picture complements, at times even qualifies the dialogue or verbal text.

The Rehearsal Process

Excluding informal conversations among the actors and me along with individual meetings, rehearsals proper, which were held in the late afternoons and for roughly two hours each, extended for a two-month period before the television filming, and for another two weeks before the stage production. Those two weeks, intended both as brush-up rehearsals and a time to make such adjustments as would be necessary for the move to the stage and a live audience, turned out to be the most creative period of the entire rehearsal process. At that time, some 20 percent of the blocking was changed, not only because of the move to the stage but also as a result of rethinking the characters and their "status" at certain moments in the play. Thus, the break between the television filming and this latter period of rehearsals, and the chance we had for reflection, enhanced as it was by the fact that we could actually view the production as it existed on-screen, allowed for a certain quantum leap in the conception of *Old*

Times and its subsequent enactment. What held steady, deepened if unchanged in its general design, were the basic portraits of the three characters outlined earlier in this chapter. Still, the characters remained flexible, full of contradictory desires and impulses, capable of a variety of responses for any given situation.

The segment where Anna in the flashback warns Kate about the park at night is a case in point, complicated as it is by the fact that, if this moment is to be taken as a flashback, there is a question of whether the personalities, even the speaking styles of both women should revert to that moment in time, some twenty years ago. Or, if Kate is the playwright behind the scenes, does she only "play" the submissive daughter here, whereas Anna, from her own perspective, is the dominant mother in earnest? And to what degree is Kate playing, or both Kate and Anna playing for Deeley's benefit? Again, the issue is the nature and the extent of the flashback.

We first tried the scene as if it were taking place in the past for both women, with Kate the daughter straining at her confines, Anna the mother almost hysterically insistent that her daughter not venture out. Then, as Anna gets into her description about the park, she realizes that she has overreacted to Kate's "Oh, I don't know. We could go out." In her desire to protect her daughter, she actually delivers a parody, however well intended at first, of parents warning of the dangers of the outside world, where men and women wait behind trees, traffic threatens at every moment, and—almost inexplicably—"swing doors" proves distasteful as do "all the chandeliers."

As a result, in this first rehearsal Anna's hysteria soon turned to laughter. The speech became a comic routine, and halfway through, both women, like girlfriends hugging each other, laughed in unison until the pause. Then, recovering her breath, Anna, suddenly dismissing the comedy, simply reminded Kate, no longer her daughter but her friend, that what Kate really wants to do is little different from what she herself wants, to stay at home.

But as our concept of the two characters deepened, especially as the notion took hold that the evening is being managed, scripted by Kate and, as a corollary, that Anna represents the attractive but domineering, possessive side of her personality, we made a radical change in the speech. Now, Kate's suggestion that they "go out" became purposeful, a set-up to test Anna's response. Afraid that other men and women will take Kate from her, desperate to reestablish a microcosmic world where she can live alone with Kate (as anticipated in the description of the two women with heads together at the cafe), and experiencing the park as if she herself were Kate, Anna reveals her own terror of the outside. The speech has the quality of a neurotic's nightmare, even as Anna tries to fashion herself as a savior shielding Kate from tragedy waiting should they step from the room. Deeley, watching from stage-right, stands for all men who "come out suddenly from behind trees." Incomprehensible by any rational standards as objects of terror, for Anna the swing doors and the chandeliers are, no less than the "shadows everywhere," horrendous threats. After the pause, she pleas in desperations for Kate to stay home, but the "you" who will "want to run home . . . and into [her] room" is clearly Anna herself. Observing in Anna what she had anticipated, Kate is still saddened by the performance, although not shocked that this once-attractive side of herself has revealed its darker half. Her "What shall we do then?" allows Anna's her wish: they will both stay in and Anna, now the compliant mother, will wait upon her daughter.

At other times, a version once tried was rejected and then reinstated, but with additions or qualifications. Kate's "No. I'll run it myself" is a prime example. Our initial instinct was that this line constitutes her first direct challenge to Anna's authority, to that routine from the past where, one imagines, Anna always drew Kate's bath. The challenge itself seems to be anticipated when Kate gives a noncommittal "I'll think about it in the bath" to Anna's suggestion of McCabe as the most appropriate male guest for the evening. Flushed with her recent successes—Kate has agreed to stay in, has agreed with Anna's opinion on clothes, and on the idea of inviting a man over—Anna is shocked at the apparent change in mood. Conversely, having been excluded from the women's conversation during the flashback, Deeley is pleased at what he takes to be Kate's rejection of Anna. As she delivers her final line before exiting from the stage, Kate appears firm in her conviction, almost combative, clearly showing that she knows what effect the lines must have on Anna. Thus, "Shall I run your bath for you" has graphically reminded Kate of just how much Anna tried in the past to control every aspect of her life.

However, this version soon appeared too heavy, too much a "curtain line." Yet when we tried it in a lighter fashion, with Kate's suggesting nothing more than that she is grateful for Anna's offer but, in wanting to draw her own bath, means no offense—this night for some (at most) inexplicable reason she simply wants to "do it herself"—the new version seemed too light, not important enough, anticlimactic in an act that so far has moved from one climax to another. Nor did the "light" version match the mime closing the act, as Anna looks fondly after Kate on her exit, before reluctantly turning back to face Deeley, who, as he raises his glass, smiles at her in a smug fashion.

It was only three days before the first stage performance that we resolved the problem. A bit disturbed by Kate's halfhearted response to her suggestion of McCabe, Anna reaches out—Kate was halfway between Anna sitting on the stage-left sofa and Deeley standing on the left side of the stage-right sofa—and takes Kate's hand, fondly, but as if pleading for her to be as agreeable now as she has been so far in the conversation. There is also a bit of anxiety in that touch, as if Anna fears being left alone with Deeley. However, Anna goes too far here, pushes Kate too far, for, equipoised between husband and friend, Kate feels that Anna's intimate touching of her hand is designed, whatever her conscious intentions, to force her to choose between them. Kate, of course, will do that later in the evening—but not just yet. Looking at Deeley, aware that he has seen Anna touch her hand, Kate now delivers the line about drawing her own bath to Deeley, as if assuring him that she cannot be owned by Anna—or by him, for that matter. Our "heavy" reading, in one sense, was restored, but with several differences: the declaration of Kate's independence is meant for both Anna and Deeley; she thereby also shows her present neutrality on the issue of their rivalry; and she reassures Deeley, whose ego has been severely bruised, that she remains his wife. The bath now becomes Kate's announcement of the intermission, as she leaves both rivals onstage, warned—if they fully catch the warning—about the potential results of their competition. Each is comforted but also discomforted by Kate's closing lines.

Most often, a version was deepened by adding elements, large or small, that sustained a reading that seemed to work. It should be noted that for any given section of the play such readings came at various times, from early to late in the rehearsal period. For instance, Deeley's menacing description of the tea he pours Anna—"Good and hot. Good and strong and hot"—led to his deliberately asking Anna if she "Like[s] the room" just as she is about to take her first sip. As a result, Anna is forced to get out her response, "Yes," only by stopping herself in the midst of taking a drink. Even when he plays the smiling host, here substituting for his wife who is offstage taking her bath, Deeley is obsessed with annoying Anna, verbally and then physically.

At first Kate delivered her "Yes I remember" after she had poured the coffee for Anna and Deeley—as Pinter's stage direction indicates—and was crossing upstage to deliver it; in effect, her response comes some time after Anna's question, "can you tell me?" (For his part Deeley had responded quickly, with his deflating "We rarely get to London.") But the gap between Anna's question and Kate's response seemed too long. We worried: Would the audience, hearing the script for the first time, even remember Anna's question? By the simple act of having Kate respond right after Deeley, and as she rises to cross downstage, we not only solved this problem but got an extra bonus. Kate's encouraging response, coming as it does after Deeley's discouraging (and self-revealing) one, thrills Anna, who, crossing upstage (to take her seat on the stage-right sofa, where Kate herself had been sitting), is further rewarded when Kate touches her hand as they pass. Noting this intimate act, Deeley is thereby "punished" by Kate for that discourteous "We rarely get to London." This touching of hands set up, and would be contrasted with, a second such intimate contact between the women at the end of the act.

Initially, Deeley and Anna sat on the stage-left divan when Kate entered from her bath, and, since there seemed no good reason for Anna to get up at this point, this meant that they also sang their song for her from that position. However, having Anna rise earlier to cross to the drum-table and deposit her teacup (so that she could then sit on the opposite divan) seemed artificial. Besides, the idea was appealing of having her holding her position on the divan, not moved or even offended by Deeley's insane suggestion that she supervise his powdering of Kate. Still, I wanted her somewhere else onstage when Kate entered, so that the singers, physically separated, might frame Kate's entrance, even while sharing the same song for the first extended time in the play. Going back over the text, we were struck by Deeley's crude, chauvinistic reference to the women as "two birds." This seemed more than enough to motivate Anna's rising and leaving Deeley. She will sit beside him, compete with him, but only if he does so on a fair, sophisticated level: slangy, sexist name-calling violates the rules.

Hence, in the revised blocking, Anna, offended by his remark, rises and walks to the drum-table, not so much to deposit her cup (though she did in fact do that) but rather to show her displeasure by turning her back to Deeley. Angered by her action, unable to rise above the occasion, he lets out the expletive "Christ," almost as if cursing himself for stooping to the chauvinistic remark. Unable to stop, Deeley insults her body as, looking at her hips, he estimates that she "must be about forty . . . by now." Kate enters on Deeley's next line, where he angrily assures Anna that, since she is now forty and cursed with wide hips, he would not recognize her at present if she walked into the Wayfarers Tavern. By bringing Kate on earlier than Pinter's stage direction indicates, we allowed Deeley, suddenly realizing that he had been overheard, to feel guilty, and this guilt led to the motivation for his initiating the song celebrating his wife, "The way you wear your hat." On her part, Anna "senses" Kate's presence, as if she can feel this other part of herself now onstage. Rescued by Kate's entrance, and realizing that she has overheard her rival at his worst, and most chauvinistic, Anna enters joyfully into the song contest, glad to battle again an opponent whose present wound is self-inflicted. I should add that our change of beverages from coffee to tea played into her first line, "The way you sip your tea." Clearly, then, the object of each rival in the song contest is very different: Deeley is apologizing; Anna is—albeit foolishly—capitalizing on an opponent's mistake.

All of *Old Times* is "difficult" in the sense of being a challenge. Moreover, it is so tightly constructed that there is no let up, no gratuitous moment when the conflict is relaxed, let alone forgotten. I do not think the challenge exists because the play's language is "symbolic"—in the way we use that term in referring to Shakespeare—or self-consciously "deep." Nor does the play labor in some allegorical fashion to sustain distinct levels of meaning that would complicate every passage or moment in the performance. Pinter is not heavy-handed in this fashion. Rather, *Old Times* covers the gamut of what we say during a social occasion, from shallow, "cocktail" remarks to the portentous, even pretentious, moments that disclose more about the speaker than the intended subject of his or her remarks. Since each of the three characters has a different object or agenda for that evening, and—equally—since the playwright refuses to label or explain away that object, the play is, in the sense I define above, "difficult."

Nevertheless, there are also some passages, some moments that in themselves proved difficult, in the most conventional sense of the word. The cinematic flashbacks, already mentioned, were the most obvious. Just when one—be it actor or spectator or reader—

is getting used to the structure or style of presentation, a present-tense social evening, a happening, in which a visitor from the past intrudes, he or she is confronted with two extended sections for which there seems no logical transition or, for the actors, motivation. Coming right after Kate's question "Do you like the Sicilian people?," Anna's "Don't let's go out tonight" seems as abrupt as does Kate's "Is it raining" in act 2. Both lines initiate flashbacks, and while the ensuing dialogue between the women can to some degree be seen as a conscious effort to act again as they used to, in part because they find such self-styled regression pleasurable, in part to annoy Deeley, still, the change seems abrupt. Even if Kate is only testing Anna, or even if Anna is hallucinating that she is with her roommate twenty years ago, the fact is that both characters speak in the present tense, as if the past were present. My concerns were not only how to offer the actors motivation, or at least a reason for this change, but also how to prepare the audience. Would they be able to accept this violation of the play's (otherwise) dominant style of presentation? A change of lighting seemed too crude, and, besides not being called for in Pinter's directions, would reduce the effectiveness of the one radical lighting change at the end of act 2. From a "literary" standpoint, or from the perspective of the play in its entirety, these flashbacks made sense, fitting nicely an interpretation that stressed the power of the past over the present, or calling attention to the interior and psychological, rather than the realistic nature of *Old Times*.

The challenge was met in part by just "doing it," going into the change, but also in part by having the two women change their voices as they got deeper into the flashback. Kate became a little girl—even this was compatible with the notion that, for larger reasons, in both instances she is consciously impersonating her younger self—her voice higher, younger, "girlish." For her part, Anna became very much the "mother," with a particularly strong maternal edge to her delivery, that of the older woman who knew what was best for her daughter. In the second flashback, where she is less confident, Anna is a mother trying desperately to be her daughter's equal, younger, a girlfriend rather than a parent.

To a degree, also, we simply allowed the two flashbacks to stand on their own, however precariously at the time of their enactment. After all, it was Kate's final speech, where she reveals that, all along, she had been testing Anna, before making her decision to delete this character from her self, that would ultimately justify both the flashbacks. All the time Kate has been reviving or visiting the past only to put it in perspective, and hence the flashbacks represent the most blatant of these authorial "visits." Pinter's "silence" before the first flashback also helps the transition, for, like the one before the "two usherettes" speech, this one seemed to indicate not so much a halt in the conversation as a passage of time during the evening itself. On this same argument, we took the liberty of expanding the "pause" before Kate's "Is it raining out?" (which precedes the second flashback) to a silence.

Almost without exception, the solution (though hardly THE solution) reached for in any of these difficult passages strengthened the immediate play and, in some instances, interpretations of *Old Times* itself. For instance, when Anna caps Deeley's story of the party with "I've rarely heard a sadder story," does she mean that his efforts are pathetic or unintentionally self-revealing? Or does she show sympathy for him, this man who lost a date to a female friend and, by his own admission, was left with nothing more than the "indentations of four buttocks" on the sofa? Our judgment here was that, essentially, Anna is being cynical, that she puts Deeley's story in its rightful place with her adjective "sadder." Indeed, she delivers this word with a critic's smile on her face, though unseen by Deeley since her back is now to him as she crosses downstage to deposit her tea cup. Still, the response may not be entirely cynical. The double meaning is preserved: whatever ulterior motives Deeley had in telling the story, it is still sad in the sense of "touching" or "effective," if one understands the mentality of a man whose need is to possess women.

Kate's spartan lines were always difficult, for, on the surface, they seem so simpleminded, obvious, even at times self-centered in that rather than keeping up with the conversation Kate tends to talk about herself, about her mood or what she prefers. For instance, after Anna and Deeley are finished with Anna's encomium to the country home, and have shifted to the issue of the word "lest," Kate suddenly blurts out with "Sometimes I walk to the sea. There aren't many people. It's a long beach." What is behind this apparent non sequitur? Perhaps our initial reaction is that she is daydreaming and has not kept up with the conversation. However, what does the combination of the line's three sentences signify? Does she like the sea, or the fact that there aren't many people, or that the beach is long (as opposed to being short)? After much debate in rehearsals, the line was read as her effort to get the rivals back to their object, which is not so much to attack each other—as Deeley's quibble about "lest" threatens to do—as to reveal themselves through their competition. Anna's line after the pause suggests that she, if not Deeley, gets Kate's message, for against the picture of the lonely, long beach, she juxtaposes the London of their girlhood, the populous city (however redundant that phrase is) which she hopes Kate will "miss" as she herself does.

Another puzzler is Kate's "Yes, I quite like that kind of thing, doing it," which occurs after an awkward pause generated by the bickering of Deeley and Anna over the latter's mistake (perhaps a purposeful one) of complimenting Deeley for having a "wonderful casserole" instead of "wonderful wife." Deeley uses the occasion to distinguish the country from the city: in the former, one needs "substantial," non-"vegetarian" food to "keep [one] going." Again, Kate's ambiguous line might represent an effort to return the combatants from the fight to the object of the fight: herself. Not denying she likes to cook, and thereby dispelling Anna's slur that Deeley has reduced Kate—or Kate in turn has allowed herself to be reduced—to a hausfrau who does little more than cooking casseroles for guests, Kate implies that this is just one among many "things" she likes to do. Refusing to specify when Anna asks her "What kind of things?" she likewise resists Deeley's reductive definition of those things as "cooking." This time, Anna shows a too eager hand when she seizes upon the issue of cooking to recall the past when the two busy women "every so often dished up an enormous stew."

Kate's silence here speaks loudly; she is not just a cook, neither Deeley's at present nor Anna's fellow cook from the past. If Kate is the ultimate odd man out, then Deeley and Anna, as hosts, have a difficult time fathoming this visitor, in the same way Stanley in *The Birthday Party* has difficult dealing with his two visitors. Clearly Kate, who is not the cook or servant to either husband or friend, is talking here about a topic larger than cooking. Yet later, Deeley, as if unable to take a hint, or unwilling to give up the issue of cooking itself, reintroduces the subject of the vegetarian casserole that he takes pleasure in reminding Anna they had prepared for her husband. His subtext would be that real man, manly men, do not let their wives go on vacation without them, eat meat, are not vegetarians, and that Anna's husband is therefore a "women" (in Deeley's chauvinistic coloring of that word). By not coming with his wife, he has further insulted their efforts to be good hosts since they have gone out of their way to accommodate his food preferences. This time Anna closes the topic, and decisively so, by informing Deeley that not only is her husband not a vegetarian but that he is "something of a gourmet."

To underscore just how central the visual dimension is to this play that, at first, seems little beyond conversation, indeed might even seem "talky" on an initial reading, I should point out that the physical "business" of *Old Times* itself proved difficult. As described earlier, the ceremony of pouring coffee and brandy was more intricate than difficult, especially given all the business we added to Pinter's otherwise simple stage directions, such as Deeley's insisting that Kate, rather than he, return his rejected coffee cup to her side of the drum-table.

Similarly, the "cigarette-lighting" routine took countless run-throughs. Kate is already on stage-right, her cigarette lit, when first Anna and then Deeley move from stage-left to join her. Jarred by Kate's threat—"You talk of me as if I were dead"—each becomes suddenly (and deservedly) insecure, needing to reassure Kate that she is not a mere object or topic of conversation. In their anxiety and confusion, mistaking Kate's initial "were" for the past rather than as the optative tense, they hurry to assure her—illogically—that in the past she was not dead. But Kate abruptly reminds them: "I said you talk about me as if I were dead." Part of their misguided effort to correct what they mistakenly think is Kate's own misconception is to get close to her, and quickly so. Here they do so by sharing in the routine of lighting (and joining her in) a cigarette.

The ceremony needs to go quickly and smoothly. Still, there must be time for Anna to take a seat so that Kate, as she lights her cigarette, can appear "shyly poised" over her, for it is this tableau that enrages Deeley, driving him to utter a petulant "Stop that," the subtext for which is: "You look like two lesbian lovers, at a moment of intimacy, and I won't have such abnormal behavior in my house, or from my wife." After practicing the routine for what seemed forever, we were finally able to establish its rhythms. Kate, cigarette in hand, takes the box from Deeley, who had lit his cigarette almost as soon as he got to the right side of the sofa, indeed at the same time Anna takes a seat on Kate's left. During Anna's "You weren't dead. Ever" Kate moves upstage-left of her and gracefully offers her a cigarette, hands the box back to Deeley, and takes a lighter, "flicking" it and lighting Anna's cigarette on the important line "shyly poised over me." Angered by what he sees, Deeley snatches the lighter from

Anna's hand—*his* lighter, a large, somewhat gaudy silver object, "masculine" in the same way that the excessively large brandy snifters signify him. He snaps at them, "Stop that," the line underscored as he returns his lighter to its proper place on the table. Even as it serves the two rivals as an act of reassurance, or of assuring Kate of what she herself needs no assurance, that she is very much alive, the basic act of lighting a cigarette becomes a bone of contention, for Anna mistakenly sees Kate's lighting of her cigarette as a recreation of their past intimacy, or such intimacy as she imagined existed between them. Deeley, caught off guard, can only cry out like some parent or policeman: "Stop that!"

The silence that follows then has a double function. First, Deeley's abrupt line makes more conversation difficult, indeed almost impossible. Second, time passes during that silence, or at least enough time for Kate to come from behind the sofa and sit on Anna's left while Deeley, characteristically, goes for another drink to soothe his damaged ego. As if pulling the topic out of a vacuum, shaken as he is by the tableau of the two women sharing a smoke and thereby unable to make a convincing transition to another subject, Deeley launches into a celebration of his student days which includes, as something of a reprimand for Kate, an unflattering portrait of her as a compliant woman, who, unlike Deeley, lacked "any sense of fixedness." Growing out of the rivals' separate fears of offending Kate, a revealing moment in itself and hence a "text" beyond the mechanics of the social routine of smoking, this "three-on-a-match" also leads to a silence, which, in turn, generates Deeley's second, and most unsuccessful long speech (so far) in the play.

Some dimensions of the play could only evolve more slowly. The tempo of the interchanges, particularly between Deeley and Anna, gradually developed its own rhythms in rehearsal. At times the two practically fall on each other's lines, as when Deeley asks Anna if men can also experience "ripples." Here Anna delights in leading Deeley on, meeting his anxious "You mean the ripples" with a noncommittal "If you like," and then, with Deeley's "Do men ripple too?" on its heels, repeating the taunting with a quick "Some, I would say." Only Deeley's "I see" can bring a pause to this wild, verbal goose-chase. Similarly, the prepositions "in" and "out" come with rapid fire, when Anna plays with Deeley on the subject of where (in or out of the tub) and how (with Kate in or out of the bathtowel) to dry a woman who has just bathed. When Deeley suggests that Kate is delighted with Anna's visit because she has few friends, Anna snaps back with the logical but ambiguous "She has you." Without missing a beat, Deeley tries to correct his first comment, observing that Kate has not made many friends since her marriage, and again Anna jumps on his qualification with "Perhaps she has all she wants." When Deeley tries to contribute to this now disputed issue of Kate's friends with the observation that his wife "lacks curiosity," Anna is just as abrupt with her own explanation: "Perhaps she's happy." The entire interchange is conducted with a speed unlike that of any normal conversation. Again, a pause mercifully draws this staccato exchange to a halt.

There are also moments when the characters speak with deliberate slowness, relishing every word, drawing out each nuance, even adding pauses beyond those indicated by Pinter. This is particularly true for the longer or set speeches, although not for all of them. Anna's opening speech, for example, starts with a bang, as she relives the days in London; at this point she is as full of passion and energy as Deeley appeared exhausted near the end of his interrogation of Kate, especially after he had learned that the two friends "roomed together." Yet as Anna moves downstage, toward the "performance area" in centerstage, she slows her delivery markedly on the passage about the two women, "heads bent," sitting quietly in the café. The mood is reverent; indeed, Anna's hands are folded in prayer as if the calm moment she describes is a sacred one. Even more slowly she reaches for the right word, rejecting "disturb" in favor of "distract," and, having said "listened," repeating and then expanding on it: "listened to all those words."

Conversely, Deeley's "two usherettes" speech begins slowly, earnestly, as if he were reliving a dream. Yet once he makes the connection between the woman in the movie and Kate now sitting before him so that the speech in turn moves to the present, he races through the narrative as he insists on his rights as a husband by recounting the history of his sexual conquest (the "true-blue pickup"), driving himself toward the ending before finishing almost postcoitally with a look into the future: since Robert Newton [once] brought them together, it is only Robert Newton who, if it ever happens, can "tear [them] apart."

It is the pauses and silences that define these rhythmic units, that serve for what in music would be called "bars" to the dialogue. In this sense, *Old Times* is like a composition with frequent changes in tempo between and among its segments. Even within a segment the tempo constantly changes. It is the pauses and, though less rarely, silences that signal such variations in the speed of delivery. This became especially evident in the final days of rehearsals. At times during a pause one can see through the character's expression or movements (or both), and hence *feel* him or her racing inwardly, trying to assess what has just been said and, at the same time, to prepare a response, to say something inwardly that will allow him or her to substitute a more sophisticated and hence less revealing facial or physical reaction for the more raw, unsubtle emotions the character senses he or she is currently displaying. At other times, the pause allows a character to relax, to savor a victory, or, as is often the case with Anna, to forget the competition for a moment and dwell luxuriously within a memory that has just been rekindled. Much of our rehearsal, accordingly, was spent rehearsing *Old Times*'s numerous pauses and silences. Conversely, rehearsal of the dialogue often was structured around the distinct portions of the text bounded by two pauses, or a silence and a pause. In the later stages of rehearsals, we could practice that larger portion of the play contained between two silences.

Some individual lines also stood out, either grabbing our attention immediately in a way that allowed us to get at what seemed to be the heart of the situation, or remaining puzzles until late in the rehearsal period. In the middle of her story about the man in the secretaries' room, Anna comes to a stop, then suddenly corrects herself. She had said the man had come over to her "quickly," but now realizes she was "quite wrong . . . he didn't move quickly . . . that's quite wrong . . . he moved . . . very slowly." Whatever her object in this speech may be, however much she—along with Deeley who listens to her apprehensively from the stage-left sofa—is reliving the moment, here she suddenly becomes very conscious of her role as a narrator editing her own story. Metadramatically, Anna drops her disguise as a character and becomes an actress, having just fouled up an important line and, onstage, before her audience of two—and the audience in the house as well—now correcting herself, getting the line "right." In Brecht or in Pirandello, such a self-reflexive moment would be almost commonplace, but in the autonomous, hermetically sealed world of *Old Times*, it is glaring.

Startled ourselves by this moment, we speculated, increasingly, that at one level the evening is very much a game involving three players, that whatever the psychological or even philosophical stakes involved for Anna, Deeley, and—more subtly— Kate, each is very conscious of, takes delight in, and is desperate to "win" this game, where the weapon of choice is language, where one can appreciate an opponent's skill even as he or she tries to best that opponent by an even greater verbal display. The play is a game where there are rules, penalties, a game that has two playing areas (the sitting-room and later the bedroom), and an agreed upon time-limit of two acts or, roughly, one hour (*Old Times* is a short play with two thirty-minute halves or acts). To be sure, this is serious play, not just a "game" in the more reductive sense of that word. *Old Times* is about important issues, for both the characters or players involved as well as the audience, or spectators. Yet it is also a game, serious in the way games can be, especially games that clearly serve as metaphors for life itself, even as the stage is a microcosm for the world that, in its own often unacknowledged way, is also a "stage."

The pleasure that my actors took in the dialogue written by a fellow actor, who knows the particular needs of actors in that special way understood by a playwright turned actor, was inseparable from the pleasure that Deeley and Anna take in their competition, and that Kate, the unannounced player, finds as her two teams challenge each other. All this is at one with the pleasure that, during the stage production, I saw the audience take in the dialogue itself. Whatever its psychological, or thematic implications, Pinter's dialogue, like that of Wilde or, in our day, Stoppard, is also pleasurable in itself, "witty," and "well-crafted" in the best sense of those otherwise abused words.

Other lines seemed buried deep within the fabric of the play, almost like subtextual phrases felt by the character and only with difficult becoming accessible to the audience. For example, at one point Deeley corrects himself by changing his question "Why isn't she married?" to "I mean, why isn't she bringing her husband?" Kate replies testily, "Ask her." Is Deeley suggesting that Anna is unhappily married and hence "needs" Kate, or (worse) that she is still in love with Kate and that this situation has ruined her marriage? Kate's annoyance grows over the next several lines, and when Deeley counters her "Everyone's married" with "Then why isn't she bringing her husband?" Kate's "Isn't she?" puts Deeley on the defensive for the first time in the interchange, and leads into a pause. Since Anna has been corresponding with her friend Kate, how would Deeley know whether or not Anna, if she is married, is bringing her husband? Collecting his wits during the pause, Deeley answers Kate's unanswerable question with a very logical one: "Did she mention a husband in her letter?" Kate's simple "No" is the puzzling line, or rather word here. It could be a lie (we learn later that Anna is married) and hence a chance to frustrate Deeley further, or it could be an abrupt way to end the conversation. We decided to take it as a simple fact: Anna has not mentioned her husband in the letter, and Kate, therefore, cannot be sure whether or not she is married. Nevertheless, the "no" now echoes deeply in the context of her earlier comment that everyone is married. Anna was attractive; attractive women tend to get married, or so Kate assumes. Perhaps Kate even hopes that Anna is married, that their own days as intimate roommates did not inhibit Anna's desire to be married. Knowing that Anna had deep feelings for her, Kate perhaps hopes that, if Anna is married, those feelings have been dissipated by marriage. And so, however much she may have controlled the question-and-(non)answer session so far, Kate cannot answer Deeley's question with a preferred "yes." Her own inevitable "no" disturbs her; for a rare moment in the conversation her guard is down. Noticing this, Deeley seizes the opportunity, the initiative, asking Kate, since Anna was her "only" friend, to speculate on what he'd be like. Her refusal of his invitation to speculate is a rather halfhearted, uninspired "I have no idea," and it is not until her next line that Kate returns to her more forceful, witty self, one that can play engagingly with the overanxious Deeley.

Some lines stood out because they seemed to break out of the play's little world and acknowledge the audience, such as Deeley's "Am I alone in beginning to find all this distasteful?"— a line that, during rehearsal, we could only pray the audience would not find applicable to the production itself. And in a play where each line of dialogue seemed to form a close-knit pattern with every other line, there was the occasional line that stuck out, almost like the "one-liner" applied so pejoratively to the less-than-well-made play. Anna's abrupt retort to Deeley's encomium for Robert Newton was one of these, the sort of response all of us dream of giving to a windbag who usurps the conversation at some cocktail party: "F. J. McCormick was good too." Deeley scores a parallel one-liner with his "We rarely get to London," and later with his "He can't make it. He's out of town," although it should be observed that generally his one-liners are more self-revealing than Anna's and, as a consequence, less focused or thereby effective.

Rehearsals, more than any read-through of the text, also highlighted the oddities of grammar and syntax in *Old Times*, the labored, often archaic constructions that, it is interesting, come mostly from Anna. Deeley's anguished *"What?"* may reflect his confusion over form as much as syntax with her "There are things I remember which may never have happened but as I recall them so they take place." The sentence's two halves bear a curious, nonparallel relationship, and the "but" and "so" give the already involved passage a strange, rhythmic quality. Kate's "It is a very long time" is grammatically sound; she means something like, "No, I can't remember because it has been a very long time since I last lived with Anna in London." It should be noted she has not yet informed Deeley that they were roommates. However, in rehearsal our Kate invariably wanted to say "was" (as in, "It was a very long time ago") rather than Pinter's "is."

Deeley, of course, is capable of lapsing, consciously and at times unconsciously, into dialect, and when this occurs, his grammar becomes awkward, or redundant. Jealous of Anna's description of her life in Sicily, he tries to establish his image as an equal to her husband, a world-class businessman, but his repetition of the phrase "matter of fact" belies the emasculated man underneath the posturing: "As a matter of fact I am at the very top of my profession, as a matter of fact."

The cliché holds: rehearsals are a learning process. One studies the text by doing the play; in the case of Pinter—particularly—the play as a piece for performance cannot be fully known in theory, or in the study. Hence, by the final day of rehearsals, *Old Times* was, in part, the work envisioned in my director's concept, but only in part, for just as often as that concept has been sustained by rehearsals, it had been qualified, rejected, and—usually—deepened.

I had not realized, for example, just how raw the antagonism between husband and wife is in their opening conversation while Anna stands upstage. Kate despises this man who, under the guise of polite questions, the small-talk one makes with a mate while waiting for the guest to arrive, is desperate to analyze Anna through his wife's memories so that he will be that much more prepared to assault her when she arrives. However much she may successfully hide her own designs for the evening from him, Kate here just manages to conceal her disgust with Deeley. Though he is not completely insensitive to the fact that he is offending her, Deeley, for his part, cannot stop himself. His obsession to know, to be able to catalog any visitor to this house and hence to control that visitor, cannot itself be controlled.

All of us involved with the play, women as well as men, also began to understand Deeley's "illness," to look sympathetically at the horrible gap between his behavior and those emotional needs that he cannot fathom and therefore cannot satisfy. From the start, he seemed in deep decline from the man Kate once knew, and in his references to his father and mother and, later, to the male friends of his youth, Deeley himself exposes his own impossible dream of returning to a period of innocence, real love, and friendship. For us, of the two rivals he was clearly the evening's "loser," and to a large degree he deserves what he get. Nevertheless, Deeley never fell below sympathy, even our empathy, and it is this kinder, more humane man to whom Kate refers when, near the end, she talks of the women's once finding his face "very sensitive, vulnerable." The compliment may have a negative ring—by implication, Deeley is no longer sensitive or vulnerable—but Kate goes on to assure him that he wasn't "crass" like other men they knew. For us, this Deeley of the past was not an afterthought on Kate's—or her playwright's—part, but someone there all along, however buried or muted on this particular evening.

In this same light, Anna, in rehearsals, never became the scheming vixen, the vampirish "dyke" that some critics and some productions have found. On the other hand, Pinter's "woman's play" was never, in our experience, chauvinistic, in the sense of glorifying, without any qualifications, female bonding. Kate herself has been variously described as a spoiled brat, a self-centered, clearly limited individual who is absurdly over-prized by Anna and Deeley, or as cold and calculating. Instead, we found her "human," in a word, trying to assert her real self, grateful to and yet rightly suspicious of the play's two claimants. Her rejection of friend and husband at the end is a painful move, but necessary. For trying to possess her, Anna and Deeley get what they deserve, are justly punished, put in their place. Still, their needs are all too understandable, and inevitable, and it is sad at the end to see these skillful artists, these engaging combatants, reduced to silence. It is no less hard to distance oneself from any of the three characters: we all need to be loved, to love. Unfortunately, these twin, complementary emotions are not easily separate from the desire to possess, to control. To know oneself is easier said than done.

Clearly Anna and Deeley are antagonists, and their combat is both exhilarating and—no less—terrifying, for there is something primitive in this battle between the genders, where the motivation for victory is both sexual and philosophical. But, increasingly during rehearsals, we felt a bond between the two and, at times, even a love, or vestiges of a former love. At the very least, Deeley and Anna appreciate each other's ability. After the same object, using the same weapons, possessed of an equal intensity, both with legitimate claims to a portion of the past, gifted in their enactment of memory, in a phrase "fellow artists" and "fellow performers," each can see something of himself or herself in the other, is mirrored in the rival. In a way, they live to compete with each other, and this is why, I think, both sometimes lose sight of Kate, their object, in the heat of competition, and why, no less, Kate must remind them of her presence. At the end, Anna reveals that she was the woman at the party, that Deeley looked up *her* skirt, but this tawdry "affair" does not explain the larger relationship between them. During the song duet, I suggested to the rivals that perhaps they once lovingly sang these same songs, in precisely the same order, to each other, and that now, even as they direct them toward Kate, they are aware of the irony of the present occasion.

In several ways, Anna, no less than Kate, is the type of woman Deeley wants, even idolizes. Until Kate's final speech, Deeley and Anna monopolize the dialogue, engage in numerous competitive "duets," and in act 2 literally own the majority of "stage time." When they are "on," battling each other, it is easy to forget Kate. Hence, the very special relationship that exists between the two actors assigned the roles of Anna and Deeley feeds into relationship, the closeness between the two characters. Deeley first describes Kate as having a "classic female figure," but, moving upstage and close to Anna who sits on the stage-right sofa with Kate, he stops and directs to her a possible rewording of the phrase, "or is it a classic female posture," as if he is asking her opinion. Even though he has earlier made fun of her old-fashioned vocabulary, here he recognizes Anna's own skill with words. Even if just rhetorically, he solicits her opinion but—catching himself—without stopping long enough for her answer.

If they acknowledge each other as a worthy rival—surely a prerequisite stance that any good fighter must adopt toward his or her opponent—there are times in the play when Deeley and Anna, besides losing sight of Kate, lose sight of each other. Our feeling was that at certain moments each, as an artist and a performer, becomes so absorbed in recreating a particular memory, in playing a part, that he or she forgets, even if just for a second or so—albeit sometimes longer—that a social evening is in progress. In part, this reflects the pleasure in hearing one's own voices, the pleasure in choosing the right word or phrase. When we found such moments in rehearsal, we would often bring the character downstage, away from both a rival and Kate upstage, allowing them to stand "alone" in the centerstage performance space, or, taking things one step further, moving them toward the drum-table, and hence close to the television viewer or the first row of audience for the stage production. The last third of Anna's opening speech is delivered downstage-left; the pivotal part of Deeley's "clock speech" occurs as he touches "six" on the down side of the drum-table. Even the most formal part of Kate's big speech, when she describes the funeral "rites" for Anna, is delivered downstage, facing the audience, her back to Anna and Deeley. Earlier, as Deeley sits next to Anna for the final part of her story about the man in the room, she is clearly aware that the speech is having its desired effect, that Deeley (more than) suspects that he is the subject of her story. Yet as Deeley plies Anna with rather prosaic questions on the details, it is clear that she is still absorbed in the past and is still relishing her own skills as a narrator. Hence, while Anna sits a matter of inches from Deeley, he is also not there for her. She is a thousand miles, and at least twenty years away.

However, if the two stellar performers at times lost sight of each other and, in such self-absorption, lose sight of their object, Kate remains an onstage audience, aware of both, watching and listening to them, aware, if she is their creator, if they are figures in her dream, that she has summoned them to life, is the author of what they are thinking, of what they are saying even in the pauses and silences. They perform, if not always for each other, constantly for her, and—no less—for the audience. In a way, Kate is our onstage surrogate.

We see Old Times as a play, to be sure, but a play, a fiction, that touches on our own reality. Rehearsals move on to performance; the next chapter charts that performance in terms of further discoveries we made in the presence of (and very often because of) the audience.

4

Old Times Onstage

I think it is something of a romantic fallacy to say that a play changes in performance, that it improves, even becomes more profound. This does happen, of course, but more often than not the cast goes, indeed ought to go into a performance with the play basically set, with the same play that existed during the final week of rehearsal. Performances, to be sure, allow the actors to get "tighter," to work out rhythms, their interaction with fellow actors. And sometimes a director, urged by an actor or by his or her own good sense, will make adjustments, particularly with elements of the production that are just not working with the audience. Still, it is difficult, not to mention dangerous, to discover a play during performance.

Rather, I think the major change that occurs during a performance has more to do with the presence of an audience. Rehearsals, dress rehearsals, even dress rehearsals attended by an audience of friends, are not the same thing as opening night, or any subsequent performance in the run. The audience's presence, their responses, even their lack of response, somehow completes an equation, *ratifies* the performance that, up to this point, has not been a real performance but only a tryout, practice, a period of finding the play. Again, the rehearsal process, an exciting process to be sure, a "period of discovery" (to invoke the theatrical cliché), is ultimately not the same thing as a performance. Without making comments from the house, and yet "making comments" as they sit, sometimes stirring in their seats, occasionally turning to each other, commenting by the way they look at the stage, follow the actors about, by the way they sigh, even breath, commenting simply by the fact that they are there—the audience offers a reading, an interpretation, myriad intepretations—to be more accurate—of the performance. Alert to this ongoing analysis, and one that takes a different form, sometimes marginally, sometimes radically, every night, the director and the actors *learn* about the play from the audience, moving deeper

into its world, into its characters, even though the production—
again, with exceptions—remains essentially unchanged from
what they saw and heard during that final week of rehearsals. I
comment here, therefore, on some of the things I learned—we all
learned, since during the run of a play the audience's reaction
becomes a major topic of conversation between director and
actors—about *Old Times*. It should be noted that viewing the
television film, along with getting the reactions of audiences to
it, constituted a different kind of learning, and this will be an
issue in chapter 6.

Like the women's two cinematic leaps back to the London of
their girlhood days, the stage direction that has Anna present
and silent onstage—facing the window upstage, her back to
Deeley and Kate as they talk about her centerstage—is one of
those radical touches, those "twists" on reality as a set-designer
friend calls it, that sets Pinter apart from most other playwrights.
Conversations during rehearsals as well as with the audience
after performance offered a wealth of conflicting interpretations.
Was Anna simply in another part of the room? Another part of
the house? Is Anna something lodged in Kate's memory that she
is trying to suppress? Is she the past, an almost allegorical figure
waiting to break into the present? In larger measure, is the entire
evening Kate's dream, a scenario of her own making, and thus is
Anna an element of that dream waiting to make its entrance? Or
is she Deeley's nightmare, the intrusion on what he takes to be
a male-centered, male-dominated world by this "monster" from
the past, or by this side of his wife, at once passionate—and
thereby desired by him—yet liberated and hence the object of
his fear?

Noting these reactions, we decided to underscore Anna's presence by allowing the couple, at times singly, at times together, to
look in Anna's direction at appropriate moments, such as on
Deeley's "She remembers you." But, to complicate the issue, or
keep the interpretations in suspension, neither Deeley nor Kate
ever looked directly at her. In addition, Anna continued to face
upstage for the first part of her speech, from "Queing all night" to
"or the ballet, that night," and then turned suddenly downstage
toward Kate on "you haven't forgotten?" eager, almost frantic that
she confirm the romantic picture of the young secretaries and
their life in London.

No less an assault on the expected stage conventions, the mime
at the end—predictably—led to a variety of conflicting responses.

Judith Williams, the chairperson of the Theater Department, suggested that Deeley's motive in putting his head in Kate's lap was not just that of a child, seeking comfort from a "mother" he knew was mad at him, but also somewhat sexual—a last, desperate, public (since Anna is watching) attempt to be intimate with her. Thus, in the stage production we added a variation. Confident that Kate will now accept, even forgive him, foolishly imagining that he is once again the sensitive man his wife has described, even hoping that, by not rejecting him (Kate moves her arms as if to welcome Deeley when he sits beside her), she will be "sexually forthcoming," he turns his head slightly in her lap so that it presses against her. The move is overtly provocative. However, Kate, reacting, readjusts Deeley's head so that it rests, once again, more like that of a child than a lover. Then, after a few seconds, she takes her arm away, and he, responding to this signal that such intimacy as she has granted him is over, straightens up, rises, and backs reluctantly to his chair. He sits slowly, his posture soon adjusting to the "slumped" position.

Other dimensions of the production, of which we were aware in rehearsals, indeed, had purposely inserted into the characterization, became even clearer in performance, often taking on more significance than we had imagined or even intended. Most obvious was the degree to which the relatively silent Kate is actually in control of the evening, and hence the way in which the entire evening represents her scenario, with those too conscious artists or filmmakers, Deeley and Anna, becoming actors unaware in her script. Sometimes that control, Kate's power, came with a single phrase, such as the "bombshell" (the adjective we used in rehearsal) she drops when she tells Deeley that she and Anna "lived together." With a masterful strategy she prepares him for this revelation minutes earlier with her seemingly casual remark that Anna was her only friend, that she "had none. None at all. Except her," which deliberately turns the conversation from herself to Anna, forcing Deeley to confront once again the real object of his inquiry and his fear. He takes the bait, but his question, "Why her?" is met with a glaring, inconclusive "I don't know." Then, to this man starving for data, Kate throws out a titillating piece of intimate information: what attracted her to Anna was the fact that Anna was a thief.

Kate assaults Deeley even more directly when he mocks the nationality of Anna's husband. After a pause, she rises, then extinguishes her cigarette in the ashtray, which she places on the stage-right table. The voice now coming from the opposite side of the room, silent for so long during this final encounter between the competitors during act 1, asks her friend about the very life-style for which Deeley envies Anna, and in so asking begins a process that will close out this first act and by which Deeley is excluded.

Some of Kate's lines unnerve both Deeley and Anna, although in different ways. Kate tells them that she was interested in some of the arts, not all, but now cannot distinguish between the ones she enjoyed and those in which she has no interest. The line may be part of a pattern whereby Kate, playing by rules not fully understood by her would-be competitors, sets up responses in them, much as a playwright "moves" characters into various psychological postures and interactions. For if Deeley takes the line as an indictment of the couple's present culturally sterile life, or even as a criticism of his modest work as a filmmaker, Anna is so disturbed at the possibility that Kate has forgotten such important details from the past that she launches into a longish speech about their days in London, one that, in its first part, almost sounds like a reprise of her opening aria.

At one point, Deeley condemns Kate for lacking "curiosity." But Anna's retort is a simple, "Perhaps she's happy." Anna surely means that Kate is happy now that she is here, yet for Kate, an audience of one observing this centerstage battle between the two antagonists, the line has a different ring: Kate may not really need friends, male or female, neither Deeley nor Anna. That audience then speaks as Kate from her sofa upstage voices the first of several objections to being treated like an object, the subject of someone's gaze or conversation: "Are you talking about me?" The pronoun "you" can just as well be single as plural; even Deeley may answer for both Anna and himself with his "Yes."

Shortly after her bath speech in act 2 Kate delivers one of the most curious lines in the play. After just celebrating the rain for blurring the harsh edges of the city, she asks Anna if it is raining outside. Out of context, unmotivated in terms of the present-tense of the play, it seems like a line out of the past, as if Kate, perhaps for one final time revisiting the London days with Anna, were here purposely testing her friend. Or she may be responding sympathetically to a woman, once so dominant, indeed dominant in the first act until the closing conversation about the bath, who is now clearly on the defensive. More than Deeley, Anna, as if instinctively feeling a change in Kate, now realizes the deeper implications of the "bath" speech. In effect, Kate's question

stands as a vastly shortened redoing of the cinematic leap back-
ward initiated by both women near the end of the first act. And
there is an ironic logic to Kate's decision to stay in: since it is
not raining, and since the harsh edges of the city cannot be
blurred, then the flat is preferable. I realized in performance how
wonderfully applicable the cliché "less is more" can be for this
character whose dialogue is so simplistic and minimal.

No less performance highlighted the extent to which Deeley
degenerates as the evening wears on. Even as he neurotically
tries to establish an image of himself as a world traveler, someone
with his "eye"—curiously, the eye, rather than the hand, in this
play about the Sartrean gaze—on "a number of pulses, pulses all
around the globe," Deeley cannot conceal his longing for the
luxurious life he imagines Anna and her husband lead, a world
of pleasure and sexuality where the women have "the longest
legs in the world, the most phenomenally soft voices." This naked longing seems light years away from Deeley's witty self-con-
fident account of the movie, even though that speech was no less
an example, if a bit more subtle, of wish-fulfillment.

His third major speech in the play is clearly his most desperate
and, in light of his object, most unsuccessful. Here he lapses
into a "hip," some have even suggested colloquial Irish style,
wondering if he "should bejasus saddle [himself] with a slip of
a girl not long out of her swaddling clothes." Deeley's chauvinism is ragged here, as he contrasts himself, sure of what he
wanted even as he "juggled" his future, with Kate who lacked
"any sense of fixedness, any sense of decisiveness." Unlike the
first half of the usherettes speech, here there is little doubt to
whom he refers. Yet as he moves toward centerstage, as if to
envelope Kate even more graphically in his condemnation of
this woman who was "compliant only to the shifting winds," he
begins to come unhinged, stumbling over the distinction between
his winds, "*the* winds," and Kate's, and showing his irritation at
a woman's persistence in following not his winds but, "with no
understanding whatsoever, the winds that only she understood."
Then, the word "figured" distracts him as the image of a woman's
body comes into his mind, and when he mockingly nods toward
Anna, asking whether "posture" would be a more acceptable,
less inflammatory word than "figure," she shows no sign of acknowledging him. The pause is deadly since Deeley very much
needs someone to reply to him. Finding no one, he moves, awk-
wardly, toward the upstage window, as if banishing himself from

their company. Grasping at the word "position" to sum up his negative attitude toward Kate's indecision, he corrects himself, substituting the more pretentious and yet no more accurate phrase "categorical pronouncement." Deeley's phrase "twenty years ago" seem to imprison him in the past, in direct contrast to Anna for whom the past is not dead and who in fact imagines that her own effort to revive this evening is successful, at least in contrast to Deeley's present sorry spectacle. The play's third silence appears to entomb him.

In his "clock" speech, near the end of act 2, he is clearly at his weakest, and yet, paradoxically, in his failure he seems to become more humanly appealing. As Deeley approaches the end of his "journey," he confesses that he is no longer sure if the woman he took to the party and, later, to a café, was Anna or Kate. The speech ends quietly, in a burst of poetry, the woman sitting across from him "having coffee" and saying "little, so little." Deeley's paradoxical failure and modest victory suggest that in a very deliberate way *Old Times*, Pinter's "woman's play" champions masculine values that liberated women have always admired and which men have often distrusted, precisely because they seemed "womanish" rather than "manly." A play about the conflict between genders, *Old Times* at length erases distinctions between male and female.

That Anna is an artist, conscious, like Deeley, of crafting words and pictures, was always clear, but in performance this love of her craft, this addiction to fashioning reality through the past began to seem an even more grievous character fault. She veritably loses herself, for example, in the account of the two women at their coffee, heads bent. Onstage, our Anna physically matched her own text by folding her hands as if in prayer. Her substitution of "distract" for "disturb" came across as too painstaking, an attention to sound and to the slightest change in meaning that suggests she has forgotten her object in the speech, reliving the past for Kate and thereby excluding Deeley, and now takes a spurious pleasure in the exactitude of her scene painting.

Similarly, after describing the women cooking, then eating "an incredibly enormous stew," and then staying up late reading Yeats together—here, the object is clearly to distinguish their intimate, and intellectual former life from the cold, poetically barren marriage—she seems to retreat into herself, and self images, as she echoes her more public "more often than not" with an equally private "every so often," preceded, as it is, by a "yes"—a sort of signal that she has hit upon a particularly fertile phrase. When she returns to the original, "more often than not," it has been enriched, ornately encased by its variation.

Such behavior enables Kate to realize that Anna has only one narrow mission: to return to a past where she would possess her. Anna, in turn, is blind to her fall from grace in Kate's eye. Fresh from what she takes to be a victory over Deeley in the "Is Charlie coming?" sequence, she falls prey to her own misreading of Kate. As much to wound Deeley with her intimate knowledge of his wife as to recreate the past for Kate and herself, she delivers a set speech on Kate's shyness, how she "would fold away from" people, removing herself from both their conversation and their touch. Anna even provides a biographical explanation: Kate, we learn from her, was a parson's daughter, like Bronte, that is, in "secrecy" rather than in "passion" (presumably Anna's province). On Anna's "She folded herself from them," Kate, offended, rises, leaving her, crossing to and then stretching out on the stage-left divan. But Anna, lost in her performance mood, is herself not "disturb[ed]" or "distract[ed]." Even Deeley is unaware of Kate, captivated as he is by Anna's account. Herself forgetting Kate's earlier objection to being treated as if she were the dead object of someone else's gaze, Anna blindly proceeds to describe how she "would choose a position in the room" from which she could see Kate's "face." To underscore her story, she rises, crosses to Kate, and stands upstage of the divan, literally recreating the tableau of seeing Kate's "face, although she could not see [hers]."

Clearly Anna's greatest mistake is her last, when, eager to portray herself as the loyal friend for whom no sacrifice is too great, she claims that "all I wanted for her was her happiness. That is all I want for her still." The speech is more complex, more self-centered, and therefore self-reflexive than its speaker intends.

Together in their craft, and in their blindness to the stature of their audience, Anna and Deeley, in performance, appear at times almost like lovers, not so secretly admiring each other's ability, understanding the other, taking pleasure, for example, in forming a duet as they sing "They Can't Take That Away from Me" when Kate enters from her bath. When Deeley confirms Anna's "Doesn't she look beautiful" with his own "Doesn't she," the exchange parodies the introduction by twin masters of ceremonies for the winner of some beauty contest. Anna and Deeley, in effect, become the opening act, the presenters for the featured attraction. Earlier, when Deeley, playing the movie director, portrays Kate taking long walks, wearing a raincoat, her hands "deep in pockets," he even seems to call upon his "partner" Anna to fill in the missing but obvious details with "You know" and "All that kind of thing." And this sense of partnership is rekindled when he later crosses over to Anna and gives her a compliment: "We're forcing her to think. We must see you more often." It is as if the evening, at least from Deeley's perspective, has moved 180 degrees from that earlier testy interchange about the volcanic island. From this perspective, it is Kate who is the odd man out, as Deeley now leans on the arm of the stage-left sofa, eagerly, (almost) amorously, responding to Anna's "But she was always a charming companion" with "Fun to live with?"

Most of all, it is Kate's final speech that can only be realized in performance, that seems the "audience's reward" (as one of the actors called it) for spending the evening in the house, watching one fairly taciturn and two chatty characters onstage, in a play where nothing seems to happen, where the facts are alternately plentiful and scarce. For Kate's description of Anna is marked by a wealth of specifics and poetic description we have not heard before, and indeed which cannot be matched by even the most detailed, rich dialogue earlier of Anna or Deeley. In a play where, up to this point, the language has been teasing and suggestive, a semitransparent cover for something we assume is below the surface, Kate's language is so graphic that the exaggerated detail in turn mocks our sense of realism. The dirt on Anna's face is handwriting, "earnest inscriptions," or an ink that, "unblotted," has run down the page.

Earlier subtle, verbal, manifest in her telling silences, Kate's dominance is now patent and physical—terrifyingly so. Now, she takes Anna's place, standing above her friend sitting silent on the divan. Anna is a thief, once more, but now a pathetic one who tries to "borrow" a "trick" that only the master can perform with any seriousness and conviction. At one moment cold, general, abstract, the next Kate's language is specific. As Anna disintegrates, pupils vanish and bones break through a face that now must resemble a skull.

With "But all was serene," Kate crosses to the drum-table, resting her hands on it as if she were some speaker at a conference. I checked my initial impulse to have her deliver the speech, in Brecht's style, directly to the viewer or audience. She speaks here of the past as if it were a play, something that, however powerful when it first happened, now in retrospect seems without substance, something no more substantial than a performance which can now be assessed by an audience. While the speech is formal, seemingly without emotions as Kate speaks of Anna's death as being without witnesses and hardly worthy of "last rites," in performance Kate's personal sadness—albeit a weakness to her mind—shows through as she chokes back tears on "I felt the time and season appropriate."

With "it was time for my bath," she breaks from the reflective mood at the table, and moves gracefully upstage-right, to sit with Anna on "sat naked beside you and watched you." In a play about time, here Kate enacts in the present her narrative describing that moment twenty years ago when, refreshed from her bath, she returned to look once more at her dead roommate. But the event is a fiction, even as the actual past, as established by Anna and Deeley, is now challenged as a fiction.

When Kate changes the topic to Deeley, her language itself changes: the description of the man seems gossipy, almost prosaic, even crude in its sarcasm. Much to Anna's surprise, Kate talks to her—several members of the audience made this observation—as if they were two women friends chatting about a man (or men in general) standing before them, almost (but not quite) close enough to hear what they were saying. For Kate, however, Deeley's sexual act is as repulsive as Anna's own efforts to possess her. Yet even when she describes her revenge, plastering the man's face with dirt, Kate's phrase "pretty pansies" (the flowers the roommates had planted in the windowbox that now supplies the dirt) struck the audience as odd, curiously "feminine" or touching, as a final vestige of the bond once existing between the women.

When Kate rises, stationing herself equidistant between the two seated figures and looking at Anna, reveals that "He suggested a wedding instead," her tone becomes clinical, and sarcastic to a degree that we have not yet heard in the play. The word "wedding" is pronounced contemptuously and then even further qualified by the reductive "change of environment," which thereby belittles the present set, the converted farmhouse, secluded by the sea where Deeley once fancied he had rescued Kate from London and Anna's clutches. Kate's "He asked me once," nominally meant for Anna, is delivered toward the audience, although in both the stage and television productions she did not address them directly. Deeley is here reduced to "He" and "him," and Anna to "who." For a second time in this speech, her voice starts to break, to lose its detachment on "I told him no one," although she recovers in time for the final line, "No one at all." With this phrase Kate buries Anna with the same finality that just seconds before she has buried Deeley.

In the silence afterward, I could only hope that the audience, not knowing that the mime follows, would not applaud, although if they did, I would have understood why, for Pinter's most radical break with convention is not to close *Old Times* on Kate's "curtain line" but to allow it to run on, first with the rivals' mimes, then with the photographerlike flash of light that suggests a camera has taken the final picture which, upon being developed, will become the possession of those guests who this evening have witnessed the reunion of wife, husband, and friend.

5

The Actors: Kate, Deeley, and Anna

Kate (by Stephanie Dugan)

DEELEY'S line from *Old Times*, "I was off center and remained so," aptly describes the love-hate relationship I maintain with the works of Harold Pinter. Although it is now more of a love-fascination relationship, it was born of the constant, obsessive search for THE ANSWER in Pinter's plays, and of the final joyous realization that there are no answers. I have grown dependent on this exultation one feels in discovering the Pinter void—the place where rational actor-thought is useless and where one is left teetering on the brink of the Pinter "abyss." *Old Times* was my first experience with that abyss, and here, then, I chronicle my "fall."

My first look over the edge was when Sid asked me to play the role of Kate in *Old Times*. I opened the script and found a yawning gap of words; I found nothing to fill in the innumerable and maddening "blanks." I refer not to Pinter's pauses and silences, but to the puzzle which occurs because of the ever-changing and dual realities omnipresent in the work.

I read the play and when I finished I had no sense of who Kate really was, or, more frighteningly, how I, the actor, was to connect to her. I knew that I was intrigued by Kate's final monologue and that some of her thoughts really captured me, yet I had no feeling as to how they connected to the rest of the play. I felt that the script was filled with contradictions, irritating contradictions. "How is an actor supposed to create a through-line with this skeleton of a script?" I found myself asking almost daily. The most illuminating question I could raise was: Is Kate what the other characters say she is? The rehearsal process helped me make this decision.

The first stages in producing *Old Times* were spent sorting out the text and attempting to delineate the reality of the characters. Many of our rehearsals involved theorizing about Kate's and

Anna's identities and their relationship. Fortunately, we "discovered" the material as we progressed, and tried not to force answers. There were times when I felt answers were being forced, answers which, necessarily, dictated my character to me in theoretical, nonplayable ways. Feeling as if I had to "find" Kate in playable terms, I frequently rejected these answers. However, I need not have worried about being pinned down since we were always in a state of interpretational flux. We allowed answers to the questions of what the play was about to change every day: Was there a struggle between Anna and Deeley for Kate? Were Anna and Kate formerly lovers? Were they the same person? Were the characters creating the past as they went along?

My actor-process was influenced by these questions and answers we tossed around every day. I feel that I discovered Kate in two stages—the early process, in which I used the text to guide me, and where my interpretation of Kate as victim dominated my thinking, and the later stage, in which rhythm guided me and Kate became the controller/creater.

First of all, let me say that Kate is a fascinating, elusive character one never quite finds in the text. She is to be found in the playing with the other actors. In this sense, the actress playing Kate must find her by relying on Anna and Deeley, or so I thought. This difficulty is precisely where I started. Kate keeps herself from the actor in much the same way she does from Deeley and Anna. Still, I kept returning to the script, hoping to find something cohesive, something to help me grasp her inner life and motivations.

Since my initial reactions to Kate were that she is innocuous and that she says surprisingly little about herself, I began to base my decisions on what the other characters say about her, namely that she "was always a dreamer," that she is shy and secretive. Pinter rarely allows Kate the luxury of refuting what Deeley or Anna says. When she does manage to disallow a comment about herself, she seems to lack the will to stick to her guns. For example, after she charges that Anna and Deeley are talking of her as if she were dead, they very easily dissuade her. What's more, she allows them to do so, without a struggle. I wondered why. My conclusion was that she must be their victim. Why, though? Why would she permit them to create her in this fashion? Why would Kate let Anna and Deeley "have" her at every turn? She struck me as a rather helpless peacemaker, trying to balance Anna and Deeley in order to hang onto them both.

As an actor, however, I had a very difficult time subscribing to this version of Kate. It was even harder playing the victim. How do you actively play passivity? I found the answer in Kate's trying to love both Anna and Deeley equally, and to help them love each other. When they couldn't, in the second act, I had to do away with them both. Kate is rather like the battered wife who takes one abuse after another, and then is finally handed a gun. She uses that gun on both Deeley and Anna. The final monologue became a regrettable but necessary evil that I, as Kate, was compelled to perform. Usually, the sadness of this killing caused me to cry.

I never stopped struggling with this interpretation of Kate, for I never felt satisfied, probably because I felt that Kate was not an active participant in the unfolding drama of this trio. At the time we had videotaped *Old Times* I felt I had failed as an actress.

Luckily, we still had the live performance to rehearse for, because it wasn't until then that I began to grow into the character. I think I was feeling as if the pressure were off, although that, of course, was completely untrue. Live performances are certainly more stressful than taped ones. Somehow, I suddenly felt that I could stare into the Pinter abyss and feel comfortable. I credit discovering the rhythms in the play as the breakthrough in character development. By rhythms, I refer to the quickness of non-pausing dialogue which is suddenly halted by a silence or a pause.

As I began to sense the tension build by contrasting pauses and unrelenting dialogue, I realized that this was the key to Kate. For example, that the quick dialogue in the opening moments between Deeley and Kate gave Kate the control over the scene. What had once seemed to me a dialogue to which Kate merely succumbed as victim now was a sign of her authority. This turn-about happened one day in rehearsal when the actor playing Deeley and I were running this scene. The speed with which Deeley questioned me infuriated me, and, as Kate, I now realized Deeley's obsession in demanding answers to his questions about Anna. Until right then, I had not understood just how crucial this information was to him. Now I could play with him, bait him, tell him half-truths. It was at this point that I became aware that Kate was the powerful one. Her silences were the source of her power.

Naturally, this discovery was welcome for it provided the missing link and changed my whole approach to the role, and to the moment by moment playing of her presence onstage. Kate became a contender, both a conscious and unconscious manipulator, someone who reveled in her power to make her ineffectual husband and friend alternately left out and included.

The playing of Kate became incredibly active, exciting, my first scene with Deeley a series of purposeful and deft dodges of the facts. I never wanted Deeley to know any truth about Anna, or about Anna and me. The reason why was unimportant. Deeley was a bore as well as a boor around whom I could dance. When Anna "arrived" with that sudden aria she delivers upstage, I gave her my unadulterated attention in order to nettle Deeley, shake him a bit. Later I delighted in Anna's and Deeley's battle of song lyrics, accepting it as a matter of course. The stakes got higher as Anna and Deeley continued to fight for me in a useless battle of their wills. *My* will was my own. *Their* wills were my own. I reminded them of this when I announced that I could run my own bath. I was bored with their game.

In this frame of mind, my reactions to their conversation about me became amused rather than alarmed. In my monologue at the end I was like a god squashing her creations. With this through-line sustaining my character, I rarely felt sad when doing the monologue. Mostly, I felt relief to be free of these two petty beings. This concept of Kate's character was at one with the answer to the question of how would Kate have this evening end if she could have anything. My answer was that she would go off to her dream place in the desert, where "you can look through the flap of a tent and see sand, that kind of thing." By "killing" Deeley and Anna, she could go there, to the east, if only in her dreams.

I came out of this Pinter experience feeling exhilarated; I understood Kate as a different kind of victim. She was the victim of her own dissatisfaction; her overwhelming need to be free was ultimately self-destructive in that she had to destroy two aspects of her self, those two dimensions of her own will found in Anna and Deeley. I also realized something about myself as an actor. I had wanted to find THE ANSWER so that I could get on with the job of acting in *Old Times*. That answer, however, lies miraculously in the playing of the play. Salvation in Pinter is accepting the unanswerable questions and letting yourself tumble into his abyss.

I have since directed two of Pinter's one-act plays, *A Kind of Alaska* and *Victoria Station*. My primary reason for choosing to direct Pinter was my new-found fascination with his rhythms. I was curious to see if they had the same effect on my actors that they had on me. Having always felt Pinter to be beyond me, I wanted to bring a sense of "graspability" to my actors, a sense of security which I had not captured until late in my rehearsing of *Old Times*. When I started working with them, there was the same look of intimidation in their eyes. Still, they found the rhythms in the two plays just as we did. My *Old Times* experience has had a lasting effect on my work in theater, for Pinter has forced me to explore character using an entirely different approach. I guess that is THE ANSWER.

Deeley (by Thomas Pender)

Approaching the role of Deeley in Harold Pinter's *Old Times* involves a conscious disregard for traditional methods of character development. Indeed, virtually all Pinter's characters present the actor with an atypical set of problems. The central trick in tackling a role in a Pinter play is to realize and accept two conditions.

First, the playwright gives the actor and director considerable leeway in creating a background for his character. Little exposition is given, stage directions (other than "pause" or "silence") are few and far between, and the meaning—if any—of a play seems deliberately witheld. Interpretation, in the sense of "what really happens," is wide open. Indeed, a continual problem in rehearsing a Pinter play is to resist the temptation to talk too much, to analyze too much, to waste valuable rehearsal time trying to break the playwright's code.

Second—and this is especially true in *Old Times*—whatever background or subtext one does create for his character may not necessarily agree with the background created by fellow cast members or the director. The decisions I made for Deeley, and the character history I wrote, did not, I am sure, always support the decisions made by the actors playing Anna and Kate. This might seem a curious way to approach a play—we are, after all, continually taught to deal with a cohesive through-line of action—but one must realize that *Old Times* deals primarily with the writing of history, the subjective recreation of a shared past, and the resulting struggle comes about precisely because of disagreements involving this past.

This is a critical, and subtle, point. We certainly did not ignore each others' choices. We did not act "in a vacuum," or refuse to make connections with one another. That would be bad acting, selfish acting, and should not be condoned under any circumstances. What we did, or at least what I tried to do, was to make a clear distinction between conflict and tension. Conflict, in my approach, involved the struggle specifically related to my version of the past and my attempt to impose this "reading" onto my fellow characters. My Deeley had a very real picture of the events of twenty years ago when he first met Kate and Anna in a ratty cinema in London during a showing of *Odd Man Out*. His churlish commentary on his and Kate's first dates, and his attempt to define the nature of Anna's life in Sicily also are ammunition in this conflict. That was a polished fiction for me, a past carefully built up over two decades. And it was as irrelevant to Kate and Anna as their versions of the past were to me. Anna, perhaps more honest than Deeley, might as well be speaking for him when she says, "There are things I remember which may never have happened but as I recall them so they take place." The conflict of *Old Times* is not shared.

But the tensions in *Old Times*, and I think in all of Pinter's plays, are far more abstract and therefore more easily shared and understood by the characters. The tensions exist in the here and now; they involve the struggle for the occupation and control of immediate stage space and time. The true connections among the actors in *Old Times* rely on this immediate interplay. How do we move, where do we sit, what objects do we touch—how do we physically and vocally impose ourselves onto, and into, the others' space? This is the stuff of acting (and we must remember that Pinter himself began as an actor), and this immediate interplay is what makes the plays such fun to act. The tension created by physical confrontation—regardless of the reason for this confrontation—is the essential element in the play. The very title of *Old Times* is a "flag of convenience." *Old Times* is not really about "old time"—that is history, and thus changeable, open to reinterpretation. What is the true history of what happened to Anna, Kate, and Deeley twenty years ago? It doesn't really matter.

But what is the play about, we ask? Audiences respond strongly to the work, but, as Leonard Powlick points out, not being able to verbalize what the play was about does not preclude responding to it.[1] Pinter's plays, to use Kenneth Burke's phrase, "dance,"[2] and it is tension that makes the plays dance. But tension is not the same as conflict; the chief fallacy in approaching Pinter's plays lies in confusing the two.

Nonetheless, the actor must create a solid background for his character, even when the playwright seems unwilling to provide significant clues. My personal interpretation of Deeley's current situation and employment is that he makes grade-B travelogues. Whether or not this was significant to the actresses playing Kate and Anna I do not know. Likewise, I did not try to intrude into their characters' histories. Even though I felt comfortable with this chosen occupation for Deeley, I soon realized that his career was not nearly of so great a concern to him as his fiction, his "screen-play" of meeting his wife in a movie theater twenty years ago. Anna is perfectly willing to play along with Deeley's picture of her present life in Sicily, and she has few qualms as to Deeley's descriptions of her present world. But for her, too, the past is a crucial sticking point. Anna's version of the past will be heard. But Kate, the "quiet one" for most of the play, only comes alive in the present. Then, with one fell swoop, she not only demolishes the combined Anna/Deeley past, but also refutes the very idea of immutable history.

In *Old Times*, Deeley and Kate open the play awaiting the arrival of Anna, a former roommate of Kate's. Deeley doesn't want Kate there for a number of reasons. She is, first and foremost, a rival. Deeley travels in his job, he sees the world, but Kate remains safely sequestered in the country house. Deeley had little concern in the past with losing Kate because his world, or his version of the world, is all she knows. But Anna (who already is onstage, albeit with her back to the action) is in a position to present Kate not only with a different view of the outside world, but also a different version of the events of twenty years ago. To defuse this potential threat, Deeley asks Kate numerous questions about Anna—is she vegetarian, will the casserole prepared for the evening meal meet their guest's satisfaction, what does she drink, was she Kate's best friend? In acting this first scene my primary concern was the development of an "inquisition" of sorts. How could I keep Kate offguard? How could I use my line of questioning, and my physical behavior, both to anticipate and prepare for the struggle ahead and to undermine Kate's own recollections of her past? One simple, tension-related piece of business seemed to convey this primary motivation for my character. Early in the play, when Kate is preparing coffee for Anna and stirring rather noisily with a spoon, I clicked my wedding band against my brandy snifter. My "comment" on the way she prepared coffee seemed the truest of possible gestures I could use to undermine Kate's actions. It drew a response from her—it created a perfect "Pinter pause"—and that simple piece of noise led us to achieve the proper tension of the moment.

A clear sense, and expectation, of exclusion is established at the outset. Throughout the play each character, at one point or another, will be cast as the "odd person out" in this little triangle. At the beginning this character is Anna. She starts the play with her back to the audience, looking out; she alone is not smoking; her "figure remains still in dim light at the window." Anna begins the play as "object"; Deeley and Kate talk about her literally behind her back. This is a curious conversation because Deeley, who never has met Anna (or so we think), immediately casts himself as the historian in the play. Through secondhand information, and with the bored acquiescence of his wife, he situates himself as the arbiter of record. The quality of Kate's and Anna's friendship, the very essence of Anna's being—"she was a thief," Kate informs us—are only revealed through Deeley's insistence. Kate has volunteered nothing. The information cannot exist but for Deeley's questions, and only he will verify the answers. Deeley tells Kate that he "shall be very interested." "In what?" asks Kate. "In you. I'll be watching you." "Me? Why?" "To see if she's the same person." While visually the play opens with Anna the "odd person out," Deeley's history-writing also focuses attention on his wife, Kate, as an "odd person." Kate, it appears, had no friends, no visitors, in her past life in London. There is almost a perverse Pirandellian *constuirse* at work here. Deeley *constructs* an image of the two women living together and, at least initially, he meets no resistance. "It is so, if you think it is so. Right you are, if you think you are," the women seem to say. They humor him. But as Deeley's reconstruction of past events becomes more and more personal, and his fallacious technique of applying the past to the present continues, he meets resistance from Anna, who will provide her own version, and interpretation, of the past.

Anna's first speech also is an attempt at "history making." She begins with a long monologue describing the carefree life the two young girls lived in London:

Queuing all night, the rain, do you remember? . . . What did we eat? . . . We were young then, of course, but what stamina, and to work in the morning, and to a concert, or the opera, or the ballet, that night, you haven't forgotten?

Deeley is unimpressed. To Anna's query if "those cafés and all those people" still exist, his response is a terse "We rarely get to London." I deliberately chose to undercut her monologue as much as I dared—I acted bored at times, I leered at her backside. Anything I felt I could do within the bounds of propriety to discredit her story seemed fair game. Her story is of no interest to Deeley, nor are her descriptive techniques. Deeley chides Anna's very use of language. To her use of the words "lest" and "gaze" Deeley bluntly responds that people simply don't use those words, or at least they haven't for a long time.

Anna's history doesn't exist for Deeley, nor his for her. But history, like theatre, never exists; it can only occur. Once the immediate event has past it necessarily becomes open to interpretation, to revision. There are few truly "hard" facts in any history, and in the "past-in-the-making" of Pinter's trio the only true point of convergence is the film *Odd Man Out*. At some point, roughly twenty years ago, the three characters agree to having seen the film, a black-and-white thriller starring James Mason as an Irish revolutionary who is wounded in a bank hold-up and separated from his comrades, thus becoming an "odd man out," and the object of a massive search by the police. The exact nature of the encounter at the cinema, however, is not quite clear. Nor, perhaps, need it be.

Deeley writes the "first draft" in the *Odd Man Out* scenario. He paints his version of the story with the brush strokes of a cinematographer. The neighborhood is described, he tells us where Kate was sitting in the theatre, he describes the usherettes and their mutual lust. Deeley gives himself a poignant past, complete with reveries about his first tricycle, bought by his father in a shop nearby. More significantly, Deeley presents what he sees as the definitive critical appraisal of the film. "I thought Robert Newton was fantastic. And I still think he was fantastic. And I would commit murder for him, even now." Deeley of course casts himself as romantic lead in this scenario, and it is his critique of the film that serves as his come-on line to Kate. "I said wasn't Robert Newton fantastic, and she said something or other, Christ knows what [Kate's criticisms apparently are not worth mentioning] but [she] looked at me, and I thought Jesus this is it, I've made a catch, this is a true-blue pickup." But definitive criticism, like "true" history, is a human conceit.

Anna, listening to Deeley's pompous recollection, does not at this point dispute the events of his supposed first meeting with Kate. She does something even more threatening: she questions Deeley's critical judgment. "F. J. McCormick was good too," she says, and the gauntlet is thrown down. Twelve lines of Deeley's remembrance are immediately undercut by a single statement from his wife's former roommate. Anna, we see, will play along with the *facts* Deeley presents, but she will not accept him as undisputed arbiter of *interpretation*. When Deeley questions Anna about her life in Sicily—"How's the yacht?"—and her husband—"What's his name? Gian Carlo or Per Paulo?"—she plays along with his inventions. Facts are not so important here; analysis is. We in the audience, like the actors playing Deeley and Anna, can easily fall into Pinter's trap if we concentrate too hard on what really happened in this dim past. But this jockeying for position, this "writing of history," is merely a dramaturgical convenience. It provides an excuse for the characters to remain onstage; it creates tension. And clearly nothing results from Deeley's and Anna's confrontation. They are equally matched, and if it seems that Anna is "ahead on points" as we near the end of the play, it is only because she happens to be the one in control when the true action of the play, Anna's denunciation of the past, reaches its conclusion. Kate's only reply to this initial salvo is that she does remember the film—"Oh yes. Very well." Exactly what she remembers is not told us—Pinter will withold that until the very end of the play.

Deeley continues the story of his budding relationship with Kate. He advances the scenario to the point where they end up in bed. Kate does not comment on Deeley's version of the story— no doubt she has heard it many times before—but Anna raises the key question of the validity of any memory. Thus she marks the beginning of both Deeley's and her downfall. Anna tells us that some things we remember may never have happened. The game of *Old Times* is decided at this point. Both Deeley's and Anna's claim to control of dramatic action is nullified; they will continue to play the game of tension, but there will be no outcome, no result, of this confrontation. That will have to come from outside the world of the past. That will have to come from Kate.

Kate is so serenely confident at this point that she has no qualms about excusing herself to take a bath. Let Deeley and Anna fight out the irrelevancies, she seems to say. I will go refresh myself. Here is a crucial action by Kate. For the only time in the entire play Pinter has a character completely leave the scene of battle. The scene between Deeley and Anna during Kate's absence is wonderfully "dramatic"—it contains some of the finest sexual sparring in all of Pinter's work. But the object of this battle—and by now we clearly see that the battle is over Kate— absents herself. This specific action thus informs the text. The nonchalant absence of Kate tells us that any results and conclusions must await her return.

Refreshed from her bath, Kate is ready to wrap up the action of the play. Now we hear her version of the past. For Kate, the big city, London, where the three characters' shared past occurred, has only one essential quality—it is a place of meaningless motion and hard edges, a venue for the illusion of solid facts. "I deplore that kind of urgency," Kate says. She prefers the soft immediacy of the country. "The only nice thing about a big city is that when it rains it blurs everything, and it blurs the light from the cars, doesn't it, and blurs your eyes, and you have rain on your lashes. That's the only nice thing about a big city." It is at this point that Deeley begins to sense what really is happening in the crucial present. He attempts to "seduce" Kate as she returns from her bath by singing to her ("The way you wear your hat . . .") and in fact enters into a competition with Anna for the now-dominant Kate. Kate, for her part, senses that she now is in control of the stage action. She flirts first with Deeley, then with Anna, until neither is sure with whom she eventually will side.

This leads to perhaps the strongest confrontation between the two would-be suitors. Now Deeley's and Anna's argument over the past takes on an urgency heretofore unseen. This was perhaps the most enjoyable, and difficult, part of the play for me. Attacking Anna's husband and her life in Sicily, attempting to defuse her recollections of Kate ("You say she was Bronte in secrecy but not in passion. What was she in passion?") was true fun. Deeley here is allowed full use of his rhetorical tricks, his physical presence. Moments later he is allowed, in one final speech, to see his posturings and inventions collapse. In Deeley's last sustained speech he circles the stage away from Kate. As he moves farther and farther away from the object of his fiction, his story loses focus and energy. On the "return trip" back to Kate and Anna, Deeley is a defeated man. His past has lost the polish of earlier fictions. He now realizes both that the past cannot truly be known and that by avoiding the present he has brought defeat upon himself. In eighteen lines of text, the true meaning of the play hits Deeley with resounding force.

The past for Kate is important, as cold as the tea served her by Anna. Anna offers to reheat it, but reheated tea, like the rehashing of past lives, does not appeal to Kate. The last words in the play are—and have to be—Kate's. Finally she gives us her version of the past, and while her story is no more or less accurate than Anna's or Deeley's, it produces results. "I remember you lying dead," she says to Anna. "I leaned over you. Your face was dirty. You lay dead, your face scrawled with dirt. . . . When I brought him [Deeley] into the room your body of course had gone. . . . I dug about in the windowbox, where you had planted our pretty pansies, scooped, filled the bowl, and plastered his face with dirt." Pansies are annual, not perennial, plants. Anna is summarily reduced to a withered stem; Deeley is buried. Performing this final scene was perhaps the most draining experience I have had onstage. My vulnerability was such that one simple vocal cue from Kate, the slight break in her voice when, speaking of who had slept in the bed before Deeley, she said ". . . no one. No one at all," was sufficient to make Deeley break down.

All that I have written does not, of course, negate the importance of the script in Pinter's play. A very strong effort was made to convey the lines verbatim, and whatever discoveries we made about the characters had to be supported by the text. What we must keep in mind, however, is that the text may in fact support numerous interpretations. However varied the histories the actors and director write, the central moments of tension in the play remain unmoved. They are the key to the play. The attempt to try and decipher the past in *Old Times* is enjoyable and necessary, but it can lead a cast away from what is perhaps a more crucial issue.

Different casts and directors will no doubt come up with quite different scenarios regarding the precise relationship among the three characters, and, like the "histories" of Deeley and Anna, they may all be equally valid. In *Old Times* there is no past, or, more accurately, there are three. And each version of the past, though equally valid as history, is equally irrelevant as far as present action is concerned. As much as anything else, Pinter's plays are about people making up plays as they go along. The plays are playwriting competitions among the characters, contests designed to show off the skills of the combatants. The plays—and, I think, this production—"work" because the immediate tensions are so clearly established. Despite the seeming obscurity of the play as a whole, there is an amazing concreteness in the moment-to-moment tasks the actors must perform. And with these immediate tensions there also is immediate gratification for the actor. To lose in a Pinter play is to be demolished, banished from the stage. To win a "point" is to hear the cheers of the crowd. We act these plays both desperately and triumphantly.

Anna (by Sandra Langsner)

As a "Professor of Theatre Arts," a title for an artist which to me is an oxymoron, I am a collector of books on acting theory, of plays and biographies about great directors and actors. I have the utmost respect for my books and mourn the loss, destruction, or displacement of any one of them. However, at some point in time, after the closing of a play in which I have acted, I will inevitably come across a battered, dog-eared, coffee- and food-stained, yellow (pink, blue, or green)-highlighted script. My first impulse is always to throw out the damned thing. What I'm trying to say, of course, is that since my relationship with a play script as a scholar or director is so totally different from my relationship with it as an actor, my very treatment of the paper the play comes on is different. I look at that script and feel that I have literally leaped into the pages and eaten from them—jumping over, crawling through, chewing, tasting, pushing and pulling my way through each curve, dot, and cross of each letter, each work, each phrase. When the play is finally over, I have devoured the contents and am ready to eliminate the remains.

As a director and actor, I have always been attracted to difficult scripts—that is to say, scripts that do not readily answer even simple questions as to time, place, date, and relationships among characters. During the process of "playing out," the lines the playwright has given me, and as the revelations of the text burst forth, discovery is as thrilling to me as perhaps anything that I have ever experienced. Pinter's *Old Times* was one such experience.

As I look at my haggard script for *Old Times* I see that part of my life spent trying to get inside the head and body of a woman as different from as she is similar to me. I believe that the experiences of all characters lie inside ourselves, and that if we use Stanislavski's simple "Magic If" we can reveal all the nuances of the character we are exploring.

Therefore, some thoughts on Pinter from a very uneducated, not very well-Pinter-read actress.

I had seen several productions of his work, including the movie of *Betrayal* with three of my favorite British actors, and had come to the conclusion that one must play Pinter realistically, although the "time" taking place in the play is not always linear. Nor, for that matter, are references to time—particularly in *Old Times*. In hindsight, for me the title of the play has most of the answers to a lot of the questions that came up during the rehearsal process. Whose story is this? Did this really happen? To whom? Who exactly is Anna? For an actress, the answers to such questions were imperative in order to play the play—but I am getting ahead of myself. Let me begin at the beginning of this project.

Upon first reading the script, hoping I would have a choice as to which of the two female characters I would play, I was more attracted to Kate only because I am usually typecast in stronger, more domineering roles. I felt that Kate was the more vulnerable of the two women, the victim of Anna's and Deeley's demands on her life. But, in the process old tricky Mr. Pinter turned me around several times. I found by the end that the opposite was true—Anna and Deeley were victims of Kate. My God, she kills them in her final speech: Anna literally, and Deeley figuratively when she emasculates him.

Even blocking Pinter poses some very interesting questions for the director and the actors. Since along with his famous and brilliant pauses Pinter has written in some very definite blocking and "business," we had some guidelines. I feel very strongly that if the *playwright* gives the actor such business and pauses, that they are just as important as the lines and must be considered most seriously as part of the story. What is unspoken in Pinter is usually the meat of the play; finding what happens during those wonderful pauses is like eating the marrow from the juiciest bone.

In the beginning, I was not always clear during the blocking process why I was moving from one place to another. This had nothing to do with the director. Rather, there were aspects of *Old Times* that did not reveal themselves to me until way after rehearsals. Being a relatively well-trained actress with a strong need for motivation, I was confident that I would eventually discover a reason for my actions. In time I realized that the key to playing Anna was in clarifying my relationships to Kate and Deeley—but again I'm getting ahead of myself.

At first, each rehearsal was a mind-blowing event where, in my hasty need to know precisely what this play was about, I would invariably come with a new, seemingly brilliant, and usually very literal interpretation of what EXACTLY was going on. I remember one rehearsal in particular where I was so overwhelmed with my "luminous" realization of what was REALLY GOING ON in the play that I was sure it MUST HAVE BEEN THE ONLY

VALID INTERPRETATION OF OLD TIMES *EVER THOUGHT OF—PERIOD!* Of course, that most brilliant interpretation changed at the very next rehearsal.

At first I was convinced that Anna and Kate were two sides of the same person: Kate was the physical reality in time and place, while Anna was the visiting "spirit" of what Kate could have been had she not married Deeley. I was certain that Anna was fighting Deeley for her independence by using the memory of herself as a single girl living in London. In turn, Deeley was shooting down her logic by presenting Anna with a completely different interpretation of what really happened at the movie theater where *Odd Man Out* was showing. But this interpretation only worked to a point, and then started to fall apart. There was nowhere to go with it because no matter how abstract a character is, she must have some basis in reality. I found that I could not play an abstraction, a memory, and that the character kept getting vague and would eventually float away during the moments where the interpretation fell short of the text. For example, if Anna is only an aspect of Kate's former personality, how could she exist without the presence of Kate as at the opening of act 2? I started to become confused for I could not possibly play two characters at once. I *had* to come up with a consistent, solid interpretation which made Anna her own person, with her own needs and personality. Eventually, I gave up trying to figure out what the play was about and decided to focus entirely on my relationship with each of the other two characters.

In the past, I have taken several different approaches to developing a character. Sometimes, the meaning of the play is so linear and the character relationships so clear that all I have to focus on in rehearsal is memorizing lines, blocking, playing clear objectives, and responding to the environment around me, both physical and psychological. Sometimes a certain type of rehearsal clothing will help me, for example, a scarf or a short skirt or a certain kind of high heel. Perfume often helps me to develop a sense (no pun intended) of the character, both viscerally and physically. And then there are times when I haven't a clue, as in *Old Times*, and so I have to do what I call "Zen-ing it," that is, memorizing the lines and blocking by rote and allowing whatever I am saying and what others are saying to me to help in developing my character. This I do without trying to bring any "homework" or research into rehearsal. I found that one trap with Anna is to portray her as a "strong" and "domineering," almost motherly figure, when in point of fact this is not the cast at all. Anna is almost childlike in her very clever, witty competition for Kate's attention. This competition, by which she tries to validate her past, completely destroys Anna.

Old Times is obviously a competitive sport, at first seemingly played by Deeley and Anna for the prize, Kate. However, as we find out in the end, Kate is the only winner. I discovered that the stakes would change as we worked our way from the whimsical and witty exchanges at the beginning of the first act, or "First Half," passing through "Halftime" into the "Second Half." Suddenly, at the end of act 1, we were no longer playing a well-mannered, friendly game of football; we were playing something else. There was a new player, namely Kate when she insists on drawing her own bath. I felt that during the competition with Deeley, I racked up more points by the end of act 1, and then something changed in act 2. Sitting in Deeley's bedroom, I was now unsure of the game. We were no longer fighting to create a past of places and events, but one of personalities and behavior. In Deeley's opening comments about the Wayfarers Tavern, he takes control over my past by bringing me into his. He is essentially changing the rules of the game, and upping the stakes considerably. As I realized that my ego, my total existence was becoming the stakes, the game became much more desperate.

Finally, toward the end of the play, I felt myself losing the desire to win, or even to play the game anymore. Wanting Kate to remember how it "really" was, I began to repeat myself in a frantic attempt to stay whole: "I took her to cafés, almost private ones, where artists and writers and sometimes actors collected, and others with dancers." These were the exact words and phrasing I had used in my lighthearted opening monologue. I had lost my cool, my strength, and now was fighting for my life. My fatal mistake was in telling Deeley that I had "found" Kate, that it was I who "essentially" had created her.

In the end, as Kate slowly killed me with her last monologue, everything became clear—I knew what I was fighting for. I was finally ready to "play" the play. The horror was revealed. In a way, my original interpretation could be realized, not by me, but by the audience. In playing her, Anna had to be as real to me as I am to myself; otherwise there was nothing to fight because this self is precisely what Anna is fighting for.

As I write this I realize that Anna is very much a part of me, that I often experience her struggle in my everyday existence as I fight to keep my own psyche intact through other's experiences of me, with me, and through me. I know that only through the playing of Anna could I understand what the play *Old Times* is about. I believe that we really only exist as a reflection in the eyes of others, and that their remembrances of "old times" are what define us. We are in constant battle for a definition of self and yet we can't battle alone. Even if we could, we don't want to. Sometimes we are in control of our memories; just as often another will take control. We will even give ourselves up completely in this desperate struggle for definition. Anna chose to find herself by visiting the "past," hoping against hope that she could come out of it whole and intact. In the sacrifice of her "self," Kate is reborn.

6

The Camera as Guest

IF *Old Times* is a play about power, where the weapon is the word, then the television camera stands as the fourth player, matching the verbal warfare onstage with its own quiet but potent visual presence. Roughly three-quarters of what was seen in the television film of our production was preplanned. I had at my disposal three cameras, which, because of the size and limitations of our studio, were confined to the downstage area, with a camera at each side of the set, and a third aligned with stage-center. The camera used, the angle and distance, whether the camera was stationary or moved—all this was in large part determined during preproduction by my director's concept.

During an earlier visit to the People's Republic of China, I had been intrigued by the added authority given directors of classical Chinese theater by the convention of having halfway onstage musicians who, with their instruments, could underscore lines or movements the director found to be especially significant. The music would also complement the actor's delivery with a variety of melodies and percussive effects. I felt a similar authority in directing *Old Times* for television. For unless I chose to film the entire production with a stationary camera mounted downstage, what was shown and how, and how much the audience was allowed to see, constituted a reading of the text. Even allowing for the actor's coequal authority and the relative independence of the viewer (however constrained by the camera and hence less free than he or she would be at live stage production), here, nevertheless, was an authority that brought with it great obligations. This preplanned camera work, therefore, became not just an extension but a confirmation of the directorial concept.

Still, if much of the camera's role was predetermined, the fact remained that changes in blocking and concept during rehearsals led to a rethinking of its role. There were also technical considerations that limited our options. Since we filmed the production twice, in postproduction work we always had a choice among shots. Sometimes one option was clearly preferable; at other times we were forced to use one shot when an alternate had proved inadequate. Given limited studio time, we also did some reshooting, as well as some special effects—almost entirely close-ups—that could not have been done while the performance was in progress, since we planned the schedule so that two alternative filmed versions of Old Times represented continuous shootings. With a few minor exceptions, we did not have to stop the performance, once it started, to make adjustments or corrections. Shooting segments often out of sequence is common practice in most television and film productions. However, given the structural tightness of Old Times, the fact that the "order" of the evening's events (or nonevents since everything is determined by what one character says in response to whoever spoke last), a continuous shooting seemed to be demanded by Pinter's work.

I should also point out that blocking for the television production was influenced by the medium itself. Since we did not have the facilities or even room to move the cameras onto the set, or to locate cameras upstage, some movements or crosses that looked appealing to the eye had to be redone for the camera. No less, the amount of lighting required by the camera was a factor; the actors had to play to the areas of light onstage—around the sofas, in centerstage, for example—and to avoid those areas that, albeit sufficiently lit for the eye, would appear darker from the camera's perspective. In one sense, the camera was a guest in the sitting-room (or bedroom), as well as an extension of the director choosing at any moment to focus on this or that character, rather than more neutrally on the entire set. But that same guest, far from being unobtrusive, also made certain demands on the three "hosts."

If the actor's movement was therefore subject to certain limitations peculiar to television, the actor's voice was not, for early in the preproduction stage I decided to use body mikes, rather than an overhead or roving microphone. Actors could speak naturally, in a way more intimate, less "theatrical" than they would have to in the stage version. And while sounds of nonspeaking characters were recorded—Anna at times laughs while Deeley speaks, and Deeley has a series of nonverbal sounds to register his displeasure at the guest or at both women when, say, they exclude him from the conversation—the sound technician, because of the body mikes, could isolate the speaker, giving him or her something of a special pipeline to the ear of the television viewer. Always close to the character speaking, literally on his or her person, the body mike relayed sound in the same way that each of us while speaking can listen to ourself. Hence, if the picture, the visual image, represented in part the performance as seen by the director, with such focus and emphasis as the director wished the viewer to entertain, the sound, as heard by that same viewer, had the effect of being the intimate property, the possession of the character speaking. The viewer, in a sense, looked *onto* the set, from various positions downstage, although with medium and close-up shots, along with zooms, that same viewer could be given the feel of entering the set, moving onto the stage. Conversely, the viewer tended to hear the performance through the body of the character speaking, except when the camera chose to focus on the listener and exclude the speaker. Even on these occasions, when the viewer saw the reaction to rather than the delivery of a line, the speaker was still "present" in a sense through the intimate sound of his or her voice off-camera.

The black background on the upstage and upstage-left walls lent a peculiar atmosphere to the image on-screen. Since there were no doors or windows upstage, no pieces of furniture against the walls, a character shot against this neutral backdrop tended to float in space, or as in a dream, timeless, the body as specific and human as the room upstage seemed ambiguous, indeterminate, without a trace of the human artifacts we normally associate with a home in which people live. An intimate medium—the close-up, for example, seen by the viewer in the privacy of his or her own real-life living room—yet one in which that same viewer is less free than in the live theatre, television seemed at once cold or abstract and yet also "live," its sense of happening before our eyes not disturbed by the camera. Still, even this live production was qualified by the feeling that it had all happened before, earlier, elsewhere. In a sense, this paradox duplicated the mood of *Old Times* itself, a social evening progressing from one topic of conversation to another, from the serving of the casserole to the after-dinner drinks, but one where the past, all that had already been, was no less present, indeed weighed upon, challenged the present.

Like Polonius with his categories and subcategories for comedy, history, and tragedy, we had our own roster for the camera: medium close-ups, medium-long shots, and so forth.

While every shot, no matter what its designation, was unique in that it recorded a distinct moment, a specific line or piece of action from the play, the three basic shots—long, medium, and close-up—each had something of individual "feel" or atmosphere.

Often, the long shot allowed the viewer to be an onlooker, the dispassionate observer. At the start of act 1, for instance, we see Deeley and Kate from a distance, small figures overwhelmed by the set, as if they were part of it, frozen until Kate's first line. The only movement was the smoke from Kate's cigarette rising above the sofa and to the top of the screen. Subsequent medium and close-up shots would allow us to voyage into this room at present so distant and cold. There was another long-shot at the end of the testy dialogue between Deeley and Anna just as Kate enters from her bath in act 2. The combatants were statues, their conversation halted, as at the top of the screen Kate appears, the one sign of life in a room momentarily "dead."

The long shot was also used when it was necessary to show all three characters in action, as when Kate orders Deeley "to go": here we see Kate move to the top of the screen, with Deeley isolated on its right side, as Anna moves, in sympathy with Kate, to the left. This feeling of impartiality in the long shot informed much of the quarreling between husband and wife at the start. As Kate's corrects Deeley's "your best and only" with "my one and only," her intimate description of Anna clashes with the physical distance on-screen separating husband and wife.

The two flashbacks started out as long shots, so that we could see Deeley on one side of the screen excluded from the two women seated at a sofa or a divan on the other side. Frequently, when Deeley would make a comment meant simultaneously to discredit Kate and show to Anna just how intimately (he thinks) he knows his wife, we would go to a long shot, to display the reactions of all three characters, as on Deeley's line "She's so totally incompetent at drying."

Keeping the camera at long range but moving it to follow a speaker had the effect of identifying the viewer with the character speaking, of allowing the viewer to move with him or her, as when Kate crosses to Deeley on her line "Do you want me to ask your questions for you?"

Close-ups, of course, put all the focus on the speaker, making the visual image as intimate as the sound. Here, the face—the eyes, the movement of the mouth, the expression—loomed on-screen, usurping it, and fleshed out the dialogue and its delivery.

Besides placing the emphasis on Deeley's need to know about

Kate's relationship with Anna, rather than on the relationship in itself, the close-up of Deeley provides a certain literal meaning to his "In you. I'll be watching you." Some of his lines which seemed more like Shakespearean asides than dialogue directed to another character required close-ups: Deeley's expletive "Christ" when Anna does not react to his scheme for their mutual powdering of Kate; or his reaction to Anna's use of the word "beguiling" ("What the hell does she mean by that?"). The close-up was also used for Deeley's incredulous "What?" to Anna's confusion (purposeful or not) of "casserole" with "wife." When Anna corrects herself with "I was referring to the casserole. I was referring to your wife's cooking," the close-up allows us to weigh the evidence: Was her slip intended or accidental, and is she now being honest or sarcastic?

Long shots of the quarrel between Kate and Deeley in act 1 tend to hide the physical evidence of the degree of her hostility to him, but when Kate's anger shows through as her reserve gives way to a more naked response, we went to a close-up, as on her "Oh what does that mean" to Deeley's innuendo in labeling Anna her "best friend." As she capitalizes on the mistake of "casserole" for "wife" by jumping back to the topic of food, this time to the meals she used to cook with Kate, Anna is seen in close-up as she talks about the "enormous stew" the two women "dished up." For Anna, the spat with Deeley is momentarily forgotten and through the close-up the viewer realizes that she is racing back to revel in the past.

Indeed, we used proportionately more close-ups of Anna than of the other two characters, as a way of showing just often she, embodying the past, retreats from the present situation to that inner self, signaled by the close-up, that delights in recalling her days in London with Kate. This effect was achieved when close-ups were used for part of Anna's story about the man in the girls' room. Even though she is sitting inches from Deeley, the close-up of her face isolates Anna, suggesting that, whatever her object in the narration, she is also reliving the moment. On the other hand, a close-up of Deeley as he asks Anna "What kind of man was he?," shows, glaringly, that he takes her story personally, that it has had its desired effect.

Above all, the close-up served as a punctuation, an exclamation point. When Kate hits on Christy, after rejecting three other men as potential visitors, we see Deeley's reaction in close-up. The contrast is startling: the face on-screen is not that of the man Kate describes as "gentle," "sensitive," and blessed with "a lovely sense of humor." No less, moving between close-ups punctuates an interchange. The close-up of Anna's deflating "F. J. McCormick was good too"—after Deeley has praised Robert Newton's performance—is followed by a close-up of Deeley as he reacts, conceding that McCormick was good but reminding Anna that it was "his" actor, not "hers," who brought Kate and him together.

Medium shots frequently have the advantages of both long-shots and close-up, being at once dispassionate and (though with some qualification) intimate, or "inner." The moments of bonding between the two women were usually done in a medium shot, especially in the first flashback where we held the medium shot—both women were on the stage-left sofa and shot from the waist up—for several pages of dialogue. Deeley, silent and off-camera, was only "implied." Just as often, a medium shot ironically showed two combatants, granting each an equal position on-screen. As Kate tempts Deeley with the revelation that Anna used to steal underwear from her, and Deeley, momentarily forgetting his object in the scene, becomes absorbed in the fact, this bone Kate has just handed him, we see in a medium shot Deeley in the foreground, Kate in the background yet, despite being further from the viewer, occupying an equal half of the screen. A medium shot was also used for that moment when Deeley offers and Anna accepts a glass of brandy, the "truce" between the rivals, itself a jab at Kate (who has just served coffee), underscored by giving the (seemingly) courteous husband and (suspicious but) charming guest the right and left halves of the screen, respectively.

These somewhat distinct feelings or atmospheres associated with the length of the shot could then be combined, juxtaposed, made to comment on each other. As Anna, for example, becomes fatally absorbed in the account of Kate's allowing her to wear her own underwear to parties, the camera goes from a long shot of Kate and Anna, with Deeley standing and listening on stage-right, to a close-up of Anna. The narrator has forgotten her audience and hence the effect that this tale of voyeurism might be having on Kate. Moments earlier there is a similar effect, with a similarly fatal consequence for Anna, when the camera again moves in on her as she talks about Kate's shyness. The parallel camera moves, from long shot to close-up, thereby reinforce the situation in which the narration seduces the narrator. We have visual evidence, in effect, for the basis of Kate's subsequent withdrawal from her friend. We see the three characters in a long shot as Deeley asks Anna to look at Kate's smile, but when he links her present smile with the one, he claims, he first saw when they left the theater after seeing *Odd Man Out*—a smile that, as we have learned in act 1 from Deeley, was a prelude to his seduction of Kate, his "true-blue pickup"—the camera suddenly focuses on Kate, who is now no longer smiling. She is wise to Deeley's object, for both Anna and herself. Actually, this change from long shot to close-up had been anticipated in act 1 when the camera moved from Anna, as she speaks of going about the art galleries, concert halls, and cafés of London, before informing Deeley that once the two women "saw a wonderful film called *Odd Man Out*." At about the word "film" the picture changes; Deeley's face, at first casual, then alarmed, fills the screen in close-up.

Less startling, the movement from a long to a medium shot still has its own special effects. As Deeley converts past to present, from the younger Anna whose skirt he looked up, to the middle-aged woman before him, the camera also moves from a long shot of the two on the stage-right divan to a medium shot as Deeley leans into Anna, reminding her that these days there is no longer the same "palpable profit" for him in staring at her legs. When Kate, stage-right, interrupts the conversation on stage-left between Deeley and Anna by rising and crossing to the table, there to light her cigarette, the action is caught in a long shot. However, once she gets their attention, indeed silences the conversation, Kate, smoking, is seen in a medium shot. In essence, she monopolizes the camera. Likewise, we see a long shot of all three characters as Anna, again on stage-left, protests to Kate that she has not implied that Kate was "dead" in the past, yet when Kate corrects Anna—she had said that Anna talks about her "as if she" is dead, now—a medium shot of Kate replaces the long shot. Again, Kate draws the focus, literally as well as figuratively, to herself.

The movement from a close-up to a long shot frequently has the effect of breaking out of a moment of self-absorption, of replacing an inner or intimate moment with the larger context framing, qualifying that moment. Deeley delivers his sarcastic announcement that Christy "can't make" dinner since he's "out of town" in close-up; we see his face screwed up in anger—he is jealous of this imaginary character. The real motivation for Deeley's interruption is not hidden from the viewer. Then, as Kate reacts to Deeley, matching his sarcastic response with one of her own, a very British and proper "Oh what a pity," we go to a long shot, and see both women as they look at Deeley with pity, even condescension. In similar fashion, Deeley's "I wish I had known you both" is delivered in a close-up, as he desperately tries to break into Anna's reverie about being a girl in London ("We were girls together"). But when Anna with her penetrating "Do you?" exposes Deeley's line for what it is, we observe her in a long shot that also registers Deeley's almost inarticulate reaction, his effort to validate his wish with a halfhearted and (for him) abrupt "Yes."

At the end of his story about the Wayfarer's Tavern, Deeley, almost wistfully, tells Anna that, after the party where he lost the two women while getting a drink, Anna seemed to disappear from the area, that he never saw her again. We watch Deeley in close-up, lost in his tale, sad, in a way, that Anna, the chief character of his story, has vanished. Yet a sudden long shot, showing Anna as she responds to his almost plaintive question "Where were you?" pulls us and Deeley back to the present situation. Anna's "Oh, at concerts, I should think, or the ballet" reminds him that she is something more than the woman he claims to have picked up at the party, that she has led a cultured life of which he has not been part. The long shot also reminds us that Deeley's narration passes the time for Anna while she waits for Kate, for after the silence it is Anna who observes that "Katey's taking a long time with her bath." Abruptly thereafter, the topic moves to Kate's bathing habits, and the Wayfarer's Tavern is never mentioned again.

Again, the shift from medium to long is a more subtle one. Deeley's story of the party ends in a medium shot, and as he speaks of the "indentations of four buttocks" on the sofa, we observe both Anna's reaction—she finds the gross comment evidence of what she takes to be Deeley's pathetic state—and Deeley as he touches the divan, his fingers inches away from Anna, as if he were absurdly searching in the present for the indentations from the past. On the pause there is a switch to a long shot, in part because this allows the camera to cover Anna's rise from the sofa and a partial cross downstage. We see Deeley in the background for a moment and then, as Anna moves toward the camera to deliver her critique, perhaps even eulogy to what Deeley has just said ("I've rarely heard a sadder story"), we see his reaction as well. Within a few lines the camera will return to a medium shot on Anna, then a close-up as she nears the drum-table, and finally a medium shot when she crosses and sits on the stage-left divan, at once a parallel to, and a contrast with— since they now sit on separate sofas—the earlier medium shot when both occupied the stage-right divan. In effect, for this opening segment of act 2, the long shot serves as a transition between its two halves, which, in rehearsals, we dubbed "Wayfarer's Tavern" and "Powdering Kate."

Earlier in this segment, Deeley, having finished with his description of the divans and taken a seat on the stage-left divan, launches into the Wayfarer's Tavern routine; the camera in a medium shot focuses on him, excluding Anna. But when she tries to trip him up by asking "When was that," we see both characters, on their opposing divans, in a long shot. Deeley's response is an ambiguous "years ago," prompting a quizzical "I don't think so" from Anna. Failing to satisfy her requests that he be specific, Deeley seizes the conversation by launching into a longish account of the tavern, trying to overwhelm Anna with a host of details, from specific names (such as Luke) to an elaborate description of Anna's outfit. When he does this, the camera reverts to a medium shot that again excludes Anna. We hear her short questions, her doubts about the veracity of the narrative from off-camera, but, except for the one long shot, because of this medium close-up Deeley otherwise monopolizes the camera.

The speed of these changes is also a factor. Sometimes the camera's distance is adjusted during a single line. When Deeley tries to force Anna to be more specific about the date when she and Kate saw *Odd Man Out*—just as she had asked for particulars about the Wayfarer's Tavern—her reply "Oh . . . long ago" is divided at the pause between a long shot on the "Oh" (as Deeley and Kate wait for Anna's response) and a medium shot of the two women, excluding Deeley, on Anna's ambiguous "long ago." The response's second half is thereby as much for Kate's benefit as it is designed to repulse Deeley's demand for specifics. When Deeley makes a similar demand of Kate, he gets an equally ambiguous (and split) "Oh yes" and "Very well." After the camera has focused on Deeley for his reaction to Anna's reference to *Odd Man Out*, it returns to Anna, during the silence, to show her, despite what she has done to Deeley, still lost in memories of the past. We hear off-camera Deeley's non sequitur which breaks the silence, "Yes." Suddenly, the camera turns to Deeley for his next line, "I do quite a lot of traveling in my job." With the exception of his opening "Yes," he has managed, however illogically, to divert the camera from Anna to himself.

At times there are sudden changes among all three basic camera positions. For instance, there is a switch from the "camera 3" to "2" to "1" within the four lines of dialogue including

Anna's reproof to Deeley's generalization about women's bodies which, once accepted by him, drives him to suggest that together they powder Kate, and Anna's sarcastic questioning of what Deeley takes to be a "brilliant idea." The three adjustments in camera angles here duplicate the frantic, irritated give-and-take of the rivals. A parallel shift among angles occurs during the song contest in act 1. Deeley is seen at a sharp angle from camera "3" as he sings "When a lovely flame dies," and then, as Anna completes the line, she is shot from an equally sharp angle from camera "1." Or as Anna confesses that it was her "skirt," she is seen in close-up, and then, as she qualifies the fact that she "remember[s]" Deeley's look with "very well," there is a sudden change to a long shot, just before the qualification. As that long shot is held, Kate interrupts Anna, adding to her "I remember" with one of her own: "But I remember you. I remember you dead." When the medium shot returns, Kate abandons Deeley for Anna, and then initiates the first half of her final speech, whose subject is her killing off of her friend.

Perhaps the most graphic sign of the camera's power came from the either/or decision of whether to focus on the speaker or the listener. The general principle here was: Did the dialogue, whatever the speaker's object, reveal more about the speaker than the listener? Or was the speaker realizing his or her object, whether it be exposing, or punishing, or retaliating against the listener?

With the exception of the one moment when she insists she did not have enough money, Anna's defenses are strong against Deeley's claim that he bought her drinks once in the Wayfarer's Tavern. Hence, Deeley's dialogue, rather than achieving its object of drawing Anna into his fiction, exposes his own wishes, the insecurities of a man whose ego is bolstered by a tale of picking up women. In this instance, therefore, we used a medium close-up concentrating exclusively on Deeley, with Anna as only a voice off-camera occasionally penetrating his narrative.

Since we can well imagine the effect on Deeley of Anna's suggestion that she must come to visit Kate more often, the camera focuses on Anna herself, so that her lines, whatever their surface meaning, only underscores her own desire to possess her friend. What Anna says became more of a personal wish, a need, than a threat. Since Deeley's question "Did she mention a husband in her letter?" disturbs Kate, aggravating her own fears about Anna's visit with the possibility that she is unmarried, a medium shot includes both Deeley's asking the question and Kate responding with thinly disguised emotion on her single, but revealing "No." Then, once Kate's mood has been established, the camera excludes her and turns on Deeley as he goes into a sustained speech about what Anna's husband would be like. We see him relishing his "victory" over Kate, the fact that he has disturbed her.

When Kate and Anna discuss the possibility of inviting Charlie to their apartment, we look at the two women, without Deeley, but with the next name, McCabe, the camera turns to him. In effect, here the difference was split between speaker and reactor. Deeley's "Well, you know what she's like when she gets in a bath" stimulates Anna to recall her own, more poetic memories of Kate, and hence the camera shows her listening to Deeley's lines, using them, rather than being disturbed by them, as Deeley hopes she will. When Anna draws that picture of Kate floating from her bath, "unaware of anyone standing" beside her, we see Deeley struggling with the image, at once intrigued and confused by what his rival says.

As Anna and Deeley debate the issue of whether or not Kate is able to make friends, the picture is of Kate alone on-screen, reacting, offended by these rivals trying to best each other, and thereby forgetting that they are treating Kate like an object. With Kate's inevitable, and caustic "Are you talking about me?" the former speakers return to the screen.

In postproduction work we increased these moments when Kate appears on-screen, listening to the debate off-screen. In the midst of Anna's speech about the man in the room, for example, we cut to Kate as Deeley interrupts with "He'd come back" and kept the focus on her to the pause, just after Deeley's seemingly gallant or concerned, but clearly possessive objection, "A man in the dark across my wife's lap." When Deeley tries to cancel Kate's question to Anna ("And do you like the Sicilian people?") with "I've been there," the camera also remains on Kate, angry at Deeley for this naked display of his jealousy, angry at him for usurping what should have been her response from Anna. When the question is repeated, the camera moves with Kate as she crosses toward Anna on the stage-left sofa, and remains on the two women, after the silence, all during the segment where Anna suggests they stay in tonight. All this time, we know Deeley is sitting by her side. Still, he is excluded from the screen. The camera literally focuses on the speaker's object, rather than the speaker, when Anna first describes Kate waiting "not just for the first emergence of ripple." Off-screen we hear Anna's saccharine description; on-screen we see Kate deeply affected by—while Deeley struggles to understand—the image.

In general, the focus on the reactor, or listener, had different meanings for each of the three characters. Anna was often seen translating the speaker's dialogue for her own use, responding to Deeley's comments but then using them as springboards into a personal vision, a sense of the past that ultimately had very little connection with his object. Deeley unwittingly revealed himself during the reactions, at a primitive level that, with varying success, he could conceal, or at least thought he had concealed while he himself was talking. With Kate, the issue is her witness to what is going on between Deeley and Kate. At times, of course, she is affected by what they say. More often, however, she watches them, like an audience, or, as I have suggested before, as if they were players manipulated or scripted by her.

In a play with three characters, an odd number, where at any given time one could become the odd man out, "two" and "one" become the operative numbers.

Whereas in the stage production all three characters remained onstage at all times, in the television version we could play variations on those same numbers, with two characters on-screen and one at best "implied," at worst nonexistent. During the song contest, for example, Deeley and Anna frequently monopolize the screen, one at the right, the other on the left, singing not so much to Kate but across to each other. Thus, the contest, whatever its ostensible object, also becomes a duet, like that between lovers, a re-creation by both singers—through each has a very different perspective on the situation—of the clichéd movie singing team.

As we have seen already, during the two flashbacks, Anna and Kate are alone on-screen; and whereas he is present but silent in the stage production, Deeley in the television version is nowhere to be seen. When he tries to barge into these flashbacks, to enter the time zone of memory, he is nothing more than a bodiless voice from somewhere off-camera. At one point in the second flashback, the camera generously, albeit briefly turns on Deeley, for a moment of silent, pained reaction.

At one point we see both Anna and Kate on-camera, as Anna recounts how shy Kate was. But when Anna embarrasses her— Pinter's stage direction is "Kate stares at her"—Kate, who has been silent during the shot, rises and walks off-camera. When Anna turns to Deeley, the screen again holds two characters, and for a time we can only speculate, having seen Kate's stare, what

Kate must be feeling off-camera as she reclines on the stage-left divan. In similar fashion, Anna walks off-camera after handing Kate her tea, and as Deeley cuddles with his wife on-screen, we can feel, but cannot see Anna's sense of rejection just a few feet— but it might as well be a million miles—off-camera. At one point in the song contest, Anna moves close to Kate, seated on the stage-right sofa, as she sings "Oh, but you're lovely / With your smile so warm," and as the camera moves to accommodate the two women, it "loses" Deeley standing on stage-right. However, not entirely so, for part of his shadow is cast on the left side of the screen.

Like a fourth character, the camera can also move about the set. Sometimes, it dutifully follows the movement of a single character, excluding the other two, as when Deeley at several points during the first act gets up to cross downstage to refill his drink. When he crosses up to his sofa to reclaim his seat, the camera in turn follows him back. Still, the fact that it moves with him, rather than covering the movement with a single, still long shot, underscores the action itself: Deeley needs a drink at this point. Likewise, when a character goes downstage to that same drum-table, to escape a difficult situation, or to retreat for a time in order to prepare for the next battle, the camera, by following the movement, underscores its significance.

While it is true that every movement and every moment in *Old Times* is significant—Deeley just doesn't pour Anna's tea to be polite—moving the camera stands as a way of highlighting representative moments. On the other hand, holding the camera steady, at long distance, for the act 2 mime suggests that the characters are "caught" in a box defined by the television screen. The camera has come to rest, is still, will not even change from the current "2" position (downstage) to options "1" (stage-right) or "3" (stage-left). Only Anna and then Deeley try to move, to exit from the screen at its top-left corner (upstage-right from the theater's direction), yet, finding that exit barred, they will at length come to rest. As the lights turn to full briefly in the final seconds of *Old Times*, we see characters frozen in position; the twentieth-century medium of movement, of the motion picture brought into the sitting-room, remains, in essence, as still as a photograph.

When Deeley moves to the drum-table, there to begin his story about the two usherettes, we shot him from the "3" camera so that he occupies half the screen on the right side, while the two women, seated on the stage-right sofa, occupy the screen's other (left) side. This is Deeley's most potent speech, and even as he lumps the two women together—the usherette fondling herself before an audience of one—they are also lumped together on-screen. This division on the screen, between Deeley and the two women, became a motif in the television production. As Deeley stands on stage-left, describing his wife taking long walks in the country, we see on the screen's left half Anna standing, Kate sitting.

More often than not, Deeley is thus confined to stage-left, or the screen's right half, and when Kate or Anna venture to that side, the move is especially graphic, as it is during the first flash-back where the women occupy "Deeley's" sofa, while Deeley is isolated downstage in the arm-chair. On-screen, we see the women in their familiar position on the left side of the screen, but, no less, they are on Deeley's side of the stage. Excluded from their conversation, he goes to the drum-table, refills his drink, and then crosses to stage-right, that is, to the women's side. A subsequent long shot positions Deeley at the unaccustomed left side of the screen, the women at the (no less) unaccustomed left side.

There are also variations on this division and balancing of the screen's two halves. Alone on stage-left, as she describes Kate's confusing Friday and Saturday to the husband and wife sitting on the stage-right sofa, Anna is seen on the screen's right side, almost huddled there, with an expanse of sofa stretching to the screen's left side. The imbalance suggests that something is wrong, and indeed it is for, whatever her intentions, Anna works at cross-purposes in describing Kate as being impractical, lost in her dreams. No less, Deeley blunders in endorsing the portrait, as if it were confirmation of his need to see Kate as a helpless woman needing a man's strong presence. Though not fully understood as such by them, the song contest that follows might even be taken as an attempt by each of the rivals, dimly aware that they may have offended her, to win back Kate. The imbalance on-screen thereby serves as a visual prelude to the entire sequence.

There were also vertical divisions of the screen, with one character in the foreground, occupying the screen's lower half, and a second character in the background, in the screen's upper half. The most striking of these is perhaps a still shot of the two women: Anna seated and Kate, who was standing by the window, appearing to rise vertically from the top of her head. Together, the women form a single bar extending from the bottom to the top of the screen, while Deeley confesses off-camera that he is no longer sure which woman was with him in the café.

While Kate is arranging the table in preparation for Anna's visit, we see her at the bottom of the screen, her back to Deeley, who sits on the stage-left sofa near the top of the screen. Deeley is cross-examining Kate, yet it is the viewer alone who can see her face, which registers a disgust with Deeley, even a sense of superiority to this man so eager to pry into a past life of which he is almost absurdly unaware. And since Deeley "up-screen" is further from the camera, he appears smaller, more distant, while Kate's larger image is, in a way, more human. This configuration is repeated when Deeley, parodying the accent of an American cowboy, is seen at the top of the screen, assuring Anna, who is at the bottom, that anytime her husband "finds himself in this direction" his "little wife will be only too glad to put the old pot on the old gas stove." Like Kate earlier, Anna is literally and figuratively closer to us; at the top of the screen Deeley seems small, both literally and figuratively.

Complementing the triangular arrangement of the furniture, cameras "1" and "3," located at either end of the stage's down side, allowed us to use very angular shots, with the foreground figure, who would loom very large on-screen, forming the top of an inverted triangle, and with the two characters upstage, or some combination of characters and furniture, serving as the distant base, the other two angles of that triangle. The triangle was exaggerated by the fact that both sofas and, in act 2, both divans, were placed at (roughly) forty-five degree angles to the square corners of the downstage area. These angular shots looked "arranged," unnatural in a sense, as if the geometric configuration in itself were more important than its human components. Because of this, such shots served as punctuation for special moments in *Old Times*. Hence, the triangular shot was used when Kate announces that she will run the bath herself this night, or when Deeley, constituting the triangle's upside-down "top" downstage, intrudes on the conversation of the women, forming the base at the top of the screen, with his irrelevant account of the "great crew" he had in Sicily. Anna (downstage) and Deeley (upstage) form the top and left angle of the triangle as they begin the song contest, and when Kate's launches into what, in rehearsals, we called her "cross-examination" of Deeley with "What do you think attracted her to you?," he is the triangle's base, while she, standing above, appears superior to him and forms the right angle on-screen. As Deeley crosses back and forth downstage, frantically agreeing that the "province" of a husband dictates that he alone can speak about the nature of his wife's passion, while the two women sit on the divan, he forms the base, they (alternately) the right and left angles as we switched from camera "1" to "3" and back again.

Kate is the base on the screen's left side, as Anna, above her, and in the screen's upper-left hand corner, tells of borrowing her underwear to go to a party. Here, of course, Anna's revelation is too intimate, and while Kate has earlier signaled her displeasure by leaving Anna on the stage-right divan and crossing to the one on stage-left, this time Anna apparently has not received the message. Unable to help herself, she continues with her discourse about Kate's shyness. The tension Kate feels is registered in part by her self-imposed isolation on the stage-left divan, but also in part by the sharp angle used for Anna's speech. Deeley stands further upstage of Anna, forming an extension of the line leading from the screen's lower right-hand to its upper left-hand corner. Both he and Anna look down at Kate, from an angle; we are below her, on her other side, watching the rivals as they, in turn, watch Kate.

The angular shot was especially prominent at the end of act 1. Kate's exit had been covered by a long shot, from the number "2" camera, and hence the picture on-screen is rectangular, Deeley standing on the far left, Anna seated on the far right, as Kate crosses upstage-center, makes a right turn at the window, and moves offstage in a line from the screen's top center to its right side. But when Anna, after Kate's exit, turns back to Deeley, there to confront his sarcastic raising of the brandy glass, we changed to a steep angular shot from the "1" camera. In medium length, Deeley appeared in the screen's lower left corner, Anna at an angle to him in the center, while in the screen's upper right corner is empty space, stretching in the direction of Kate's very recent exit.

All these various techniques and dimensions provided by the camera, as well as the larger aesthetic properties of the medium of television which influenced the production of Old Times and, in turn, distinguished it from the stage production, figured in their most concentrated form in the several set speeches of the play, in the "monologues" Pinter provides for the three characters. A distinct part of the rehearsal process in that the actors got off-book on the dialogue first, so that we could use our time together most efficiently by rehearsing the monologues separately later in the rehearsal process, these monologues also were set apart by their camera work. Camera location, focus, movement, as well as the relationship between and among the employment of the three cameras were determined by each actor's reading and subsequent delivery of the text.

At the start of Anna's first speech, she appears at long-distance, facing the upstage window, a still figure, albeit speaking, framed by Kate (on the left of the screen), Deeley (on the right of the screen), both frozen on their respective sofas. Slowly the downstage "2" camera moves in on Anna, her figure becoming larger, so that when she turns to face the couple on "you haven't forgotten," she appears in a full-faced close-up on the screen. As she faces and then crosses to Kate with the details of their living together in London, a medium close-up puts Anna in the screen's center, and Kate's head, turned in her direction, in the lower left corner. Leaving Kate and moving to stage center, as she recounts being in the cafe with her roommate, Anna is next seen at long-distance. Yet as she becomes involved in her memories, a close-up is used, broken only by her question, directed to the couple upstage, "and does it still exist, I wonder?"

For her speech about the man crying in the room, Anna is first seen in a close-up, as if, forgetting the presence of Kate (on the upstage-right sofa) and Deeley (on the upstage-left sofa), she has retreated into herself to make sure that, by reliving the episode, she will present the details accurately. This close-up is broken momentarily with a long shot on Anna's reference to "Katey still on her bed" and then, just as quickly, restored. When Anna moves after the pause towards Deeley, as if she were imitating the man who "moved . . . very slowly" across the room toward her bed, the camera backs up, catching Anna and Deeley in a medium shot. Once Anna sits on Deeley's left, we changed to the "3" camera, showing both figures from an angle: Deeley silent but reacting inwardly in the foreground, Anna, nearer the top of the screen, lost in her narration, almost as if she has forgotten its object. As a result, she seems to tell herself, rather than Deeley, that she "would have nothing to do with him, absolutely nothing."

Deeley has most of these set speeches in the play, and this presented a special challenge in filming. For if he is, as I have suggested above, at his most potent in the two usherettes speech, he is most confused and unfocused in his final speech. His several speeches in between represent progressive stages in his decline. It was important, therefore, both to distinguish the speeches and to highlight a pattern whereby this man, at first so confident, albeit neurotically so, so given to the factual, the actual, and particulars, gradually loses his monopoly on the present. No less, he loses his certainty with language, and his ability to control reality with reductive descriptions and seemingly inflexible categories.

The two usherettes speech, for example, opens at the drum-table, and, as if the camera itself were his possession, his slave, Deeley, as he crosses up to the two seated women, is followed in medium close-up by the "1" camera. The transition in his narrative from the neighborhood where the film was showing to his stepping inside the theater ("marched in" to use Deeley's macho phrase) is signaled by a change to a long shot, which then, on his mentioning that there was "only one other person in the cinema," changes back to a medium close-up of both women. The result is that there is a gap between what Deeley is saying and what we see on-screen. Once again, the camera returns essentially to Deeley, and if the women appear on-screen, it is only because he has moved close to them, as he does when he points at Kate with "there she is." For a few lines, as he moves away from them and toward the up-side of the stage-left sofa, the camera moves back to a medium-long shot. Then, just as quickly, it returns to its focus on Deeley when, describing how he picked up Kate outside the movie, he circles the sofa before sitting down, triumphantly and aggressively, with the prediction that it is only Robert Newton who can "tear" Kate from him.

Moments later, stung by Anna's suggestion that F. J. McCormick "was good too," and confused by both women's ambiguous replies to his questions about the film, Deeley delivers a less impressive speech, and most certainly less subtle, as he describes his sexual encounter with Kate. Curiously, he justifies their relationship by suggesting that Robert Newton himself would have approved of it; then, a second later he seeks Anna's opinion on what the actor would have thought. This time, the camera is not so slavish; instead, Deeley's rise, cross to the two women—that is, he compulsively must leave his seat and return to their side of the stage—and address to them from a few feet downstage are covered by a single, neutral long shot. No obedient camera this time. Indeed, there is only one camera change in the speech, a medium close-up as Deeley, kneeling before Kate, speaks of touching her "profoundly all over."

In act 2, the camera again becomes Deeley's property with his

"China" speech, although this time there are important adjustments in its servant's role. As he speaks of "the great argument going on" at the party, the "3" camera offers a close-up of Deeley. It backs up, obediently, when he rises and, still talking, makes his way to the drum-table to refill his tea cup, so that he is now seen in a long shot at the table, with Anna visible upstage, watching him. When he reaches her sofa and sits, there is a change to the "1" camera with Deeley in the foreground (of the lower-left corner) speaking of "the great multitude of men" surrounding him and Anna in the background (upper-right corner of the screen) listening, half intrigued, half suspicious of his object. But as Deeley becomes involved in his story, uncharacteristically forgetting his object, there is a change to the "3" camera and a close-up of his face that suddenly excludes Anna. It is as if Deeley is now lost in his own past, fictitious or not. Only when he returns to the subject of the "two girls on the sofa" is Anna recovered, this time by a medium "1" shot. And to punctuate the end of the speech, as Deeley speaks of the indentations of the four buttocks, there is a change to a medium "3" shot, that is, a reverse parallel to the abandoned "1" shot. When Anna rises with her "I've rarely heard a sadder story," that medium shot turns to a long shot as she crosses to the table, there to deposit her tea cup. Here, therefore, we combine something of the principles of the camera from the two usherettes speech with the variations offered by Deeley's account of his sexual life with Kate.

During his last speech, the camera, rather than following Deeley around as he makes a clockwise circle of the stage, "waits" instead for him, shooting from the "3" position as he moves from "noon" to "six" with his cocky tale about his "kinky" days, and then from the "1" position as he moves from "six" toward "eleven" (the right side of the stage-right sofa) where Anna sits—and waits. Deeley moves, while the camera, stationary, rotates just enough to keep him in the center of the screen. Except for one vertical shot of the two women at the end of the speech, Deeley is the center of attention—but ironically so. If the camera simply does its work, changing only from "3" to "1" when necessary, Deeley himself changes radically: the confident man at the start is, at the end, suspicious for the first time of the details of his own story.

While some have seen it as an instance of her egoism, Kate's "bath" speech is the first graphic signal that her identity, as she perceived it, will be different from that understood by her rivals.

Not an expression of a self-centered individual, therefore, the speech is instead an assertion of the self that would otherwise have been possessed as an object by Anna and Deeley. The first half involves a close-up of Kate, in fact the most sustained close-up of the television production. On "that appeals to me" there is a change to a medium "3" disclosing her onstage audience of two, for here Kate's warning points to Deeley's scenario for her (one of "harsh lines" and "urgency") as well as to Anna's London. A medium changes to a long-shot as she sits on "somewhere like that," but, just as quickly, returns to a close-up of Kate when she goes into the particulars—or the few particulars she chooses to dispense at this time—of her new eastern home. With "cars," we get a medium close-up of Deeley, and then one of Anna on "blurs your eyes," with the speech ending on a final close-up of Kate as she announces "That's the only nice thing about a big city." In effect, the camera duplicates the structure of Kate's speech: an initial expression of the self she is defining; a more conscious inclusion of Deeley and Anna in her remarks; a return to her self-portrait as she envisions an alternative place to both London and the country; then a second, more pointed address to Deeley and then Anna; and a final return to her self.

Kate's—and the play's—final speech is, for the camera no less, the most complex in the television production. In all, there were some eighteen camera changes. It opens with a long-shot, from Kate's "I remember you" through the pause to "I remember you lying dead," so that we can see both Anna's and Deeley's reactions to Kate's sudden interruption of Anna's smug "I remember you well." As Kate turns to Anna on "You didn't know I was watching you," there is a change to a medium shot (from "3") of the two women. Anna, struck by Kate's remark, takes a seat on the stage-left divan, as both Kate and "her" camera follow her there. Deeley is now out of the picture; the women have moved, in effect, to their half of the stage. With Kate's "It would have been graceless" and the subsequent reminder to Anna that she is talking about her room, not Anna's, we get a close-up of Kate, which is then relieved by a medium "1" shot of both women as Kate speaks about the events subsequent to Anna's waking. When Kate moves to Anna's left, speaking harshly about Anna's attempts to steal her tricks, both women are seen at a sharp angle, with Kate in the foreground, from the "3" camera. As she graphically describes Anna's grin sticking in her mouth, Kate is once more seen in a close-up. The feeling her is that Anna is alternately in and out of the picture, that Kate includes her only in the sense that, once recognized for what she is, Anna can now be dismissed. This alternation also allows for the contrasting moods of Kate's steel-like coldness and Anna's growing sense of desperation and humiliation.

As Kate speaks of looking in vain for tears in Anna's eye, the camera, accordingly, offers a medium shot from the "1" position. All this time, as Anna appears and disappears from the screen, with Kate remaining on-screen at all times, Deeley is literally out of the picture. With "but all was serene," as Kate crosses to the drum-table, we get the first long-shot since the opening of the sequence; Kate walks into the camera from stage-left. And while Deeley and Anna are visible near the top corners of the screen, they are little figures, for it is Kate who stands at the screen's bottom center as if speaking directly to the audience when she discusses Anna's "last rites." This long shot changes to a close-up on Kate's "I felt the time and season appropriate," so that we can see the anguish on her face. The lines themselves are something of a direct address to the audience, as if they were too complex, too profound, to be overheard by "mere" characters.

The spell downstage, the moment of intimacy with the audience, is broken with Kate's announcement that it was "time for [her] bath." Her cross upstage is covered by a medium shot from "1" that in turns changes to a long shot just before the pause. After the pause, and with Kate now sitting beside Anna, we return to the "1" medium, this time showing the two women sitting side by side on the stage-left divan, Anna dark and depressed, Kate full of life and energy, as if she were a schoolgirl imparting secrets about men to a girlfriend. As the speech changes in midstream from Anna to Deeley, we get a medium-long "3" shot that includes Deeley on Kate's "He liked your bed": Deeley now looks like Anna, devastated, shocked at this sudden, powerful outburst from Kate, and, like Anna, fearing the worst. For the first time in the speech, there is a close-up of Deeley, exclusively, on "he was a man," which is then lost in a medium "2" shot of the women as Kate reveals this man's own self-centered and tawdry notion of the roles of man and woman in the sexual act. Deeley moves slightly toward the chair on the right side of the stage-right sofa on "He resisted"—a beat after Kate has described plastering his face with dirt—and this move is caught in a long shot of the entire set, so that we, along with the women, watch and move. With the sarcastic "He suggested a wedding instead," we see all three characters from a sharply angled "1" shot. Then, after the "slight pause" on the clinical "Neither mattered" Kate appearas in a close-up that is held through the pause and includes her final lines. What she says, rather than the reactions, or even the feelings of the rivals, is all that matters now to her. In a cyclical return to the first lines of the bath speech, the camera here is Kate's, and Kate's only. Her "No one at all" said, there is an abrupt long shot to cover Kate as she sits, equidistant between two still, "dead" figures on her right and left.

Ultimately, the television film itself represented no single performance but rather, at every moment, the best choice among options, as in postproduction work we stitched together a bit of film here, a bit there, at other times splicing together two different takes of a single line. In this sense, the television film was unreal, representing some Platonic "ideal"—or as ideal as we could make it. This fact became especially evident when, on more than one occasion, we took the audio from one tape and matched it with the video of another, since in the audio for the latter the actor had delivered the line in a way less impressive than in the former. The reverse was also true. A particularly striking visual was substituted for a less impressive one that, in reality, had accompanied the audio. In several instances, we went one step beyond even this sort of matching. At one point all visuals of a given character proved unsatisfactory, and so we took out the audio of another piece of film where a character on-camera was seen listening to a voice off-camera, and substituted that video, in effect transforming a moment where the focus was on the listener for the one planned earlier in which the speaker alone would appear on camera.

If there were world enough and time—if we could have taken, say, twice as many takes of the performances—we could have avoided situations in which we lifted a single word from one audio and substituted it for a mispronounced word in another. Only someone who had been present during postproduction work, we like to think, would have been able to detect the insertion. I should add that such "surgery" was infrequent and, when performed, most often represented a bow to necessity. But, aware of it, I also realized how unreal the resulting television film could be. If we had not shot in sequence, such unreality would have been magnified exponentially. If compared to television, then, the stage performance is "live" in a temporal or spatial sense, it is also live in numerous other ways. It really happens—mistakes and all.

Real—although that word is certainly relative when applied

to the theatre—or unreal, live or canned, controlled to varying degrees—whatever the differences between the media of stage and television, perhaps the most important is that of the director's relation to his or her audience. For if in the theatre the onstage action is moved about for a stationary audience, in television it is the audience that, no less than the actors onstage, can be moved. That moving audience becomes a surrogate, in one sense, for the director, seeing the play as the director would want to see it, at one point stepping back from the characters, at another staring a character in the face, now looking directly at the character who is speaking and thereby giving only cursory attention to the character listening, a moment later reversing the process. At one moment the audience can move with the actor also moving onstage; at other point, they may wait for the actor to come to them, or to leave one area and travel upstage, out of sight. At times the audience focuses on two characters in dialogue; at other moments—if the director so chooses—they can forget the characters and look on some inanimate object.

As I have suggested before, the final mime of *Old Times* has the appearance not of a television image, but of a photograph, or of a scene suddenly illuminated by the photographer's flash. But it is not the only moment. A tremendously human medium, in that the figures on-screen are not gigantic as they can be in the cinema, human also in that the "house" is, most often, the room, the very living quarters of the spectator, television can at other times present images that diminish the human presence and stress instead the composition, the pattern implicit in the picture on-screen. This is what happens in the final mime.

This same paradox of a live human medium that can also become aesthetic and nonhuman also occurs at the beginning of *Old Times* for there we see the still image of Anna, upstage, facing away from the camera, dormant, at once present and not present. Downstage of Anna, speaking to each other and hence to us, observed unaware by the camera, are Kate and Deeley in movement, in conversation. Anna waits to be called by the medium, to be activated. And when she does speak, the tables are reversed—the once live figures of Kate and Deeley remain frozen in position until Anna faces the camera and thereby turns to them. The potential for life, for tragedy or comedy, that was upstage, denying the camera, enters the set. Its overture complete, Pinter's *Odd Man Out,* his *Old Times* begins.

At the end all this is reversed. All three characters on-screen, onstage, freeze into position. Even the light, so essential to this technological medium, is reduced, made impotent. When it does returns, fitfully, it cannot revive the dead figures onstage. As the viewer turns off the set, the television set becomes a blind and deaf instrument, and it is now the life outside its confines, reflected for the previous hour within, that takes the stage.

Afterword: Doing Pinter

"IT happens"—this is what Pinter himself says about *Old Times*. The scholar or critic, by definition, will see the play from the past tense: it has happened and the ensuing interpretation will, accordingly, deal with the work as set in time, as an entity that is over, finished. Now still, an object, it becomes the subject for commentary. This is how it should be, indeed perhaps the only way it can be, for the scholar or critic. For the person working in the theatre, the director charged with mounting a production, the actor assigned the part, however, Pinter's own present tense, "it happens," will have a special, a very immediate meaning. To be sure, that same director—probably more so than the actor—will, like the scholar or critic, find a structure in the play, an overall meaning or concept, and will see the evening as "going somewhere." But, like the actor, the director, especially in the (appropriately named) *rehearsal process*, will focus much more on what is going on moment by moment in the play, what is *happening* with every word, within every line, in the space between the end of Deeley's line and the beginning of Kate's. Not to mention what happens without words during every pause and silence.

This focus on what happens, what "is entirely taking place before your eyes" (as Pinter rephrases the issue), is, properly, spoken of as "presence" in the theater. In a wonderful essay called "Presence on the Stage," Alain Robbe-Grillet applies the term to *Waiting for Godot*.[1] In the absence of Godot, of any certain larger principle informing the play, all that we—actors and audience—have is what is presently before us onstage, the *now* existing and dying and existing again with each successive moment onstage.

One of the pitfalls we tried—not always successfully—to avoid during rehearsal for *Old Times* was imposing some sort of allegorical or symbolic reading on the play. No less, "psychologizing" the characters proved frustrating. The problem is that not all of the character is there; some dimensions are buried so deeply that even subtext will prove inadequate. Besides, in the relative, "Pirandello-ish"/*No Exit* world of the play, what one is is what one thinks one is, as well as what any other two characters think you are. Then, too, this is a social evening, not a heart-to-heart talk as one might find between two characters in, say, a play by Sam Shepard. Nothing can remain certain, fixed about the characters; no one interpretation can be pushed too far.

My three actors could talk about traits in this or that character, or a change (Deeley's or Anna's degeneration, for example, or Kate's emergence). But in their essays they also comment on the verbal, even physical competition during the evening, the sense that it is a game, with all the twists and turns, the expected (when one's strategy works) and the unexpected (when someone else's strategy prevails) that we associate with games. For me, their essays convey how much they struggled with their characters, *struggled* in this most productive sense of that word, and how they learned to cherish Deeley or Kate or Anna without being able to resolve their complexities, and contradictions. Things went better in rehearsals when we forgot the "big picture"—the director's concept, this or that allegorical grid—and, while never exactly "going with the flow," learned to take the play line by line, to analyze it, if you will, but mostly in terms of what is going on in the speaker's and the listeners' minds at every moment. Like Pinter, we found *Old Times* to be something happening.

There is a pleasure in the moment here that is inseparable from the continuous pleasure in performance itself, the presence of the play in which the actor, while knowing the routine by heart, how to deliver this line, where to move on that phrase, what facial expression to employ as he or she overhears a remark, nevertheless manages to give the illusion that everything is really happening for the first time, that the character is "real." This presence is sustained by the audience, supporting this fraudulent reality by their own suspension of disbelief, balancing the conscious artifice of the happening with those associations from real life that each spectator makes with the event onstage.

This presence is not often, perhaps cannot or should not be the object of critical or scholarly studies. As I suggest above, the critic or scholar works with a "different" play, one after-the-fact of what happens. In the Preface I tried to straddle the debate about performance criticism by suggesting that it represents at most another approach to the text, that if it is more attuned to the spatial, temporal, physical dimensions of a play, to the play as something transpiring in the theatre, performance criticism is still no more valid as interpretation than those more conventional approaches that have constituted literary studies, or the self-professed unconventional or radical approaches of the present time.

With a joint appointment in our departments of theatre and English, I straddle both worlds not just on the page but on campus as well. When I say that these two departments are very different worlds, I do not intend to qualify what I said in the Preface about the ways that scholars and people working in theatre can learn from each other. The professionas are mutually supportive. Bringing such people together is fashionable these days, and gratifying after all those years during which they had almost nothing to do with each other. Usually without much justification, people in theatre often dismiss scholars as boring and irrelevant, their comments on the play as of very little value since they have no practical experience with staging, or treat the play as if it were some literary text stillborn on the page. Conversely, one of my colleagues in the English Department asked me recently if I didn't find work in the Theatre Department "intellectually sterile." "After all," he continued, "those people don't really think about the play—they're mostly concerned with pleasing the audience, with quick effects." Such divisions are, by nature, unproductive.

Yet my own experience is that the two worlds can never be brought into perfect alignment, that the scholar often talks about a text that can never be staged, and that what happens in the theatre is diminished to some extent by analysis. Perhaps the people who talk best about what happens during a performance are not scholars, not even those concerned with the phenomenology of the theatrical experience—if for no other reason than that they speak abstractly and after the fact—but those engaged in staging or in watching the plays. Even when directors or actors in theatre departments speak of their work, as I have tried to do in this book on *Old Times*, something is lost in the translation. The real speaking is done on the spot during rehearsals, in the director's moment by moment work with an actor, day by day as a line, even a moment is given various deliveries. The real speaking is done at the performance itself; a film of a performance represents a reading, an intrusion, something violating the co-presence at a given moment of actor and audience.

If writing is, by definition, after the fact, even as film is, then can we ever speak about a play, about the event that happens, about what goes on in a performance if that going-on is always more than any theory, beyond the reach of any abstraction? My response to this apparently self-inflicted dilemma—to speak about that which is ineffable—is an affirmative one. We speak when we perform the play, or—no less—we speak silently when we witness the performance. Performer and actor are on equal footing here. We also speak when we encounter the text and imagine what it would be like to direct it, or to perform as one of the characters.

You can do this right now. Here are the first six lines of dialogue between Deeley and Kate. You will probably want to ask yourself a series of questions, starting with the most basic, the most profound of all: What do you think is happening here? Not just what has happened, or what happens in the context of the entire play, not where these questions will lead, but also what *is* happening, right now. In a way, whatever has happened now becomes part of what *is* happening. Treat the six lines as a little play, as something complete, autonomous.

Kate. Dark.
   (pause)
Deeley. Fat or thin?
Kate. Fuller than me. I think.
   (pause)
Deeley. She was then?
Kate. I think so.
Deeley. She may not be now.

You will best devise subsequent questions, but some of them just might go like this. What happens just before Deeley's first line? If we are coming upon the couple in the midst of an argument, how long have they been arguing? And at what intensity? Or are they coming together for the first time this day? Has the issue of Anna's visit been raised before? At least after the initial announcement that she was going to visit? Since her first line is "Dark," Deeley has clearly asked Kate something about the color of Anna's hair. But how has he asked the question—as a matter of fact, with a not-so-hidden agenda, as little more than a way to open a conversation? Why does he ask the question in the first place? Of what possible significance to him would be the color of Anna's hair? As he asks the question, whatever his motive, what does Kate think? What colors her one word reply? Colors it to the degree that after she does reply, "Dark," there occurs one of those Pinter pauses. What happens to Deeley during the pause? How satisfied is he with Kate's answer?

If before we come upon the couple, he has said something to her like "What is the color of Anna's hair?" then why is his second question phrased with the either/or of "Fat or thin?" With no pause, Kate answers "Fuller than me" and then adds "I think." Given her definitive one-word answer to the first question, why is she more relative here, both with the "fuller" and then the qualifying "I think"? Is she really less certain about Anna's size than she was about her hair color? Or is there something about Deeley's more prescriptive "Fat or thin" that leads her to reply as she does, differently than the first time—or that annoys her? What is her strategy here?

At its most basic, Deeley's object in the scene is to find out some physical facts about Anna. But, assuming he is not just idly curious, what is his larger object? Kate's relative "Fuller than me I think" is followed by a second pause. What happens here to Deeley, the questioner, and to Kate, the answerer? What is going on in their minds? After the pause, Deeley tries to pin down Kate by suggesting that all that she really knows is that, in the past, Anna was "fuller" than her. But, without a pause, Kate shoots back, "I think so," that is, not giving Deeley the more definite, even the obvious, "Yes." Does Deeley's "She may not be now" signify a victory—he has forced Kate to admit that now, at present, Anna may not be fuller, that Kate only knows Anna from the past, indeed that her "I think so" shows that her knowledge of the past is spotty? Or is it only a victory in Deeley's mind? Has Kate been playing with him all along, giving him the definitive "Dark" and then, having set him up, unsettling him with more relative, qualified answers?

Not all these questions—and they are only representative—could be voiced during rehearsal. There wouldn't be enough time. Some the actors would raise silently, naturally, with themselves. But all such questions have to do with what is happening, the presence of two people onstage, even if that presence is here a miniplay of only seven lines, lines that, of course, will lead further, but that are in themselves complete.

Once such questions are raised, they must be immediately qualified by a no less stronger presence, at least qualified in terms of the audience for the spectators present in the house, just offstage, have one of their own present onstage, upstage, "at the window." Does Anna face upstage all the time "looking out," or at times does she turn from the window and face downstage? Does she see and possibly overheard Deeley and Kate? Or does she not? The past, the subject of this initial dialogue between husband and wife, is present, is happening, is there before us. And it will be this theatrical presence, manifest in Pinter's violation of the stage's realistic picture of a seemingly mundane conversation between husband and wife, that will make the evening happen.

This book on *Old Times* has been an attempt, after the fact of the performances and the filming, to describe what happens not so much in the text of the play but during that interaction among playwright, director, actor—and character.

Since I wrote this, I have had the chance—and the challenge and the pleasure—of directing two other plays by Pinter—*A Kind of Alaska* and *The Lover*. They have their own happenings, their own sense of presence. This fact, peculiar to the theatre, was confirmed by the audience present at the performances, for example, by the physician who, seated a few rows in front of me, broke into tears when Deborah starts to flick her cheek with her finger as she relives her claustrophobic life during the coma or by the young couple who turned to each other with "I told you so," when Richard came onstage in the role of Max, his wife's lover. About the past, and the way it intrudes on the present, *Old Times* also happens, and happens for the performer no less than the audience. I have tried to record here, after the fact, what happened.

Appendix: Pinter's *Odd Man Out*

For Deeley and Kate, the reference to Carol Reed's 1950s film *Odd Man Out* is not accidental, or causal. Sensing that he has "lost," or at best only matched Anna in the song-duet, after a silence Deeley launches into his most extensive monologue in the play when he recalls that time he "popped into a fleapit" to see the film. If the cinema itself was disreputable, its neighborhood holds fond memories for him. As a little boy Deeley went to "this very neighborhood" with his father to buy a tricycle, indeed the first and only tricycle that he ever owned. We will recall earlier that Deeley has tried to brand Anna as Kate's "one and only" friend. This established, he draws a sharp contrast between the film, which he was compelled to see in this run-down movie house, and the two usherettes, lesbians, one of them stroking her breasts, the other announcing her pleasure as an audience with the suggestive epithet "dirty bitch." But this particular showing of *Odd Man Out* was fortuitous, for the "one other person in the whole cinema" was Kate, with whom Deeley struck up a conversation outside after the showing. His come-on line, initiating what he calls a "true-blue pickup," was to ask her if she also thought Robert Newton, who played Lukey in the film, was "fantastic." If he cannot remember Kate's first response, Deeley does remember that later, over tea, Kate pronounced Newton's performance "remarkable." Deeley ends the monologue asserting that it was therefore Robert Newton who "brought [them] together" and then, strangely, illogically, that "it is only Robert Newton who can tear [them] apart."

After a pause, Anna deflates Deeley's praise of Newton by observing that F. J. McCormick, who plays Lukey's roommate Shell, "was good too." Deeley agrees, but insists that the real issue is not the relative performances of the two actors, but rather the fact that F. J. McCormick, although "good too, . . . didn't bring [Deeley and Kate] together." Deeley's next question to Anna, "You've seen the film then," seems unnecessary, or an attempt to make sure she is qualified to judge McCormick's performance in light of Newton's. It may even be a weak attempt to diffuse the tension which she, from his perspective, has created and to which he has contributed. Not satisfied with her "yes," Deeley asks her to specify the date, but receives only a noncommittal, "Oh . . . long ago." As if to pull closer to Kate, Deeley then asks if she recalls seeing the film, and his wife's answer combines a straightforward "yes" with a more enigmatic "Very well." Does Kate mean "too well" in the sense that she regrets having met Deeley under such circumstances, particularly if she had purposely gone alone to see *Odd Man Out?*

Clouding the entire story is the fact that Deeley's account of the two usherettes is delivered directly to the two women, so that the fictive characters seem to be embodied in the two stage characters before us, seated, in our production, together on the stage-right sofa. In essence, Deeley's uncomplimentary portrait of lesbian lovers, contrasted with the macho pride he displays in having picked up a woman at the movie who later became his wife—"there she is. And there she was"—may be an attempt to distinguish the heterosexual, married love he offers Kate from the forbidden passion, associated with the past, and reintroduced by Anna's presence this evening. Kate was in the "dead center" of the auditorium; Deeley jokingly recalls that he was "off center" and has "remained so." Perhaps, seeing the two women together now, he feels "off center," displaced by Anna. Thus the monologue represents an attempt to displace her in turn, to regain the center. Currently threatened with the unwanted status of being the odd man out, Deeley tries to exchange places with Anna.

After the pause following Kate's "Oh yes. Very well," Deeley, as if vindicating his superior sexual attraction, recalls a subsequent date with Kate. This time, as he holds her "cool hand" and recalls how pleased he was that something he said "made her smile," Kate is judged to be "even more fantastic than Robert Newton." After the next pause, Deeley is bolder in championing heterosexual love; as he describes a "later stage" when their "naked bodies met," he recalls wondering "what Robert Newton would think of this." He underscores the purely theoretical question, one that seems to confuse Newton as real-life film actor with the artist he played in *Odd Man Out*, with a repetition that only heightens the portrait of sexual passion: "What would he think of this I wondered as I touched her profoundly all over." Surely, the curious word, from this self-conscious word-smith, is "profoundly." Suddenly, he challenges Anna with the question, "What do you think he'd think?" Anna's response is at once specifically deflating and vaguely supportive. Asserting that she "never met Robert Newton," she nevertheless assures Deeley that she does "know [she] know[s] what he mean[s]." And this reply, with its conflicting signals, leads into Anna's account of the man crying in the girls' apartment, one that, in essence, juxtaposes a male's sexual rejection at the hands of two women with Deeley's story of masculine sexual conquest.

It is Anna who makes the other reference to *Odd Man Out*. Kate professes to have been interested in the arts "once" but just as quickly claims that she "can't remember now which ones they were." As if desperate to reestablish the rich details of their cultural life in London twenty years ago, Anna launches into her own monologue, one recalling their days spent at the Tate Museum, or exploring London's old churches and its suburbs, along with visits to galleries, theaters, and concerts. Then, having informed Deeley that it was Kate who planned such excursions by first consulting the review pages—which she "ravished" and from which Anna "could never get her away"—Anna pointedly recalls "one Sunday" when, looking up from the newspaper, Kate impulsively bolted out of the door, Anna in tow, to "some totally obscure, some totally unfamiliar district" where in a movie house, "almost alone," the two women saw *Odd Man Out*. Anna describes it as a "wonderful film." Perhaps lured into the narrative, Deeley seems unprepared for this second mention of *Odd Man Out*. Anna's detail "almost alone" is intriguing, for it may imply that Deeley was also in the theater, or that if Anna and Kate were the two usherettes of Deeley's story, then the co-presence of a single customer and the two employees, united in their passion, qualified the sense of being "alone" for either side. After a "silence," Deeley seemingly leaps to a new topic, his traveling about the globe on important business, a digression clearly designed to polish his self image, just battered by Anna's conflicting account of the episode at the cinema.

In this fashion, Pinter, himself a screenwriter, uses a "real" film, as well as references to two of its lead actors, as an object of contention between the two antagonists of *Old Times*, references that, as we conflate Deeley's and then Anna's separate accounts of the showing, include Kate herself. Moreover, as one critic observes, Deeley's "hero worship" of Newton, the "fallen film star," intrudes on his own life, his past as he remembers it, even as it anticipates the future: Newton brought them together and it will only be Newton who, if anyone, can separate husband and wife. Conversely, Anna uses the showing to remind Kate of one of those "arts" for which the girlhood friends shared a common passion, even as her account challenges Deeley's "facts." Richard Dutton cautions us that "for many people the resonant title is all that the film will convey,"[2] and, indeed, the notion of the "odd man out" might be taken as the determining principle of *Old Times's* dramatic organization. From their perspective, Deeley and Anna foresee that one of them will be excluded from Kate's affection, will be the odd man out. The irony may be that Kate deliberately chooses this odd-man role for herself as in the final moments of *Old Times* she asserts her freedom from these two claimants representing a past friendship and a present marriage. At any stage in the evening, therefore, any one of the three characters can be excluded from the other two.[3]

Nor, in a more general sense, is this reference to a film isolated. Deeley claims to be a film writer and director when, disturbed by Kate's interest in Anna's life in Sicily, he barges into the women's conversation boasting about the "great crew" he had in Sicily, particularly his "marvelous cameraman, Irving Shultz. Best in the business."[4] He appears to have made a documentary offering a "pretty austere look at the women in black. The little old women in black." Deeley's line "I wrote the film and directed it" echoes the particular signature that Orson Welles gave to his film version of Kafka's *The Trial*, where at the end the camera focuses on the projector's dazzling light as we hear the voice of Welles announcing, "I played the Advocate . . . and wrote and directed this film. My name is Orson Welles."[5] And in Welles's ill-fated film *The Magnificent Ambersons*, where he himself provided the narration, at the end a microphone appears on-screen as Welles's voice informs us, "I wrote the script and directed it. My name is Orson Welles."[6]

Curiously, Deeley, unlike Kate or Anna, is never referred to by name in *Old Times*—the "Deeley" is confined to the dramatis personae—and thus his assertion that his name is Orson Welles might be seen as a desperately comic attempt, a patent lie, to draw attention to himself and thereby disrupt the women's intimate conversation. Or perhaps Deeley even believes himself to be, or wishes he were the brilliant, controversial film-director. If the actor plays Deeley as a failure in his profession, a third-rate director trying at present to compensate by belittling his wife and overpowering this guest from Kate's past, then his identity as Welles is pathetic, and ironic. It is also unsuccessful in that, without a pause, Kate resumes her eager questions about Anna's life on the Mediterranean: "Do you drink orange juice on your terrace?" When Deeley tries to assert himself a second time, claiming that he is "at the top of [his] profession," Kate remains unaffected by his tactic: "And do you like the Sicilian people?"

From a critic's perspective, or that of a scholar studying the text, why Deeley chooses Robert Newton—and why Anna counters with F. J. McCormick—is an intriguing, possibly an important issue, but one that needs to be pursued with caution.[7] However, for actors playing Deeley and Kate and thereby confronted with the more overtly mimetic demands of bringing a fictive character to life onstage, the direct references to the real-life Newton and McCormick, as well as implied references to their characters in *Odd Man Out*, Lukey and Shell, will perhaps offer some information from the past, from Deeley's and Anna's "life" as people outside the present evening, that might be used in understanding the character, especially as that character exists as something other than, sometime not fully spelled out by the dialogue on the page.[8] The actor invariably, and rightly, will ask himself or herself: Why does Deeley think so highly of Robert Newton? What is there in the character of Shell that might attract Anna? What is there about the movie that leads Anna to pronounce it "wonderful"? Why did Deeley go out of his way, into that fleapit in a run-down neighborhood, to see the film? Why does he seem to need the approval of Robert Newton, a man he has never met but only seen on-screen, for his lovemaking with Kate?

Again, Pinter cannot count on everyone in his audience having seen the Carol Reed film, as, say, Stoppard can count on—or just about count on—everyone at a performance of *Rosencrantz and Guildenstern Are Dead* being familiar with Shakespeare's *Hamlet*. It will be enough, therefore, that Deeley and Anna, who quarrel about everything else, prefer different actors in the film. To be sure, its title will not be lost on any spectator, even those who, not knowing the film, might suspect that Pinter makes up the title. What we can count on is the fact that Pinter himself, an avid film-goer as well as film writer, has seen *Odd Man Out*, that of all the films he has seen he chooses this one to be the point of reference, not once but twice, and each time for a sustained passage of dialogue between husband and guests.[9]

The story of *Odd Man Out* (I use Roger Manville's text[10]) has almost nothing in common with the plot of *Old Times*. The film, which in its opening statement professes to be about the ways in which the struggle between the IRA and the Dublin authorities affects the lives of those on both sides, is about a robbery of local mill, which goes afoul when the gang leader, Johnny McQueen (played by James Mason), falls out of the getaway car.

At large in the city and pursued by the police, McQueen, badly wounded in a shoot-out, is also sought by his fellows in the Organization, as well as by Kathleen, in whose house he had hid from the authorities and who has fallen in love with him. After a series of near captures one dark, snowy night in Dublin, during which McQueen is alternately rejected and befriended by various people, he is found by Shell, who takes him back to the house he shares with an artist down on his luck (Lukey, played by Robert Newton) and Tobin, a former medical student. At first, Shell is determined to sell McQueen to the highest bidder. Lukey, however, wants him as a subject for a portrait, for in the eyes of the dying man the artist hopes to be able, after many failures, to paint the "truth" about being human. At the end, McQueen, aided by Shell, leaves the studio to rendezvous with Kathleen, whose plan is to have the lovers escape by a ship leaving Dubiln at midnight. But before this can happen, the two are killed when Kathleen draws their fire by shooting at the police.

Odd Man Out, therefore, cannot be a source for Pinter in the way, say, the story in Cinthio's *Hecatommithi* was Shakespeare's source for *Othello* or Plutarch's account of Cleopatra in his *Parallel Lives* led to *Anthony and Cleopatra*. Still, it is a reasonable assumption that Pinter might have had *Odd Man Out* in mind for reasons beyond its title, or merely the specific names of two of its actors. Likewise, Deeley and Anna have not only seen but remembered the film and, what is more, the specific circumstances under which each saw it twenty years ago. We might then speculate about the relationship betwen film and play. At the very least, such speculation can use the film as a mirror which, by the comparative nature of the critical act, might illuminate the play. For the actors playing Deeley and Kate, the process is similar, since their taste in films and in film actors, as "documented" by the text, might prove useful in bringing to their portrayals dimensions of real life, that subtext both implied by the play and reflecting the actors' own experiences offstage.[11]

It should be noted that Deeley and Kate choose two characters who appear only much later in the film: We first see Shell in segment 127 and Lukey in 148 of the some 185 segments in Roger Manville's edition of the film script. In fact, Johnny's encounter with the two really constitutes a short "third act" of the script, the first two acts focusing on the robbery and then, when Johnny falls out of the car and becomes the odd man out, his flight through Dublin. The mood of *Odd Man Out* itself changes radically in this final act. Earlier playing on, indeed elevating the conventions of the generic "cops and robbers" film, *Odd Man Out* with the introduction of Lukey, Shell, and Tobin becomes a more conscious "allegory" in which Tobin, the "university men"—Tobin wears a university scarf, a reminder of his aborted days as a medical student—contends with Lukey for Johnny's "soul" and "life." Meanwhile, the street-wise Shell, who has been solely interested in selling Johnny, becomes a more sympathetic character when he decides to return Johnny to Kathleen and his boyhood priest, Father Tom, who has promised Shell payment in "faith."

One can imagine, as the actor would in a very direct way, just what attracts Deeley to Lukey's character, beyond Robert Newton's performance. Lukey is the self-conscious artist, always "on-stage," a poseur with his inflated gestures and dialogue—indeed in several reviews of the film Newton was criticized for playing the character too broadly. Lukey's studio itself constitutes the film's sole nonrealistic set, filled as it is with portraits of people gazing in fantastic ways at the viewer since Lukey's point of focus as a painter is their eyes. A stagelike "throne," on which his models pose, sits in the studio's dead center, while the only reminder that this temple of the artist is also a room in which Lukey lives is a small, neatly made bed in the corner. To illuminate his models, Lukey has on hand a light that very much resembles a stage spot. The studio itself, ornate and cluttered, a "stage" in a figurative sense, is in the midst of a once-fashionable, but now decaying house: the walls are scarred, and snow filters down from a hole in the room.

One critic suggests that, like Deeley, Lukey sees both life and his subjects, like Johnny, with a manifest "detachment and objectivity,"[12] as if his models were not real persons but only material for his art. There is a superficial warmth, a joviality about Lukey that, at any moment, can be swept away to reveal, just below the surface, a very frustrated, defensive man, whose bravado is a obvious means to keep his own personal failings under cover. Lukey's two physical clashes with Shell are especially violent ones. In the first, at the studio, when Shell tries to back out of Lukey's demand that he bring Johnny to him, Lukey grabs him harshly, threatening to hit him "where it hurts." In the tavern, when Lukey spots Shell, he charges at him, breaking glass, smashing his cane on the bar, pushing bystanders aside. Fencie, the owner, reminds Lukey this is not the first time his "artistic differences" have damaged the establishment.

And, like Deeley, Lukey pretends to greatness, to be on "top of his profession." In truth, he has yet to capture a man's "soul" on canvas, or, as he confesses to Tobin, his faces "don't stay" (p. 173). Hence, Lukey needs Johnny, this man near death, the "man [he] must paint" (p. 173) and in whose eyes he will be able to see "the truth" (p. 178), "wonderful thoughts" (p. 188). Lukey's vow that the portrait, if completed, will allow "something to be said before he dies" (p. 189) seems directed as much to himself as to his subject. Tobin warns Lukey ominously that, even if he does succeed, he "might find something [he doesn't] like" (p. 189), and is offended that his roommate is willing to "take" a man's life to have his vision, to paint him while the life "dribbles out of him" (pp. 194–95). Even Lukey's professed concern to capture Johnny's "soul" (p. 188) is dubious; his real object appears to portray the man's helplessness, the "doomed" expression, to use Lukey's own word, that he may feel in himself. When, during a fight, Lukey's canvas and painting supplies crash to the floor, Shell helps Johnny from the studio, before Lukey "almost got it." After that, this complex man, so energetic and yet tormented, never returns to the film.

Anna's identification with Shell is alternately clearer and more puzzling. Lacking the formal education of his two rommmates, Shell is the "odd man" among the three, dependent on Lukey for kindness, for his very physical security, and dependent on the more genial Tobin for food. Both characters clearly tolerate Shell, or use him, as Lukey does, as an unpaid model. Just as Anna's calling F. J. McCormick "very good too" incites Deeley, so Shell is Lukey's antagonist, particularly when he disobeys, or fails to comply with the demands of his bullish roommate. Clearly, Lukey's "boisterous gaiety,"[13] as it has been called, exists for Shell only as long as he is submissive to the artist.

McCormick, it should be noted, is small in stature, thinner and more fragile than the tall, large-framed Newton. And if the complexity in Lukey's character is generated by the division between his surface and inner self, Shell's contradictory qualities are simultaneously present: without much education or the ability to be introspective, he is still clever and witty. A collector of junk, Shell, like Anna, preserves the past, literally so. And he has a way with words, is flexible with the language and, in particular, given to a poetlike use of allegory: Johnny is equated by Shell with a wounded, imprisoned bird. Even his decision to sell Johnny, his "business," as he terms it, is justified, albeit in small part, by his need to "live," a need that Father Tom also confirms.

Shell also undergoes a character reformation of sorts; his mission once leaving Lukey's studio with Johnny is to take him "home."

If Lukey remains an imposing, but isolated and lonely individual, Shell at the end is struck by the lover's deaths. The film closes with Father Tom putting a comforting arm around him as the two move off-camera. If the antagonists in the film's first two acts, before Lukey and Shell are introduced, are the police and the Organization, clearly the antagonists in its final act are Lukey and Shell, roommates at odds both in personality and in their view of Johnny McQueen.

Once we move beyond these two characters, there are other ways in which *Odd Man Out* provides a context for *Old Times*. There are elements in the film that may have influenced the play or, at the very least, that parallel dimensions of *Old Times*.

Christopher Hudgins's analysis of the play's "filmic technique"[14] has been commented on in some detail in the first chapter. It should be noted here, in specific, that Pinter twice uses the cinematic flashback: once during the conversations between Anna and Kate in which Deeley is excluded and later when the women revert to their characters twenty years before.

There are two such flashbacks in *Odd Man Out*, and they, likewise, stick out in a film that otherwise is structured by that present-tense, sequential realism common to British films of the 1950s. While he is hiding in the air-raid shelter, Johnny hallucinates, transforming a little girl who has come to retrieve her ball into a guard from his prison days, even going so far as to speak to the guard as he reviews the struggle with the plant employee on the steps of the mill, during which Johnny's opponent was killed and Johnny himself badly wounded. Mason plays this conversation as if he had returned to perfect health; his manner with the silent guard is relaxed, even friendly.

Later, in The Four Winds tavern, Johnny sees faces of all the major characters in the film in the circles formed by air pockets in the beer which has spilled on the table in front of him. The flashback has two stages. In the first appear the members of the Organization, along with the woman Rosie who nursed Johnny, all speaking characteristically and rapidly. When Rosie's husband Tom cries, "That's the man the police is looking for!" (p. 178), this first set of faces vanish to be replaced by a second, including more minor characters, such as the First Soldier and the bartender, along with Tom (Alfie in the script) and Father Tom who speak in unison: "I'm thinking of the decent man he killed." The face of Kathleen dissolves the vision; on her "Shall I come to see you, Johnny?" he snaps out of the flashback and, scratching his wounded hand on the table, cries out in pain. That cry leads directly to Lukey's catching sight of Shell and then the battle between them, during which, it is interesting, customers takes sides for and against the two combatants.

There is even a moment in *Odd Man Out* when characters offer conflicting accounts of the same past event, as do Deeley and Anna on the showing of the movie, the party to which Deeley claims to have taken her, or the episode with the man in the room, to which Kate, in her final speech, adds a third, and "authoritative" version. Shortly after we see Johnny fall from the car and the abortive efforts of his friends, fueled by their frantic disagreements, to rescue him as the police close in, Murphy, Pat, and Nolan, with Dennis as the arbitrator calling for them to "keep to the facts" (p. 107), offer very conflicting "readings" of the same event, alternately absolving themselves of blame while accusing their fellows. They argue over the interpretation of each moment of the get-away: Did Pat stop the car in time? Why did Murphy and Pat delay in getting out of the car, once stopped, to rescue Johnny? These conflicting "truths" force Dennis to order the three men to report to the Organization's headquarters for a court martial.

Old Times begins in the evening, announced by Kate's first word "dark." Later Anna, standing before the window, asks if her hosts can see that "tiny ribbon of light" shining across the darkened ocean, and it is Anna whose fear of the dark—and pleasure in a warm, well-lighted room—drives her to resist Kate's suggestion that the two women go out at night. Indeed, though in her opening monologue Anna speaks of "queuing all night" and, in general, paints a romantic picture of London at dark, when Kate suggests a "walk across the park," she, almost in hysteria, paints a grotesque picture of darkness—the dirty park, men and women hiding in the darkness, shadows everywhere, even the grotesque artificial light of chandeliers in hotel lobbies.

Once the robbery is completed, the setting for *Odd Man Out* quickly becomes the evening, to the extent that after segment 75 all shots, both interior and exterior, are night shots. It is through this inhospitable, terrifying night, during which a heavy rain changes to snow, that Johnny makes his way. Further, there is a pointed contrast between the darkness outside and the comfortable, well-lighted interiors of houses seen from the street. In segment 77, for example, as Pat, Nolan, and Murphy hide from the police in a dark alley, at the top of the frame we see the living room of a cozy apartment, a man playing the accordion, a woman listening. As Johnny races down the black streets of Dublin, we observe residents closing shades, or peeking out the windows, slamming doors, separating themselves, secure inside their houses, from the violence taking place on the street. In one long segment of the film two sisters find Johnny on the street, take him inside their house to attend to his injuries, but, once discovering his identity, send him out again, just as the snow storm becomes particularly violent. As Johnny makes his way in pain down the dark street, Maudie, after putting his cap on his head, scampers back to her doorway, leaving Johnny to make his way through the stormy night. Then there is a cut to the house's interior. Tom, the husband, assures his wife that they "acted charitable," that the "best thing" was that Johnny "took and went," and then asks Rosie if his "tea [is] ready."

There is a parallel scene in Teresa's house, to which Pat and Nolan go to escape the police. As they enter, the hypocritical Teresa makes much ado about the darkness and the rain, and at the end of the segment, after she has alerted the police, she literally pushes the two out into the night, where they will be shot. Finally, there is a particularly glaring display of this outside/inside motif near the end of the film, where Johnny lies in the bushes, the snow pelting on him, while through the upstairs window of a house we see two children open the curtain and stare out at the falling snow, their eyes full of delight as they anticipate tomorrow's playing in the snow.

It should be noted that Deeley refers to a bar twice in *Old Times*. At the start of act 2 he recalls the Wayfarers Tavern, where he claims to have bought drinks for Anna, after which he took her to a party. It is interesting that at the drinking party, in Deeley's first version, he found the men disgusting: with "their stinking and broken teeth and the hair in their noses," particularly their obsession with topics such as "China and death." Here, the men, insisting that Deeley join their discussion, "as if [he] were the cause of their argument," only managed to separate him from Anna. When he later caught sight of her sitting with another woman on the sofa, and tried to make his way back to her, she was gone before he got there, the women leaving only the "indentations of four buttocks" on the sofa. But in the second version, after Deeley has realized Kate's power, as well as the strong bond between her and Anna, his picture of the men at the same party changes radically. These "philosophers" were "not a bad bunch," in fact are called "old friends," people who "spoke their minds" and whom Deeley now misses very much. Excluded by the women, his masculinity threatened, Deeley in effect returns to such all-male fellowship as the bar affords, that nightly party where women are pretty much excluded, where men do "men's business," drinking, arguing over politics, speaking their minds, and not having to compete over women.

In *Odd Man Out* Johnny stumbles into a tavern called The Four Winds; it is clearly a male hangout, the room packed with men, the regulars, jostling for drinks, talking loudly. When the fight between Lukey and Shell breaks out, the few women present are terribly agitated. One woman in fact screams hysterically to her husband to take her home (p. 179). When Johnny is hustled out of the bar, back into the night—earlier he has pleaded with the head barman to allow him to stay at least until closing time— he is escorted by Lukey, and thus the return to the outside signals the film's final movement, the fight among Lukey, Tobin, and Shell for Johnny, and the climactic scene of Johnny's death set at the docks minutes before midnight.

Old Times is, by Pinter's own admission, a work in which he was very interested in the matter of time; the title itself underscores this. Accordingly, the three characters offer us three versions of their past, individual and mutual. As we have seen, even though each version may have been unconsciously fashioned, distorted by memory, a character's faith in the accuracy of his or her memory of the past very much determines the present, how that character acts toward and, no less, influences others. No essay on the subject of time, *Old Times* enacts time, in this medium of presence where, sharing the same time frame as their audience, actors speak and move about before us.

In *Odd Man Out*, the clock tower of Dublin is the film's most pervasive visual motif. We see that tower as the camera zooms in on the city from the hazy clouds above. In both exterior shots, as the robbers go toward the first meeting of the Organization in Johnny's room, and in interior shots, such as the room itself, we see the tower in the background. When the film changes to night shots, the clock is lit. Whether Johnny is making his way through the street or trying to find sanctuary indoors, the clock is never long from our view.

Fencie's strategy for clearing the bar is to have an assistant push the hands of the clock forward and then declare closing time. And at the end, Kathleen races to get Johnny to the boat before the deadline of midnight set by the Seaman. The final shot of *Odd Man Out* is that of the clock striking that hour. Except in its two flashbacks, which represent moments of delirium on Johnny's part, the film, like a well-made play, moves forward in time, each segment taking place in a logical temporal sequence. For Johnny, Kathleen, and the Organzation, as well as for the police, the events constitute a race against time.

Conversely, *Old Times* is given to flashbacks, to violations of the conventional "march" or "progress" of time, not just in those two moments obviously borrowed by Pinter from the film medium but, more generally, in the presence of the past in the present. For Anna brings the past with her, is in a sense Kate's past. Deeley enters that same past, sometimes using it to establish an image of himself that he thinks will, this evening, prove superior to that of women, as he understands their gender. At other times he creates a version different from the one Anna brings, so that he can supplant hers with his own. But it is Kate, at the end, who buries both husband and friend in the past. Symbolically distancing herself from Anna, while also putting Deeley in his place, she is at least free of them, of their conflicting pasts, free of time generally.

There is no clock in *Old Times*, and no one announces the minutes or hour, as the clock does so relentlessly in *Odd Man Out*. However, a "clock" is still everywhere, and nowhere, even as the film's title, spilling over from the specific references by Deeley and then Anna to Carol Reed's film, pervades the play— Pinter's enactment of the odd man out.

Notes

Chapter 1. *Old Times* in the Theatre and among the Scholars

1. Martin Gotsfried, "Harold Pinter," Vogue 158 (1 August 1971): 71. The text for *Old Times* is that published by Grove Press (New York, 1971). See, also, Michael Anderson, *Anger and Detachment: A Study of Arden, Osborne, and Pinter* (London: Putman, 1976), p. 108; and Charles Marowitz, "Can Pinter Be Beckett?," *New York Times* (13 June 1971): sec. 2, pp. 1, 3.

2. Tony Ayburn, "The Memory of All That: Pinter's *Old Times*," *English* 22 (1973): 102; and Benedict Nightingale, in *Plays in Review 1956–1980: British Drama and the Critics*, ed. Gareth and Barbara Lloyd Evans (New York: Methuen, 1985), p. 180.

3. Walter Kerr, "Is Mr. Pinter Telling Us Less than He Knows?," *New York Times* (18 November 1971): sec. 2, pp. 1, 7.

4. Steven Gale, "Harold Pinter's *Family Voices* and the Concept of the Family," in *You Never Heard Such Silence*, ed. Alan Bold (Totowa, N.J.: Barnes and Noble, 1984), p. 158. Also, Harold Hobson, "Pinter's No-Contest: *Old Times*," *Christian Science Monitor* (14 June 1971): 4; and Ronald Bryden and James Trewin, in *Plays in Review*, ed. Evans, pp. 178–79, 177.

5. Martin Esslin, *Pinter the Playwright* (London: Methuen, 1984), p. 187.

6. Jeremy Kingston, "*Old Times*," *Punch* 260 (16 June 1971): 826–27. Also, J. K., "Camera Obscura," *Newsweek* 8 (29 November 1971): 110–11.

7. John Russell Taylor, "*Old Times*," *Plays and Playgoers* 18 (1971): 28.

8. Mollie Panter-Dounes, "Letters from London," *The New Yorker* 47 (3 July 1971): 64–65.

9. Gotsfried, "Harold Pinter," p. 71. Also, Christopher Porterfield, "Memories as Weapons," *Time* 97 (14 June 1971): 76.

10. Arthur McGuiness, "Memory and Betrayal: Landscapes of *Old Times*," *Drama and Symbolism*, Themes in Drama 4, ed. James Redmond (Cambridge: At the University Press, 1982): 101.

11. Kerr, "Is Mr. Pinter Telling Us," pp. 1, 7. Also, Harold Hobson, "Remembrance of Things Past," *Sunday Times* (London) (6 June 1971): 29; Porterfield, "Memories," p. 76; John Russell Brown, "Theater without Adventure," *Times Literary Supplement* (29 December 1972): 1570.

12. Harold Clurman, *The Divine Pastime: Theater Essays* (New York: Macmillan, 1974), pp. 287–88. Also, Kenneth Hurren, "These Foolish Things," *Spectator* (12 June 1971): 821.

13. Steven Gale, *Butter's Going Up: A Critical Analysis of Harold Pinter's Works* (Durham, N.C.: Duke University Press, 1977), p. 184.

14. Jean Kerr, "*Waiting for Pinter*: A Play, No Curtain," *New York Times* (12 December 1971): sec. 2, pp. 3, 5.

15. Brendon Gill, "The Cry," *The New Yorker* 47 (27 November 1971): 89.

16. TEK, "Is Meaning a Cat or a Mouse?," *Time* 98 (29 November 1971): 70–71. Also, J.K., "Camera Obscure," pp. 110–11.

17. Stephen Martineau, "Pinter's *Old Times*: The Memory Game," *Modern Drama* 16 (1973): 295.

18. Gerald Weales, "The Stage," *Commonweal* 95 (17 December 1971): 278.

19. Kingston, *"Old Times,"* pp. 826–27. Also, Gill, "Cry," p. 89.

20. Benedict Nightingale, "Three's a Crowd," *New Statesman* (11 June 1971), p. 817.

21. John Russell Taylor, *"Old Times,"* *Plays and Players* 18 (1971): 28. Also, Hobson, "Remembrance," p. 29.

22. TEK, "Is Memory," pp. 70–71.

23. Kerr, "Is Mr. Pinter," pp. 1, 7. Also, Steven Gale, "Observations on Two Productions of Harold Pinter's *Old Times*," *Pinter Review* 1 (1987): 40–41.

24. John Francis Lane, "No Sex Please, I'm English: John Francis Lane on the Pinter-Visconti Case," *Plays and Players* 20 (1973): 19–21.

25. Hurren, "These Foolish Things," p. 821. Also, Gill, "The Cry," p. 89.

26. Marowitz, "Can Pinter," pp. 1, 3. Also, J.K., "Camera Obscure," pp. 110–11; TEK, "Is Memory," pp. 70–71.

27. Gotsfried, "Harold Pinter," p. 71. Also, Hobson, "Remembrance," p. 29.

28. Marowitz, "Can Pinter," pp. 1, 3.

29. Kerr, "Is Pinter," pp. 1, 7.

30. Gotsfried, "Harold Pinter," p. 71.

31. Weales, "The Stage," p. 278. Also, Hobson, "Remembrance," p. 29.

32. Panter-Dounes, "Letters from London," pp. 64–65. Also, Hurren, "These Foolish Things," p. 821; Hobson, "No-Contest," p. 4.

33. Nightingale, in Evans, *Plays in Review*, p. 180. Also, Kerr, "Is Pinter," pp. 1, 7.

34. J. W. Lambert, "Plays in Performance," *Drama* 102 (1975): 47–49. Also, Marowitz, "Can Pinter," pp. 1, 3; Richard A. Cave, *New British Drama on the London Stage: 1970 to 1975* (New York: St. Martin's Press, 1988), p. 10.

35. Porterfield, "Memories," p. 76. Also, Kerr, "Is Mr. Pinter," pp. 1, 7.

36. Cave, *New British Drama*, p. 10. Also, Taylor, *"Old Times,"* pp. 28–29; Marowitz, "Can Pinter," pp. 1, 3; Nightingale, "Three's a Crowd," p. 817; Weales, "The Stage," p. 278.

37. Hobson, "No-Contest," p. 4.

38. Kingston, *"Old Times,"* pp. 816–17.

39. Porterfield, "Memories," p. 76.

40. Cave, *New British Drama*, p. 10. And see Kingston, *"Old Times,"* pp. 826–27.

41. Taylor, *"Old Times,"* pp. 28–29. And see Porterfield, "Memories," p. 76; Panter-Dounes, "Letters," pp. 64–65; Nightingale, "Three's a Crowd," p. 817.

42. Weales, "The Stage," p. 278.

43. TEK, "Is Memory," pp. 70–71.

44. Hobson, "No-Contest," p. 4. See also Hurren, "These Foolish Things," p. 821.

45. Weales, "The Stage," p. 278.

46. Hurren, "These Foolish Things," p. 821.

47. Kerr, "Is Mr. Pinter," pp. 1, 7.

48. Weales, "The Stage," p. 278.

49. Mel Gussow, "A Conversaation with Harold Pinter," *New York Times Magazine* (5 December 1971): 42–43, 126–36.

50. See Kathleen George, quoting Pinter from an interview in *Sunday Times* (London) on 4 March 1962, in *Rhythm in Drama* (Pittsburgh: Pittsburgh University Press, 1980), p. 33.

51. Simon Trussler, *The Plays of Harold Pinter* (London: Victor Gollancz, Ltd., 1973), pp. 173–78.

52. Elizabeth Sakellandou, *Pinter's Female Portraits* (Totowa, N.J.: Barnes and Noble Books, 1988), pp. 169–73.

53. David T. Thompson, *Pinter: The Player's Playwright* (New York: Shocken Books, 1985), p. 51. And see A. R. Braunmuller, "A World of Words in Pinter's *Old Times*," *Modern Language Quarterly* 40 (1979): 55; George Watson, "Osborne, Pinter, Stoppard: A Playful Look at London since 1956," *University Quarterly Review* 62 (1986): 280.

54. Peter Briggs, "*Old Times*: Beyond Pinter's Naturalism," *English Studies in Canada* 1 (1975): 469–74.

55. David Savran, "The Girardian Economy of Desire: *Old Times* Recaptured," *Theater Journal* 34 (1982): 53–54.

56. Sakellandou, *Female Portraits*, pp. 165–67.

57. Barbara Kreps, "Time and Harold Pinter's Possible Realities: Art as Life, and Vice Versa," *Modern Drama* 22 (1979): 55. See also Lucina Paquet Gabbard, *The Dream Structure of Pinter's Plays: A Psychoanalytic Approach* (Rutherford, N.J.: Fairleigh Dickinson University Press, 1976), p. 240.

58. Savran, "Girardian Economy," p. 49. See also Francis Gillen, "'All Those Bits and Pieces': Fragmentation and Choice in Pinter's Plays," *Modern Drama* 17 (1974): 486.

59. Noel King, "Pinter's Progress," *Modern Drama* 23 (1980): 254.

60. Arthur Ganz, "Mixing Memory and Desire: Pinter's Vision in *Landscape, Silence*, and *Old Times*," in *Pinter: A Collection of Critical Essays*, ed. Ganz (Englewood Cliffs, N.J.: Prentice-Hall, Inc., 1972), pp. 176–78.

61. Robert W. Corrigan, *The Theater in Search of a Fix* (New York: Delacorte, 1973), p. 313. See also Briggs, "Beyond Pinter's Naturalism," p. 466.

62. Diamond, *Comic Play*, pp. 175, 164.

63. Robert Skloot, "Putting Out the Light: Staging the Theme of Pinter's *Old Times*," *Quarterly Journal of Speech* 61 (1975): 266–69. See also Christopher C. Hudgins, "Inside Out: Filmic Technique and the Theatrical Deception of Consciousness in Harold Pinter's *Old Times*," *Genre* 13 (1980): 362–63.

64. Kreps, "Time," p. 59.

65. L. A. C. Dobrez, *The Existential and Its Exits: Literary and Philosophical Perspectives on the Works of Beckett, Ionesco, Genet, and Pinter* (New York: St. Martin's Press, 1986), pp. 361–62. And see Esslin, *Pinter*, p. 192.

66. Gale, *Butter's Going Up*, p. 197.

67. Cave, *New British Drama*, p. 15. And see Ronald Hayman, *Harold Pinter* (New York: Frederick Ungar Publishing Co., 1973), p. 143; Richard Hornby, *Drama, Metadrama, and Perception* (Lewisburg, Pa.: Bucknell University Press, 1986), p. 173.

68. Hayman, *Harold Pinter*, p. 148.

69. King, "Pinter's Progress," p. 249. See also Hurren, "These Foolish Things," p. 821; Lawrence I. Eilenberg, "Rehearsal as Critical Method: Pinter's *Old Times*," *Modern Drama* 18 (1975): 390.

70. Diamond, *Comic Play*, pp. 162–64.

71. Katharine Worth, *Revolutions in Modern English Drama* (London: G. Bell and Sons, 1972), p. 98. And see Ganz, "Mixing Memory," p. 171.

72. Austin Quigley, *The Pinter Problem* (Princeton: Princeton University Press, 1975), p. 275.

73. Andrew K. Kennedy, *Six Dramatists in Search of a Language* (Cambridge: At the University Press, 1975), p. 233. See also Gillen, "All These Bits," p. 483.

74. Braunmuller, "World of Words," p. 59. And see John Russell Brown, *Theatre Language: A Study of Arden, Osborne, Pinter, and Wesker* (New York: Taplinger Publishing Co., 1972), p. 54.

75. Watson, "Osborne, Pinter, Stoppard," p. 282.

76. Braunmuller, "Harold Pinter, the Metamorphosis of Memory," in *Essays on Contemporary British Drama*, ed. Hedwig Bock and Albert Wertheim (Munich: Hueber, 1981), p. 166.

77. William Baker and Stephen E. Tabachnick, *Harold Pinter* (Edinburgh: Oliver and Boyd, 1973), p. 137.

78. Gussow, "Conversation," p. 42. And see Thomas P. Adler, "Pinter, Proust, Pinter," in *Harold Pinter: Critical Approaches*, ed. Steven H. Gale (Rutherford, N.J.: Fairleigh Dickinson University Press, 1986), pp. 130–31.

79. Baker and Tabachnick, *Pinter*, pp. 145–46.

80. Gabbard, *Dream Structure*, p. 239.

81. Katherine H. Burkman, "Death and the Double in Three Plays by Harold Pinter," in *Harold Pinter: You Never Heard Such Silence*, ed. Alan Bold (Totowa, N.J.: Vision and Barnes and Noble, 1984), pp. 138–39.

82. Kreps, "Possible Realities," p. 55. And for a more direct focus on this issue of "bedfellows" and hence sexuality in Pinter, see Stanley Kauffmann, "Pinter and Sexuality: Notes, Mostly on *Old Times*," *American Poetry Review* 3 (1974): 39–41. Kauffmann says of the New York production that it "figuratively takes place in Kate's loins" (p. 39) and speaks of the work's "genital ambience" (p. 41). See also Bernard F. Dukore, *When Laughter Stops: Pinter's Tragicomedy* (Columbia: University of Missouri Press, 1976), p. 55; Anderson, *Anger and Detachment*, p. 110.

83. Gabbard, *Dream Structure*, p. 243.

84. Cave, *New British Drama*, p. 10.

85. Trussler, *Pinter*, p. 176. And see Eilenberg, "Rehearsal as Critical Method," p. 176; McGuiness, "Memory and Betrayal," pp. 104–8.

86. Hudgins, "Inside Out," p. 357.

87. Savran, "Girardian Economy," p. 45–49.

88. Richard Dutton, *Modern Tragicomedy and the British Tradition* (Norman: University of Oklahoma Press, 1986), p. 170. See also B. S. Hammond, "Beckett and Pinter: Towards a Grammar of the Absurd," *Journal of Beckett Studies* 4 (1979): 42.

89. Diamond, *Comic Play*, p. 177. See also Ganz, "Mixing Memory," p. 170; McGuiness, "Memory and Betrayal," p. 102.

90. Brigg, "Beyond Pinter's Naturalism," p. 472. And see Burkman, "Earth and Water: The Question of Renewal in Harold Pinter's *Old Times* and *No Man's Land*," *West Virginia University Philological Papers* 25 (1979): 102.

91. Cave, *New British Drama*, p. 9. And see McGuiness, "Memory and Betrayal," p. 109.

92. Burkman, "Earth and Water," p. 104.

93. Hudgins, "Inside Out," pp. 364–73. And see Martineau, "Memory Game," p. 295.

94. Burkman, "Earth and Water," p. 104.

95. Diamond, *Comic Play*, p. 171. And see Trussler, *Pinter*, p. 176.

96. Gabbard, *Dream Structure*, pp. 235–48.

97. See Douglas Colby, *As the Curtain Rises: On Contemporary British Drama 1966–1976* (Rutherford, N.J.: Fairleigh Dickinson University Press, 1978), pp. 95–96; Eilenberg, "Rehearsal as Critical Method," pp. 388–89.

98. Kreps, "Possible Realities," p. 54. See also McGuiness, "Memory and Betrayal," pp. 103–4; Dukore, *When Laughter Stops*, p. 57; Steven Gale, "The Significance of Orson Welles in Harold Pinter's *Old Times*," *Notes on Contemporary Literature* 13 (1983): 12; Baker and Tabachnick, *Pinter*, p. 147.

99. Esslin, *Pinter the Playwright*, p. 192. And see GIllen, "All These Bits," p. 485.

100. Hughes, "They Can't Take That Away," p. 472. And see Ayburn, "Memory of All That," p. 102.

101. Sakellandou, *Female Portraits*, p. 165. And see Gabbard, *Dream Structure*, p. 250.

102. Diamond, *Comic Play*, p. 170. And see Gabbard, *Dream Structure*, p. 235; Martineau, "Memory Game," p. 289.

103. Diamond, *Comic Play*, p. 176. And see Anderson, *Anger and Detachment*, p. 111.

104. Sakellandou, *Female Portraits*, p. 171.

105. Martineau, "Mixing Memory," p. 174. And see Gabbard, *Dream Structure*, p. 243.

106. Burkman, "Death and the Double," p. 138.

107. Ganz, "Mixing Memory," p. 171.

108. Braunmuller, "World of Words," p. 61. And see Baker and Tabachnick, *Pinter*, p. 145.

109. Sakellandou, *Female Portraits*, p. 169. And see Hughes, "They Can't Take That," p. 473; Colby, *Curtain Rises*, p. 83; Hughes, "They Can't Take That," p. 475.

110. Diamond, *Comic Play*, p. 176. And see Gabbard, *Dream Structure*, p. 243.

111. Hughes, "They Can't Take That," p. 496.

112. Diamond, *Comic Play*, p. 177. And see Cave, *New British Drama*, p. 14.

113. Gabbard, *Dream Structure*, p. 247–51. And see Worth, *Revolutions*, p. 93.

114. Braunmuller, "World of Words," pp. 70, 73. And see Savran, "Girardian Economy," p. 52.

115. Martineau, "Memory Game," p. 296.

116. Skloot, "Putting out the Light," pp. 266–67. And see Hudgins, "Inside Out," pp. 373–74.

117. Dukore, *When Laughter Stops*, p. 53. For a detailed review of criticism on Pinter see Susan Hollis Merritt, *Pinter in Play: Critical Strategies and the Plays of Harold Pinter* (Durham, N.C. and London: Duke University Press, 1990.

Chapter 2. Within Pinter's World

1. The texts used for Pinter are all published by Grove Press (New York), except as noted; *Complete Works: One* (*The Birthday Party, The Room, The Dumb Waiter, A Slight Ache, A Night Out, The Black and White, The Examination, Writing for the Theater*) (1977); *Complete Works: Two* (*The Caretaker, The*

Collection, *The Lover, Night School, Trouble in the Works, The Black and White, Request Stop, Last to Go, Special Order, Writing for Myself*) (1977); *Complete Works: Three (The Homecoming, Tea Party, The Basement, Landscape, Silence, Night, That's Your Trouble, That's All, The Applicant, Interview, Dialogue for Three)* (1978); *Monologue* (London: Covent Garden Press, Ltd., 1973); *Mountain Landscape* (1988); *No Man's Land* (1975); *Other Places (A Kind of Alaska, Victoria Station, Family Voices)* (1983); *The Proust Screenplay* (1977).

Chapter 5. The Actors: Kate, Deeley, and Anna

1. Leonard Powlick "What the Hell Is *That* All About?": A Peek at Pinter's Dramaturgy," in *Harold Pinter: Critical Approaches*, ed. Steven H. Gale (Rutherford, N.J.: Fairleigh Dickinson University Press, 1986), p. 31.
2. Kenneth Burke, quoted in Porolick, "What the Hell," p. 31.

Afterword: Doing Pinter

1. Alain Robbe-Grillet, "Samuel Beckett, or Presence on the Stage," in *Snapshots Towards a New Novel* (New York: Grove Press, 1966), pp. 111–25.

Appendix: Pinter's *Odd Man Out*

1. William Baker and Stephen E. Tabachnick, *Harold Pinter* (Edinburgh: Oliver and Boyd, 1973), p. 144.
2. Richard Dutton, *Modern Tragicomedy and the British Tradition* (Norman: University of Oklahoma Press, 1986), p. 168.
3. Ibid., p. 167.
4. Bernard Dukore, *When Laughter Stops: Pinter's Tragicomedy* (Columbia: University of Missouri Press, 1976), p. 57.
5. A. P. Braunmuller, "A World of Words in Pinter's *Old Times*," *Modern Language Quarterly* 40 (1979): 66. And see also Dukore, *When Laughter Stops*, p. 57.
6. Also see Steven Gale, "The Significance of Orson Welles in Harold Pinter's *Old Times*," *Notes on Contemporary Literature* 13 (1983): 11–12.
7. Elin Diamond in *Pinter's Comic Play* (Lewisburg, Pa.: Bucknell University Press, 1985) discusses the general parallels between Pinter's two characters and their counterparts in the film (p. 165).
8. Dutton in *Modern Tragicomedy* speaks of Deeley's association with Lukey as being "in character" (p. 165).
9. On the filmic dimension of *Old Times* see Katharine Worth, *Revolutions in Modern English Drama* (London: G. Bell and Sons, Ltd., 1972), p. 93; and Noel King, "Pinter's Progress," *Modern Drama* 25 (1980): 250.
10. The script for *Odd Man Out* is edited by Roger Manvell, *Three British Screenplays* (London: Methuen, 1950).
11. Braunmuller, "World of Words," p. 63.
12. Dutton in *Modern British Tragicomedy* suggests that Deeley, an Irishman living in London, and hence not involved with the politics of his home-

land, would have a special interest in a film about the battles in Dublin between the IRA and the authorities, such as *Odd Man Out* (p. 168).

13. Manville, script of *Odd Man Out*, p. 171.

14. Chris C. Hudgins, "Inside Out: Filmic Technique and the Theatrical Deception of a Consciousness in Harold Pinter's *Old Times*," *Genre* 13 (1980): 355–76.

Bibliography

Anderson, Michael. *Anger and Detachment: A Study of Arden, Osborne, and Pinter.* London: Pitman, 1976.

Ayburn, Tony. "The Memory of All That: Pinter's *Old Times.*" *English Language Notes* 22 (1973): 99–102.

Baker, William, and Stephen Tabachnick. *Harold Pinter.* Writers and Artists Series. Edinburgh: Oliver and Boyd, 1973.

Bold, Alan, ed. *Harold Pinter: You Never Heard Such Silence.* Totowa, N.J.: Vision and Barnes and Noble, 1984.

Braunmuller, A. P. "Harold Pinter, the Metamorphosis of Memory." In *Essays on Contemporary British Drama,* edited by Hedwig Bock and Albert Wertheim, 155–70. Munich: Hueber, 1981.

———. "A World of Words in Pinter's *Old Times.*" *Modern Language Quarterly* 40 (1979): 53–74.

Brigg, Peter. "*Old Times:* Beyond Pinter's Naturalism." *English Studies in Canada* 1 (1975): 466–74.

Brown, John Russell. *Theatre Language: A Study of Arden, Osborne, Pinter, and Wesker.* New York: Taplinger Publishing Company, 1972.

———. "Theatre Without Adventure." *Times Literary Supplement* (29 December 1972): 1570.

Burkman, Katherine. "Death and the Double in Three Plays by Harold Pinter." In Alan Bold, *Harold Pinter: You Never Heard Such Silence,* 131–145. Totowa, N.J.: Vision and Barnes and Noble, 1984.

———. "Earth and Water: The Question of Renewal in Harold Pinter's *Old Times* and *No Man's Land.*" *West Virginia University Philological Publications* 25 (1979): 101–7.

———. "*Family Voices* and the Voice of the Family." In *Harold Pinter: Critical Approaches,* edited by Steven Gale, 164–74. Rutherford, N.J.: Fairleigh Dickinson University Press, 1986.

Cave, Richard Allen. *New British Drama in Performance on the London Stage: 1970–1985.* New York: St. Martin's Press, 1980.

Clurman, Harold. *The Divine Pastime: Theatre Essays.* New York: Macmillan, 1974.

Colby, Doublas. *As the Curtain Rises: On Contemporary British Drama: 1966–1976.* Rutherford, N.J.: Fairleigh Dickinson University Press, 1978.

Corrigan, Robert W. *The Theatre in Search of a Fix.* New York: Delacorte, 1973.

Diamond, Elin. *Pinter's Comic Play.* Lewisburg, Pa.: Bucknell University Press, 1985.

Dukore, Bernard F. *When Laughter Stops: Pinter's Tragicomedy.* Columbia: University of Missouri Press, 1976.

Dutton, Richard. *Modern Tragicomedy and the British Tradition.* Norman and London: University of Oklahoma Press, 1986.

Eilenberg, Lawrence I. "Rehearsal and Critical Method: Pinter's *Old Times*." *Modern Drama* 18 (1975): 385–92.

Elsom, John. *Erotic Theater*. New York: Taplinger Publishing Company, 1974.

Esslin, Martin. *Pinter the Playwright*. London: Methuen, 1984.

Evans, Gareth and Barbara Lloyd. *Plays in Review: 1956–1980: British Drama and the Critics*. New York: Methuen, 1985.

Gabbard, Lucina Paquet. *The Dream Structure of Harold Pinter's Plays*. Rutherford, N.J.: Fairleigh Dickinson University Press, 1976.

Gale, Steven. *Harold Pinter: An Annotated Bibliography*. Boston: G. K. Hall, 1978.

———. *Butter's Going Up: A Critical Analysis of Harold Pinter's Work*. Durham, N.C.: Duke University Press, 1977.

———. *Harold Pinter: Critical Approaches*. Rutherford, N.J.: Fairleigh Dickinson University Press, 1986.

———. "Nature Half Created, Half Perceived: Time and Reality in Harold Pinter's Later Plays." *Journal of Evolutionary Psychology* 5 (1984): 196–204.

———. "Observations on Two Productions of Harold Pinter's *Old Times*." *Pinter Review* 1 (1987): 40–43.

———. "The Significance of Orson Welles in Harold Pinter's *Old Times*." *Notes on Contemporary Literature* 13 (1983): 11–12.

———. "The Use of a Cinematic Device in Harold Pinter's *Old Times*." *Notes on Contemporary Literature* 10 (1980): 11.

Ganz, Arthur, ed. "Mixing Memory and Desire: Pinter's Vision in *Landscape*, *Silence*, and *Old Times*." In *Pinter: A Collection of Critical Essays*, 161–78. Englewood Cliffs, N.J.: Prentice-Hall, Inc., 1972.

George, Kathleen. *Rhythm in Drama*. Pittsburgh: University of Pittsburgh Press, 1980.

Gill, Brendon. "The Cry." *The New Yorker* 47 (1971): 89.

Gillen, Francis. "All These Bits and Pieces: Fragmentation and Choice in Pinter's Plays." *Modern Drama* 17 (1974): 477–87.

Goetsch, Paul. "Harold Pinter: *Old Times*." In *Das Englische Drama der Gegenwart*, edited by Horst Oppel, 206–21. Berlin: Schmidt, 1975.

Gordon, Lois G. *Strategies to Uncover Nakedness: The Dramas of Harold Pinter*. Literary Frontiers Edition. Columbia: University of Missouri Press, 1970.

Gotsfried, Martin. "Harold Pinter Cracks His Cool." *Vogue* 158 (1971): 71.

Gussow, Mel. "*Old Times* Ushers in New Pinter Era." *New York Times* (18 November 1971): 60.

Halliwell, L. *The Filmgoer's Companion*. New York: Avon Books, 1971.

Hayman, Ronald. *Harold Pinter*. New York: Frederick Ungar Publishing Company, 1973.

Hewes, Henry. "Odd Man Out." *Saturday Review* 4 (1971): 20.

Hinchliffe, Arnold. *Harold Pinter*. New York: St. Martin's Press, 1967.

Hinden, Michael. "After Beckett: The Plays of Pinter, Stoppard, and Shepard." *Contemporary Literature* 27 (1986): 400–408.

Hobson, Harold. "Pinter's No-Contest: *Old Times*." *Christian Science Monitor* 14 (1971): 4.

———. "Remembrance of Things Past." *Sunday Times* (London) (6 June 1971): 29.

Hollis, James P. *Harold Pinter: The Poetics of Silence.* Crosscurrents/Modern Critiques. Edwardsville: Southern Illinois University Press, 1970.

Hornby, Richard. *Drama, Metadrama, and Pereception.* Lewisburg, Pa.: Bucknell University Press, 1986.

Hudgins, Chris C. "Inside Out: Filmic Language and the Theatrical Deception of a Consciousness in Harold Pinter's *Old Times.*" *Genre* 13 (1980): 355–76.

Hughes, Alan. "'They Can't Take That Away From Me': Myth and Memory in Pinter's *Old Times.*" *Modern Drama* 17 (1974): 467–76.

Hurren, Kenneth. "These Foolish Things." *Spectator* (12 June 1971): 821.

Imhof, Rudiger. *Pinter: A Bibliography.* London: T Q Publications, Ltd., 1976.

J. K. "Camera Obscura." *Newsweek* (29 November 1971): 110–11.

Kennedy, Andrew K. *Six Dramatists in Search of a Language.* Cambridge: At the University Press, 1975.

Kerr, Jean. "*Waiting for Pinter:* A Play." *New York Times* (12 December 1971): sec. 2, pp. 3, 5.

Kerr, Walter. "Is Mr. Pinter Telling Us Less Than He Knows?" *New York Times* (28 November 1971): sec. 2, pp. 1, 7.

King, Noel. "Pinter's Progress." *Modern Drama* 23 (1980): 46–57.

Kingston, Jeremy. "Pinter." *Punch* 260 (1971): 826–27.

Kreps, Barbara. "Time and Harold Pinter's Possible Realities: Art as Life and Vice Versa." *Modern Drama* 22 (1979): 47–60.

Lambert, J. W. "Plays in Performance." *Drama* 102 (1975): 47–49.

Lane, John Francis. "No Sex Please, I'm English." *Plays and Players* 20 (1973): 19–21.

McAuley, Gay. "The Problem of Identity: Theme, Form, and Theatrical Method in *Les Negres, Kaspar,* and *Old Times.*" *Southern Review* 8 (1975): 51–65.

McGuiness, Arthur E. "Memory and Betrayal: The Symbolic Landscape of *Old Times.*" *Themes in Drama, Drama and Symbolism,* 4: 101–11. Cambridge: At the University Press, 1982.

Manvell, Roger, ed. *Three British Screenplays.* London: Methuen, 1950.

Marowitz, Charles. "Can Pinter be Beckett?" *New York Times* (13 June 1971): sec. 2, pp. 1, 3.

———. *Confessions of a Counterfeit Critic: London Theatre Notebook* London: Eyre Methuen, 1973.

Martineau, Stephen. "Pinter's *Old Times:* The Memory Game." *Modern Drama* 16 (1973): 287–97.

Merritt, Susan H. "Harold Pinter Bibliography." *Pinter Review* 1 (1987): 77–82.

Morrison, Kristin. *Canters and Chronicles: The Use of Narrative in the Plays of Samuel Beckett and Harold Pinter.* Chicago: University of Chicago Press, 1983.

Nightingale, Benedict. "Three's a Crowd." *New Statesman* (11 June 1971): 817.

Panter-Dounes, Mollie. "Letters from London." *The New Yorker* 47 (1971): 64–65.

Pinter, Harold. "A Conversation with Harold Pinter," by Mel Gussow. *New York Times Magazine* (5 December 1971): 42–43, 126–36.

Porterfield, Christopher. "Memories as Weapons." *Time* 97 (1971): 76.

Powlick, Leonard. "What the Hell Is *That* All About: A Peek at Pinter's Dramaturgy." In *Harold Pinter: Critical Approaches,* edited by Steven Gale, 30–37. Rutherford, N.J.: Fairleigh Dickinson University Press, 1986.

Quigley, Austin E. *The Pinter Problem.* Princeton: Princeton University Press, 1975.

Robbe-Grillet, Alain. "Samuel Beckett, or Presence on the Stage." In *Snapshots Toward a New Novel,* 111–25. New York: Grove Press, 1966.

Sakellandou, Elizabeth. *Pinter's Female Portraits.* Totowa, N.J.: Barnes and Noble Books, 1988.

Savran, David. "The Guardian Economy of Desire: *Old Times* Recaptured." *Theatre Journal* 34 (1982): 40–54.

Skloot, Robert. "Putting out the Light: Staging the Theme of Pinter's *Old Times.*" *Quarterly Journal of Speech* 61 (1975): 265–70.

Stoll, Karl-Heinz von. *The New British Dramatists: A Bibliography with Particular Reference to Arden, Bonds, Osborne, Pinter, Wesker.* Bern: Herbert Lang, 1975.

Sykes, Alrene. *Harold Pinter.* New York: Humanities Press, 1970.

Taylor, John Russell. *"Old Times." Plays and Players* 10 (1971): 28–29.

TEK. "Is Memory a Cat or a Mouse?" *Time* 98 (1971): 70–71.

Thompson, David T. *Pinter: The Player's Playwright.* New York: Schocken Books, 1985.

Trussler, Simon. *The Plays of Harold Pinter.* London: Victor Gollancz, Ltd., 1973.

Watson, George. "Osborne, Pinter, Stoppard: A Playful Look at London since 1956." *Virginia Quarterly Review* 62 (1986): 271–84.

Weales, Gerald. "The Stage." *Commonweal* 95 (1971): 278.

Worth, Katherine. *Revolutions in Modern English Drama.* London: G. Bell and Sons, Ltd., 1972.

Zinman, Toby S. "Pinter's *Old Times.*" *Explicator* 43 (1985): 56–57.

Index